Wingate's Lost Brigade

Wingate's Lost Brigade

Brigade

The First Chindit Operation 1943

Philip Chinnery

Pen & Sword
MILITARY

First published in Great Britain in 2010 by
Pen & Sword Military
an imprint of
Pen & Sword Books Ltd
47 Church Street
Barnsley
South Yorkshire
S70 2AS

ISBN 978-1-84884-054-6

A CIP catalogue record for this book is available from the British Library.

Typeset in 11pt Ehrhardt by
Mac Style, Beverley, E. Yorkshire

Printed and bound in the UK by the MPG Books Group

Pen & Sword Books Ltd incorporates the imprints of Pen & Sword Aviation,
Pen & Sword Maritime, Pen & Sword Military, Wharncliffe Local History,
Pen and Sword Select, Pen and Sword Military Classics and Leo Cooper.

For a complete list of Pen & Sword titles please contact
PEN & SWORD BOOKS LIMITED
47 Church Street, Barnsley, South Yorkshire, S70 2AS, England
E-mail: enquiries@pen-and-sword.co.uk
Website: www.pen-and-sword.co.uk

This book is dedicated to the Chindits of Operation LONGCLOTH who did not make it home.

Contents

Preface

This book is the culmination of research which began in 1995 when I was commissioned to write March or Die: The Story of Wingate's Chindits for Airlife Publishing. The book covered both the 1943 and 1944 Chindit expeditions, but due to the size of the second campaign, with six brigades involved, the narrative dwarfed the story of the 1943 show. I had hoped to redress the balance and devote a whole book to the men who followed Wingate into the unknown in 1943, and am grateful to the publisher for allowing me finally to do so.

I am proud to have known some of the participants, especially the late Mike Calvert who I met on a number of occasions. The first of these was in his small retirement flat in Haywards Heath. With his old cat 'Gurkha' asleep on the sofa next to me, he described how he fought and drowned a Japanese officer in a river during the retreat from Burma to India. I realized then that I was privileged to be in the company of a remarkable man and would come to understand how he came to be Wingate's most devoted disciple and the most charismatic and successful of the Chindits leaders.

Fourteen more years passed before I could finally put pen to paper to tell the story of Wingate's Lost Brigade. By then Calvert, Dunlop, Bromhead and Scott, the last of the column commanders, had passed away, as had most of my original Chindit correspondents. Only one or two of the British Other Ranks were still around; the 13th Kings were not young men when they went into the jungle sixty-five years earlier. It was to my amazement, however, that I then discovered some of the young officers who had followed Wingate. These men, barely out of their teens, included Denis Gudgeon who had fought with Mike Calvert's column, and Ken Spurlock, Wingate's signals officer, both of whom had not only been left for dead at the side of the track, but had managed to survive two years in Rangoon Jail. Barely weeks before the manuscript was due to be handed over I found Bill Smyly, the animal transport officer with Bernard Fergusson's column, who not only escaped death on the way home in 1943, but who went in again in 1944.

It has been a pleasure to make the acquaintance of these brave but modest men and I hope that this book will provide a fitting tribute to their exploits and achievements.

Philip Chinnery, London

Acknowledgements

I would like to thank the following former Chindits, without whom this book could not have been written: Private Charles Aves, 7 Column; Lance Corporal George Bell, 2 Group HQ; CQMS Duncan Bett, 2 Group HQ; Major George Bromhead, 4 Column; Private Denis Brown, 8 Column; Major Mike Calvert, 3 Column; Captain John Carroll, 8 Column; Private John Cartner, 8 Column; Major George Dunlop, 1 Column; Private Leon Frank, 7 Column; Lieutenant Alec Gibson, 3 Column; Lieutenant Denis Gudgeon, 3 Column; Private Roger Hamer, 8 Column; Sergeant Eric Hutchins, Brigade HQ; Lieutenant Harold James, 3 Column; Private Fred Morgan, 7 Column; Lieutenant Nick Neill, 8 Column; Captain Ray Scott, 4 Column Burma Rifles; Lieutenant Bill Smyly, 5 Column; Lieutenant Ken Spurlock, Brigade HQ; Sergeant John Thornburrow, 5 Column; Signaller Byron White, 5 Column; Lieutenant Alan Wilding, Brigade HQ; Sergeant Arthur Willshaw RAF, Brigade HQ.

Many thanks also to Steve Fogden, whose grandfather Private Arthur Leslie Howney was one of the men of 13th Kings in 5 Column who did not make it home. He kindly assisted me with contacts, photographs and war diaries, and in return I helped trace his grandfather to Rangoon Jail, where he sadly died on 17 June 1943.

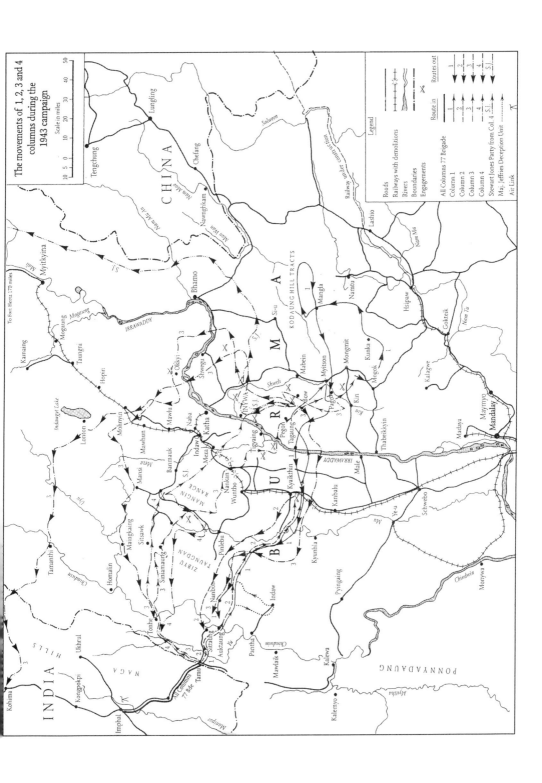

The movements of 1, 2, 3 and 4 columns during the 1943 campaign

Scale in miles
10 5 0   10   20   30   40   50

Legend

Roads
Railways with demolitions
Rivers
Boundaries
Engagements

All Columns 77 Brigade
Column 1
Column 2
Column 3
Column 4
Stewart Jones Party from Col. 4
Maj. Jeffries Deception Unit
Air Link

Route in
1
2
3
4
S.J.

Routes out
1
2
3
4
S.J.

CHINA

Tengchung
Lungling
Chefang
Nawnghkam
Salween

Myitkyina
To foot Hertz 170 miles
Mali
Kamaing
Mogaung
Taungni
Hopin
Indawgyi Lake
Lonton
Mohnyin
Mawlu
Naba
Katha
Okkyi
Shwegu
IRRAWADDY

Bhamo
Si-u
KODAUNG HILL TRACTS
Mangla
Namtu
Lashio

B U R M A

Mabein
Mytison
Mongmit
Kunka
Mogok
Kalagwe
Hsipaw
Gokteik

Nam Mã

Shweli
Pago
Kin
Pegon
Tapaung
Kyaiktin
Male
Thabeikkyin
Madaya
Maymyo
Mandalay

INYWA
Tigyaing
Meza
Indaw
MANGIN RANGE
Nankan
Wuntho
Pinlebu
Kyunhla
Kanbalu
Schwebo
Ye-u

Mansi
Banmauk
Mawhun
Maingkaing
Sitsawk
Sinlamaung
ZIBYU TAUNGDAN
Nanbon
Auktaung
Sittaung
Indaw
Pantha

Homalin
Tamanthi
Chindwin
Uyu

Tamu
All Comms 77 Bde
Mawlaik
Kalewa
Kalemyo
PONNYADAUNG

Kohima
Kongpokpi
Ukhrul
NAGA HILLS
INDIA
Imphal
Manipur
Pyingaing
Chindwin
Monywa

PART 1 – Operation LONGCLOTH

Chapter 1

Declaration of War

Clouds of wood smoke greeted the author and his guest as they walked into the Cherry Tree public house in Farnham on a wet day in January 2009. The landlady apologized and explained that they had just lit the fire and would we like a menu? The guest opted for Lamb Rogan Josh and the author a Fish Pie; while the cook banged around in the kitchen the guest, an old soldier, began to talk of events that took place sixty-seven years before.

Denis Gudgeon was a young twenty-year-old subaltern – a second lieutenant – with an artillery regiment in London when he saw the recruiting notice. The war had been going badly in the Far East and thousands of officers were required to join the Indian Army. The prospect of extra pay and adventure appealed to Denis and soon he was on a troopship leaving the Clyde. He recalled that the journey was more like a modern-day 'booze cruise' and the officers spent most of their time in the bar, hoping that German torpedoes would not come their way out of the darkness.

Denis decided that spending the whole journey in alcoholic oblivion would be counter-productive and chose to learn Urdu instead. A wise choice as it turned out, as he did very well in his Basic Urdu exam after he arrived in India and was sent to join the 3rd Battalion of the 2nd King Edward VII's Own Goorkha Rifles (The Sirmoor Rifles). He arrived on 16 May 1942, just ten days short of his twenty-first birthday.

Denis found himself second in command of 'C' Company, under Captain George Silcock. Training proceeded apace with Denis getting to know his Gurkhas and improving his knowledge of their language and traditions. Suddenly orders arrived, transferring the Battalion to the newly formed 77th Indian Infantry Brigade and they were all packed off by train to Saugor in the Central Indian Provinces. As they pulled in to the station they were met by a smiling, broad-shouldered Major by the name of Mike Calvert. He would become a great influence in the development of the young officer and his life was about to change for ever. Calvert explained that great things lay ahead of them, and by the way did Denis know anything about mules?

The War was going badly in the Far East at that time. For two years Great Britain had been at war with Nazi Germany and most of mainland Europe had fallen to the armies of the Wehrmacht. In the Far East, Japan had already occupied Korea and its troops had been fighting in China for five years. As 1941 came to an end the Japanese had such military might in the area that it was reasonable for the people of the East Indies, Malaya, Thailand and the Philippines to fear attack. On 6 December, President of the United States Franklin D. Roosevelt sent an urgent note to Emperor Hirohito, the 'Son of God', in an attempt to dispel the clouds of war gathering on the horizon. It was a futile gesture. Six Japanese aircraft carriers were already steaming across the Pacific Ocean towards the Hawaiian Islands and Pearl Harbour, where the American Pacific Fleet lay at anchor. At 0755 hours on 8 December the first Japanese dive-bombers began their bombing runs against the airfields and the eighty-six ships spread out beneath them. Within two hours, nineteen warships had been damaged or sunk, including four of the seven giant battleships in the fleet; 350 aircraft were damaged or destroyed and 2,403 men killed. It was, as President Roosevelt declared, 'a day that will live in infamy'. That evening the United States declared war on Japan and the sleeping American giant began to stir.

Great Britain had planned to announce its own declaration of war the same evening, after the United States, but news arrived that Japanese troops had begun landing in Malaya, so the Cabinet approved the declaration at once and it was delivered to the Japanese envoy at 1.00 pm. Within a week, Japanese troops were fighting British, Indian and Australian forces in Malaya and Hong Kong, and Japanese marines were storming ashore on the main Philippine island of Luzon. On 11 December, the British battleships HMS *Repulse* and *Prince of Wales* were attacked by waves of Japanese dive-bombers as they headed for the base of Singapore, on the southern tip of Malaya. Within two hours they had been sunk and 840 crew had been killed. On the 15th, troops from the Japanese Fifteenth Army advanced westwards from Thailand into Burma, capturing three key southern airfields. Their objective was to take Rangoon and then cut the main Allied supply line to General Chiang Kai-shek's Chinese Nationalists already fighting the Japanese in their vast country. The Japanese Army could also make good use of the 12 million acres of rice under cultivation in Burma, together with its natural resources such as oil and manganese. In addition, Burma would provide a springboard for the invasion of India, the largest British possession in the East.

The early months of 1942 saw one defeat after another inflicted upon the Allied forces. On 15 February, Singapore fell and 130,000 British, Indian and Australian troops were taken prisoner. It was the greatest military defeat in the history of the British Empire. In Burma, the airfield and town of Moulmein had fallen and the Japanese continued their advance towards Rangoon. The important Sittang Bridge was blown up too soon by the defenders on 23 February, marooning thousands of British, Indian and Gurkha troops on the east side of the river, in the path of the advancing Japanese. Hundreds died as they tried to swim across. On 8 March, Rangoon was abandoned and the British defenders under General Alexander began their long retreat northwards to India. Two days later the first reports reached the British government of Japanese atrocities in Hong Kong and Malaya, including the cold-blooded murder by bayoneting or beheading of hundreds of prisoners of war, including wounded men, civilians and nurses. The true nature of the enemy was now becoming apparent.

On 19 March, Lieutenant General William Slim took command of the two depleted divisions retreating through Burma, 17th Indian Division and 1st Burma Division. As they made their way up the Irrawaddy valley they destroyed the largest oilfield in the Far East at Yenangyaung, to prevent the wells falling into Japanese hands. On 29 April, the Japanese captured Lashio, cutting the Burma Road to China, and at midnight the next day the men of Burcorps blew up the Ava Bridge across the Irrawaddy River, and turned towards India. They had two weeks of hard marching ahead of them; 13,463 British, Indian, Burmese and Gurkha troops lost their lives during the 900-mile retreat, together with three-quarters of a million refugees. By 20 May, all of Burma was in Japanese hands.

One of the men trying desperately to fight a rearguard action against the seemingly invincible Japanese was Major Mike Calvert, the commander of the Bush Warfare School at Maymyo. Together with instructors from the school and whatever stragglers he could conscript, he had been operating behind the retreat, getting in the Japanese troops' way whenever possible and picking up anyone left behind. One night in April, he received a message from a loyal Burmese that there were some Gurkhas in the next village who were lost and wanted to be put back on the right road to India. They were in a longhouse that stood on stilts and a faint light shone through cracks in the badly fitting door as Calvert and two of his men approached. 'They may think we are Japs so we'll talk loudly in English as we get near the door,' he told his corporal.

> I knocked on the door, lifted the latch and walked in. The house consisted of one long room and in the middle stood a table with nine or ten chairs around it. I already had a smile of greeting on my face, but there were no answering smiles from the occupants of the chairs. They were all Jap officers. I stopped abruptly two paces inside the doorway, but my Corporal and Private, having no idea that anything was wrong, bumped into me and pushed me further into the room before they too came to a halt when they saw the yellow faces. For what seemed like hours we stared at each other. They seemed too

stunned to think of shooting. We certainly were. Suddenly I realised that there was only one thing to do. I said quickly, "Excuse me gentlemen. Good night." Then I turned, grabbed my men by the arms and bundled them out through the door and down the steps. Then we ran like hell for the jungle.

Not long afterwards, Calvert and a dozen of his men reached a tributary of the Chindwin River. They had not seen the enemy for a couple of days and the temptation was too hard to resist – they stripped off for a badly needed bath. Calvert wandered around a little headland and dived in. He was naked except for his boots, one item of clothing never taken off in the jungle. It was fortunate that he stuck to his rule and still wore them. A Japanese officer, who had also decided to bathe in the same small cove, advanced towards Calvert, determined to kill him in hand-to-hand combat. Around the other side of the cove, a party of Japanese soldiers was splashing and shouting. The Japanese officer had heard Calvert's men, but did not know their strength. If the alarm was raised they might have outnumbered the score of men in his own patrol, so he decided to tackle Calvert with his own bare hands. It was a great mistake. Calvert recalled:

He knew his ju-jitsu and the water on his body made him as slippery as an eel, but I was bigger and stronger. It is extraordinarily difficult to keep balance or move quickly in two or three feet of water. The Jap got more vicious as he jabbed his fingers at my face in an attempt to blind me. He was putting up a tremendous show and I was hard put to it to hold him. I pulled myself together. I had to kill him or he would kill me. I managed to grab the Jap's wrist and force his arm behind his back. I buried my face in his chest to stop him clawing my eyes out, then as he lashed out with his left arm and both feet, I forced him gradually under water. My boots gave me a firm grip and I shut my eyes and held him under the surface. Eventually he went limp and his body floated away downstream.

There was no time to lose. Calvert staggered around the headland and alerted his men. 'Japs, in the next cove but one. They don't know we're here but they will do in a minute. I killed their officer. Get after them now.' They grabbed their guns and found about twenty Japanese and killed them all. They only just made it – soon after they reached the cove the body of the officer floated past.

Weeks would pass before Mike Calvert and his men arrived safely in India. On the way he would have plenty of time to recall his first meeting in February 1942 with a man who would change his life for ever. That particular day had not started well. Calvert had been recalled 70 miles to Prome, while in the middle of a successful waterborne raid down the Irrawaddy to Henzada, only to find himself on the receiving end of a sharp rebuke for commandeering a riverboat belonging to the Irrawaddy Flotilla Company and damaging property of the Burmah Oil Company during his demolition operations. The fact that the property would have fallen into the hands of the Japanese anyway was ignored by the stiff-necked staff officer. Pretty fed up, he made his way back to the Bush Warfare School only to find a brigadier sitting in his office, behind his desk.

'Who are you?' Calvert glared at the stranger, who was quite calm and composed.

'Wingate' he replied. 'Who are you?'

'Calvert. Excuse me, but that's my desk.'

'I'm sorry,' said the Brigadier and he moved aside at once to let Calvert sit down. Calvert later recalled:

> I was impressed. He showed no resentment at this somewhat disrespectful treatment by a major. He began talking quietly, asking questions about the showboat raid. And to my surprise they were the right sort of questions. Tired as I was, I soon began to realise that this was a man I could work for and follow. Clearly he knew all that I knew about unconventional warfare and a lot more; he was streets ahead of anyone else I had spoken to. Suddenly I no longer felt tired. For even at that first meeting something of the driving inspiration inside Orde Wingate transferred itself to me.

Wingate did indeed know what he was talking about. From 1928 to 1933 he had served with the Sudan Defence Force, during which time he had become fluent in Arabic and gained his profound knowledge of the Middle East. Because of this he was sent for when groups of Arab rebels started raiding Jewish settlements and damaging oil installations in Palestine and Transjordan in 1936. Wingate raised, trained and led a force of what became known as 'Night Squads', Jewish volunteers who fought and defeated the Arabs at their own game, using Wingate's guerrilla tactics. This achievement earned Wingate the DSO and the undying gratitude of the Jews, who would very possibly have chosen him to lead their own army when they fought to establish the state of Israel in 1948. Wingate's next exploit was to command a force of guerrillas against the Italians in Abyssinia, which gave him more experience and a chance to try out his theories on mobile, free-moving columns of troops, operating behind enemy lines. During some of these exploits, Wingate had served under General Wavell, who was impressed with the man and his methods, and when he was appointed Supreme Commander South-West Pacific, which put him in overall command of Burma, he sent for Wingate and ordered him to take charge of all guerrilla activities there.

It soon became clear in the summer of 1942 that nothing could be done to stop the advance of the Japanese to the Indian border. All Wingate could do was study the land, and the people and the tactics of the Japanese troops. He stayed at Maymyo for a while and he and Calvert walked for miles and talked for hours. 'My conviction grew that this was a man I could fight for,' Calvert wrote later. He took Wingate to see General Slim, the commander of Burma Corps, and left them together. On the way back to Maymyo, Wingate said he was very impressed with Slim. 'Best man, bar Wavell, east of Suez.' Wingate continued his tour of Burma, using Maymyo as a base, and in March met the Chinese General Chiang Kai-shek, some of whose troops had crossed the border into northern Burma to carry on the fight against the Japanese under the command of American General 'Vinegar Joe' Stilwell, who had been appointed Chiang's chief of staff. He wanted the views of Chiang, experienced as he was in fighting the Japanese, on the idea of a long-range penetration force to be used in the Burmese jungle. Soon Wingate was recalled to Delhi to write a full paper on what he wanted and what he planned to do if he got it. The report was submitted to General Wavell and Wingate was destined to spend weeks waiting in Maidens Hotel, Delhi while it was being considered.

While Wingate cooled his heels in Delhi, Mike Calvert continued to operate behind the Japanese advance. By the time he and the remains of his Bush Warfare School men arrived in India, sick and emaciated, two months had passed and Wingate's report had finally been accepted. He had been ordered by Wavell to form a long-range penetration brigade and was looking for volunteers to join him. Although Calvert had lost a third of his body weight due to the conditions under which he had been fighting, and his good friend Captain George Dunlop was in hospital suffering from cholera, they both said yes. Instructed to get well again before reporting for duty, Calvert once again had a purpose in life. A full brigade of troops was to be trained to fight the Japanese at their own game and Wingate would lead them.

Chapter 2

A New Way of Fighting

Wingate described his theory of long-range jungle penetration thus: 'Granted the power to maintain forces by air and direct them by wireless, it is possible to operate regular ground forces for indefinite periods in the heart of enemy-occupied territory to the peril of his war machine.' It sounded simple enough, but it was a radical concept. The British Army fought its battles with a long logistic lifeline behind it; trucks would bring supplies and reinforcements to the front, and take casualties away to the rear areas. Wingate's proposal did away with this long-established system and replaced it with an aerial logistic lifeline. Once behind enemy lines, his men would be supplied by air. Their supplies, food and ammunition would be dropped by parachute into clearings in the jungle. The aircraft would be summoned by wireless, instructed which supplies to drop, and told where and when. The men would collect their supplies and melt away into the jungle to continue their task. Wireless could also be used to direct air attacks on targets of opportunity if any were found in the enemy rear areas.

The concept of long-range groups was nothing new – they had already been used in the Western Desert to disrupt Rommel's lines of communications. The drawback, however, was that the raiders had to carry their supplies with them and when they ran out they had to return home, so their effectiveness was strictly limited. Wingate's new proposal was much more far-reaching and on a far larger scale.

In 1942 very little was known about air supply and indeed there was very little equipment available in India at that time. Local firms were put to work making parachutes and packings, and the first Indian Parachute Packing Company was formed. There were very few cargo aircraft available and in the beginning Wingate could only count on the support of five planes – three Douglas C-47 Dakotas and two Hudson's which would later be replaced by C-47s. The problem of directing the aircraft to the right dropping zone at the right time was more difficult to solve. There were no portable radio sets that could be used for the men on the ground to communicate directly with the pilots as they approached. Missions had to be planned well in advance, so the instructions had to be precise. Who better to organize supply drops than the Royal Air Force itself? Wingate decided to form detachments of RAF personnel, including pilots, who understood the difficulties of flying over Burma. The pilots who volunteered for 'arduous and dangerous duty of a highly secret nature with ground forces' were extremely enthusiastic and of a very high calibre. They would be invaluable in the months ahead.

The idea was that the requirements of Wingate's force would be radioed back to the RAF base at Argatala in India, the planes would be loaded and the pilots would take off and head for the area. They would be given a recognizable datum point from which they could follow the instructions given in the signal requesting the supply drop. For instance, the signal might give a river junction as a datum point and direct the pilot to fly at a given altitude, on a given bearing for a certain distance to the dropping zone, which would be marked by a geometrical pattern of fires. Often the signal would instruct the pilot which direction and height to take after each run and he would always be made aware of any flying hazards in the area. Despite the fact that the dropping zones were seldom more than 400 yards by 100 yards the procedure was very successful.

In order to limit the length of the signals, all of which had to be sent in cipher code for security reasons, a method was worked out of compiling 'shopping lists'. Every man had a set of spare clothes and boots kept in stock at the supply base and a code was worked out for the supply of these items in detail. Items of equipment were similarly coded, although in many cases it was possible to use the ordnance or medical vocabulary numbering. This coding method of signalling for supplies was so successful that with only slight modification, it became a standard manual. Two air bases were eventually used – the main base at Argatala with its good dispersal facilities and anti-aircraft protection held three months supplies, and a reserve field nearby which was stocked with only seven days supplies. The latter was used once in emergency when the main air base was bombed by the Japanese and some stores destroyed.

Three types of standard radio sets were taken into the field. They provided communications within the column, communication between columns and headquarters and between headquarters and Corps HQ; the latter via a relay station placed on the mountain crests in the later stages of the operation. The first radio, for communications within the column, was too heavy for the job and had to be carried on a mule. It was the only one available with the necessary range, often up to 15 miles. The second radio, used for communications between the columns and brigade headquarters, had a range of between 30 and 60 miles and was a very robust set. Even if it was immersed in water during the river crossings it would work as soon as it had dried out in the hot sun. The third set had to be able to work over considerable distances and it too had to be carried on a mule.

The location of the night's bivouac would often be dictated by the Signals Officer who would want to be on a hilltop and there was often the inevitable argument with the Animal Transport Officer who would want to be in a valley near water. Usually the Signals Officer won.

The radios were powered by batteries which had to be kept charged by using charging engines, again carried by mules. They were by definition noisy machines, although this could be minimized by putting exhaust extensions into a hole covered with brushwood. One column neglected their charging so much that they almost found themselves without communications.

One-time cipher pads were used in order that the capture of one column's codes would not jeopardize the safety of the other columns. Such a system put great strain on headquarters, especially after the cipher common to all columns was thought, wrongly as it happened, to have been compromised.

The one problem with long-range penetration that could not be solved at that time was the treatment and evacuation of casualties. The only way to carry casualties the distances and at the speed required was on horses or mules. Anyone who could not be carried had to be left with friendly villagers, together with whatever medical drugs could be spared and their weapons, in the hope that they could recover in time, either to remain in hiding or make their way back to friendly forces. Occasionally there would be no option but to abandon a man at the side of a track and leave his survival to fate. Needless to say the fear of being wounded in battle did nothing to raise morale. In addition there were also diseases such as malaria, dysentery, anthrax in certain areas, plus the usual fevers which accompany fatigue in hot climates.

The Senior Medical Officer had a number of drugs at his disposal. The main cause of sickness was dysentery, but through experience it was found possible to cure this within a few hours by the use of Sulfaguanidine, in doses which would not have been tolerated in a hospital. The use of Benzedrine for officers who had to stand the greatest strain proved justified, despite the forebodings of the doctors. To aid them in their work they would carry 300 lb of medical stores on two mules for each column of 400 men. One of the main tasks for the doctors was keeping an eye on the officers and men, and advising the column commander which ones were about to crack, so that remedial action could be taken in time to forestall it.

Morale is the most important single factor in long-range operations, but everything in such an operation as proposed by Wingate works against it. The monotonous diet, the feeling of being cut off from help and rest, the problems of casualty evacuation, the heat and fatigue, the silence and oppressiveness of the jungle and of having to fight both nature and the enemy at the same time produces an abnormal strain. Only confidence can overcome low morale. Confidence in one's ability to live and fight in the jungle, confidence in one's leaders and confidence in those who are planning his activities and feeding him. However, over time such confidence is easily eroded.

There were no suitable long-range rations available in India at that time. The ration eventually decided upon consisted mostly of a nourishing and fairly palatable biscuit, compressed almonds and raisins, cheese, chocolate and tea, milk and sugar. This ration was designed to give 3,000 calories and it was intended to supplement this with a further 1,000 calories which would be obtained from wild game or from the purchase of food in local villages. Here Wingate had clearly got it wrong. A force operating behind enemy lines is dependent on speed of movement and cannot stop very often in villages to buy food. Nor does the average village produce very much that they can afford to sell, while to simply take food from the villagers would have been bad policy when the goodwill of the villagers was vital to success. The raiders would also be competing with the Japanese occupation forces, who obtained food from the villages, either by force or by paying with worthless Japanese script. Moreover, 4,000 calories is not sufficient for such an operation, where men might have to march 20–25 miles each day, a miscalculation that undoubtedly caused many casualties from fatigue and hunger.

Another difficulty was feeding the Gurkhas who accompanied the British troops on the operation. Due to religious principles the Gurkhas would not eat beef and their method of cooking rice at that time was communal. They had yet to learn to cook individual portions of rice.

It is also important on long-range penetrations to learn what can be eaten in the area of operation. There were snakes, roots and herbs that could have been eaten, but this was not fully exploited, even after Burmese troops joined Wingate's force.

If Wingate's method of resupply was innovative, so indeed was the manner in which his men would move and fight. The Brigade would be split up into eight columns 'big enough to deliver blows of the necessary weight, while small enough to slip through the enemy's net'. Four columns would comprise mainly British troops and four mainly Gurkhas (see details of column composition on page 24).

One criterion for the successful employment of long-range penetration troops was that they should be used in conjunction with a main force offensive, which would occupy the enemy front-line troops while the LRP forces wreaked havoc in their rear areas. Failure to achieve this would allow the enemy to concentrate all of his forces on the destruction of the invaders. As time went by, however, it became apparent that there would be no attempt to retake Burma in 1943 and it was only with reluctance that Wavell gave Wingate permission to launch Operation Longcloth. The object of the operation was firstly to demonstrate the correctness or incorrectness of Wingate's LRP theory. The second object was to test the revolt potential of the Burmese, especially the hill tribes, and to make arrangements and plans that would assist the eventual reconquest of Burma. Thirdly, the purely military object was to disrupt the Mandalay-Myitkyina line of communications, exploiting the resulting situation and, if it seemed worthwhile, to march on across the Irrawaddy to operate against the main Japanese communications to the north and east, Maymyo-Lashio-Bhamo. Wavell must have been convinced at an early stage that Wingate's ideas were viable, because after 77 Brigade entered Burma he ordered a second LRP unit, 111 Brigade, to be formed.

In June 1942, Wingate was allocated the following resources from which to form his columns: 13th Battalion, The King's (Liverpool) Regiment; 3rd Battalion, 2nd King Edward VII's Own Gurkha Rifles; 142 Commando Company; 2nd Battalion Burma Rifles (composed of Karens, Kachins and Chins, the Karens from the Delta, the other two from the hills); a number of RAF sections commanded by flight lieutenants with recent fighting experience;

Organization of a British Column

Unit	Number of Personnel
Column headquarters	8
RAF section	5
Medical section	5
Regimental signallers	6
Royal Corp of Signals detachment	5
Sabotage Group (Commandos)	29
Burma Rifles Platoon (Reconnaissance)	45
Infantry Company	115
Support Group	31
2nd Line Transport	57
Total	306

Notes

a) A Gurkha column comprised 369 men as their infantry company and support group were larger, at 166 and forty-one respectively. This was because they took their first reinforcements into the field with them.

b) Each infantry company would carry four Boyes anti-tank rifles and nine light machine-guns (Brens). Two more LMGs were carried by the 2nd Line Transport for anti-aircraft duties.

c) Each support group would carry two 3-inch mortars and two Vickers machine-guns.

d) Fifteen horses and 100 mules were allowed in each column. There were fifty-one first-line mules and forty-nine second line.

a Brigade Signal Section from the Royal Corps of Signals; and a Mule Transport Company. Neither the mules nor the muleteers to lead them were readily available. It was decided that the majority of the muleteers would be Gurkhas, an unwise decision as it later transpired.

In nearly every case the troops allotted were chosen because they were the only ones available at the time. India Command was at that time very badly off for British troops and those available were unseasoned. The 13th King's was a garrison battalion with a high proportion of middle-aged and married men and 40 per cent would be weeded out and replaced with infantry drafts from Deolali before the operation commenced. Wingate stated that 'There are three elements which go to make up a good soldier: physical toughness, training (in which are included intelligence and education, which alone ensure adaptability and grasp), and courage. The last, which is the most important, may be defined as the power to endure present evil for the sake of ultimate good. A hard, well-trained soldier needs far less courage than a soft and ignorant one.' Wingate set out to mould his men into a tough, well-trained force. As for courage, they would need all they could find before the operation was over.

Private John Cartner recalled the feelings of the men when they were told that they were to be commanded by Wingate:

> When we were told that he had picked us because he wanted North Country men for the job, there were the usual comments such as 'What did he want to pick us for, we were quite comfy doing garrison duties.' I personally got to speak to him once, when we were resting during a training exercise. I was sat with our Labrador dog Judy when he came by. He stopped and asked me what I thought of her and I replied that she had been very impressive during her training. She was a very intelligent dog, well-trained, and her job was to convey messages between sections. On one occasion I had to go on patrol and left Judy with another soldier. Unfortunately he lost her and we never saw her again.

The 3/2nd Gurkhas were an average wartime Gurkha rifle battalion. Only one of its officers had seen service in any war and few of the British junior officers could speak Gurkhali. It was not unheard of for a battalion commander to communicate directly with the Gurkha officers and NCOs and then brief his British officers, who would command the men in battle. Soon, 200 of the 750 Gurkhas in the 3rd Battalion were weeded out and 1,200 more arrived direct from the Regimental Centre to fill the spaces in the Battalion and provide muleteers for the columns. They arrived only a few weeks before the end of training and Wingate admitted in his after-action report that 'most of the Gurkhas entered Burma insufficiently trained'.

142 Commando Company was originally supposed to have been a battalion, but there were not enough trained men available. Its function was to provide

each column with a squad of fighting saboteurs. They were trained by Mike Calvert and soon became experts at blowing up railway lines and bridges and laying booby-traps. Calvert was a Royal Engineer officer whose knowledge of explosives had been put to good use in Norway during the retreat of the British Expeditionary Force, and in southern England when plans were being made to resist a possible German invasion. He gained notoriety together with Captain Peter Fleming when they blew up General Montgomery's flowerpots while testing security at Monty's headquarters.

The Mule Transport Company suffered from the late arrival of both men and animals and the lack of trained personnel in the art of mule tending. Gurkhas are at their best in their traditional family unit, the battalion, and the parcelling out of men as muleteers to British columns was not a good idea. However, the men themselves were physically fit, having just arrived from the Regimental Centre. This was essential as Wingate was of the opinion that 'the physical effort of mule leading is such that double pay for muleteers is underpayment'. The problem facing Wingate, of course, was 'the great difficulty in the British Army of finding the indispensable minimum of persons who could tell one end of an animal from the other'. Sadly only one or two of the mules would ever see India again. Most would be killed, eaten or set free behind Japanese lines.

The 2nd Battalion Burma Rifles comprised of native Burmese troops led by British officers, most of whom were already working in Burma when war broke out. They knew the countryside and they spoke the language of their men. Wingate later stated that they were the finest men that he had ever had under his command in the field. Their forte was reconnaissance. Carrying out patrols in enemy territory, gathering local intelligence, handling boats and living off the countryside were all tasks at which the Burmese hillmen excelled. They were also very loyal to their officers and a bond existed between officers and men that had no comparison in the British Army regimental system. Their commander was Lieutenant Colonel L.G. Wheeler, who would be posthumously awarded the DSO after being killed by a sniper some months later, on the way back to India. The Battalion would win two DSOs, one MBE, one Order of Burma, seven Military Crosses, twenty-one Burma Gallantry Medals (equivalent to the Distinguished Conduct Medal or the Indian Order of Merit) and twenty-seven Mentions in Despatches. Towards the end of the operation, after Wingate ordered his brigade to disperse and return in small groups to India, the 'Burrifs' came into their own, scouting for the enemy, walking alone into villages in search of food and seeking out boats with which to cross the Irrawaddy and Chindwin Rivers.

Wingate's brigade would be divided into two Groups. The Northern Group consisted of the following elements: Brigade Headquarters commanded by Wingate (250 all ranks); Burma Rifles Headquarters commanded by Wheeler (150 all ranks); Headquarters 2 Group (120 all ranks); 3, 4, 5, 7 and 8 Columns, each of 330 all ranks (total strength 2,200 men, 850 animals). The Southern Group comprised Headquarters 1 Group, plus 1 and 2 columns, and had a total of almost 1,000 men and 250 animals. Number 6 Column had been broken up due to sickness and shortage of men, and the remainder divided up amongst the other columns.

Wingate's plan was to take his brigade across the Chindwin River at Tonhe and over the south-north Zibyu Taungdan Escarpment just west of the line between Pinbon and Pinlebu (see map on Page 11). The Mu River would then be crossed and the Mangin mountain range climbed before reaching the main Japanese south-north supply line, the Mandalay-Myitkyina railway. The line would be demolished at various points and then, continuing eastwards, the Irrawaddy River could be crossed. Thereafter the whole force could continue to harass the enemy, with support from friendly hill tribes in the area. Perhaps the force could sit out the monsoon in the hills, supplied by air, or maybe they could continue eastwards into China and thence back to India. It was an ambitious plan.

Order of Battle: 77th Indian Infantry Brigade
Commander: Brigadier Orde C. Wingate DSO, late Royal Artillery.
Brigade Major: Major R.B.G. Bromhead, Royal Berkshire Regiment, later Major G.M. Anderson, Highland Light Infantry.
Staff Captain: Captain H.J. Lord, Border Regiment.

Number 1 (Southern) Group
Commander: Lieutenant Colonel Alexander, 3/2nd Gurkha Rifles.
Adjutant: Captain Birtwhistle, 3/2nd Gurkha Rifles.
No. 1 Column: Major G. Dunlop, MC, Royal Scots.
No. 2 Column: Major A. Emmett, 3/2nd Gurkha Rifles.

Number 2 (Northern) Group
Commander: Lieutenant Colonel S.A. Cooke, Lincolnshire Regiment, attached The King's Regiment.
Adjutant: Captain D. Hastings, King's Regiment.
No. 3 Column: Major J.M. Calvert, Royal Engineers.
No. 4 Column: Major Conron, 3/2nd Gurkha Rifles, later Major R.B.G. Bromhead, Royal Berkshire Regiment.
No. 5 Column: Major B.E. Fergusson, Black Watch.
No. 7 Column: Major K.D. Gilkes, King's Regiment.
No. 8 Column: Major W.P. Scott, King's Regiment.

2nd Battalion, The Burma Rifles
Commander: Lieutenant Colonel L.G. Wheeler, Burma Rifles.
Adjutant: Captain P.C. Buchanan, Burma Rifles.

The dividing line between the Japanese forces in Burma and the British forces in India was the Chindwin River. Wingate's problem was how to get his 3,000 men and 1,000 animals through the Corps front and across the river, and walk some 150 miles to the railway without interception. All main roads, rivers and railway lines in Burma run from south to north, forming a series of hurdles for the men to cross during the course of the expedition. Careful planning was the key. No one knew whether the Japanese would be waiting on the far bank of the Chindwin, and if they were not and the crossing was successful, whether they would be found in force around the Zibyu Taungdan Escarpment, the first obstacle to climb.

In order to confuse the enemy as to the intention of the Brigade, a diversionary force of 1,000 men and 250 animals would cross the Chindwin further south. 1 (Southern) Group, consisting of a Headquarters plus 1 and 2 Gurkha Rifle Columns, would cross at Auktaung, just south of Sittaung. A small force led by Major Jefferies, commander of 142 Commando Company, would accompany them. Jefferies would wear the uniform of a brigadier to convince the enemy that Wingate was with them. As soon as the group was across, its commander, Lieutenant Colonel Alexander, had orders to slip away unobserved over the mountains to the east, proceed at speed to the railway near Kyaikthin, attack it in passing and then cross the Irrawaddy at Tagaung, before continuing on to the mountains around Mongmit to await the arrival of the main force or further orders. It would mean a march of 250 miles through enemy occupied territory (see map on Page 11).

Chapter 3

Assembling the Circus

The monsoon was in full swing when Major Mike Calvert joined Wingate's new brigade at Saugor where, in typical fashion, Wingate had chosen a camp site many miles from the nearest road, right in the thick of the jungle. He later recalled: 'Training with this human dynamo was tough but stimulating. After marching for miles and fighting mock battles in the thick bush we would strip to the waist in the steamy rain and sit round an eighth-century well, part of an ancient temple now in ruins, listening to Wingate propound his new lore of the jungle.'

During the evenings the officers would sit around trying to think what to call themselves. They were known as the Long-Range Penetration Brigade and later as Special Force, but they wanted something better that would sum up in one word what they were trying to be and do. After training was completed and the Brigade was staging through Tamu on the Assam-Burma border, prior to crossing the Chindwin, Wingate found the answer. He asked Captain Aung Thin, one of the Burmese officers, what was the national creature of Burma. He suggested the peacock, but had to think again as Wingate considered a peacock to be unwarlike, so Aung Thin suggested the Chinthe, the mythical beast, half-lion and half-eagle, statues of which guard the entrances to many Burmese temples. Wingate thought the Chinthe symbolized the close co-operation between ground and air that was necessary for successful behind-the-lines fighting. The name soon became 'Chindit' although it was not really established until after the expedition.

Wingate always contended that any ordinary soldier could be trained to operate behind the enemy lines. There was no formal selection system as used in modern times by regiments such as the Special Air Service. However, the unfit were weeded out as the training progressed and in fact 6 Column had to be broken up as those without the mental and physical abilities to survive in the jungle were sent to other units. As the word got around that a special force was being formed, officers and men from other units came forward to volunteer. We will now meet some of them.

Lieutenant Ken Spurlock

Wingate's new Signals Officer arrived straight from a commando course held at Ambala, where signallers were being trained to work for 'V' Force amongst the Shan tribesmen of Burma. He had never heard of 77 Indian Infantry Brigade and was most surprised when he stepped off the train at Abchand near Saugor to find that instead of a proper railway station there was just a dusty shack. A soldier was working nearby, stripped to the waist and wearing some sort of Australian hat.

He asked Spurlock, 'Where the bloody hell are you going?'

Ignoring the lack of respect due to an officer, Spurlock informed him that he was looking for 77 Brigade.

'You've got a bloody long walk then, boy!' replied the soldier, pointing to a muddy track leading into the jungle.

When Spurlock found Brigade Headquarters there was just a handful of tents, and four or five officers and a score of other ranks scurrying around. Spurlock was directed to Wingate's tent by the Brigade Major. He straightened his uniform, coughed and pushed his way through the tent flap. Behind a trestle table sat Brigadier Orde Wingate, stark naked with the exception of his boots, wearing a Wolsey helmet, with a fly swat in his hand.

'Are you Spurlock?' the Brigadier enquired. When the perspiring officer replied, Wingate shuffled the papers and maps on his desk and handed over a sheaf of papers. 'The success of this operation depends on you. Take these plans away and look at them. If you think that the signals will not work we may just as well pack up and go home.'

Spurlock was taken to a tent containing a table and a chair where he sat down and began to read. The plans detailed Wingate's ideas on long-range penetration and described the composition of the columns, the equipment and the tactics to be used. From the signals point of view the Brigadier would need to communicate with each of the units in the field, as well as headquarters and the RAF in India. Three types of wireless transmitters would be required, together with trained operators who could also repair the sets as well as work them; all the problems involved in sending signals from valleys as well as mountains had to be surmounted. Finally Spurlock walked back to Wingate's tent and handed the plans back to him.

'Given the right equipment, sir, I think we can do it'.

'Good man,' smiled Wingate as he rose from his desk. 'Now follow me.'

Wingate strode off to show Spurlock where the battalions were going to be camped when they arrived. After walking for a mile or so they came to a fast-flowing river, about 40 yards across. Wingate kicked off his boots and plunged into the water, still wearing his helmet. Without hesitation Spurlock did the same and swam steadily to the other side. They climbed out of the water and inspected the clearing where some of the infantry would set up camp. Then

Wingate turned around and started to swim back to the far side. By the time the pair had got across again they were quite a way from their boots and walked back to reclaim them. It dawned on Spurlock that this had been a test and he had apparently passed with flying colours. If he had refused to follow the Brigadier into the river he would probably have been returned to his unit. After that he could not put a foot wrong and eventually became quite close to Wingate, learning first hand about his adventures in other campaigns.

Major George Dunlop

Major George Dunlop had plenty of reasons to be fed up. He had just recovered his health following the retreat from India and was posted in October 1942 to command Number 1 Column. Their main fighting unit was a company of young Gurkhas, but as Dunlop was not expecting the command, his knowledge of the Gurkha language was rather limited. Furthermore the Company Commander, who was Dunlop's Second-in-Command (2 i/c), Captain Vivian Weatherall, was posted over to Number 2 Column a couple of weeks after he arrived and it took three months of protesting before he was returned, just prior to the start of the expedition. Dunlop lay the blame at the door of the 2 i/c of 3/2nd Gurkhas who disapproved of the idea of outsiders being appointed to command Gurkha units. Events were to prove the he did indeed know what he was talking about. The Gurkha changes his loyalties slowly, if ever, and from the very first Dunlop was continually coming up against a blank wall of misunderstanding. In fact, Lieutenant Clarke was the only British officer to remain with the unit from its first formation until the return of the expedition.

The men that the British officers would need to rely on to pass their commands to the Gurkha riflemen were the Viceroy Commissioned Officer, Subedar Kulbir, and the Non-Commissioned Officers (NCOs) who had recently been promoted due to the expansion of the unit and were still learning their new roles. There had also been a fair turnover of men between June and December.

As the year came to an end the column was brought up to War Establishment with the arrival of stores and equipment, and new blood in the shape of the column doctor, Captain N. Stocks, RAMC; the RAF Liaison Officer, Flight Lieutenant J. Redman; the Animal Transport Officer, Lieutenant J. Fowler with the rest of the mules; and two young subalterns straight from the officer training unit, Second Lieutenants Harvey and Wormald. They had to learn quickly – there were two river-crossing exercises planned and wireless training to be carried out with the newly arrived Signals Section.

George Dunlop and his officers were called to Brigade Headquarters in Imphal and given their instructions which were short and to the point:

a) Together with Number 2 Column and under the orders of Number 1 Group commander, to create a diversion to the South of the main objectives (of which they were naturally not given details) in order to draw off as many Japanese as possible.
b) To meet Brigadier Wingate in the low ground beyond Tagaung Taung on the east side of the Irrawaddy River.
c) Failing further orders to go to Mongmit and raise rebellion amongst the Burmese.

They were the last orders received from the Brigadier for six weeks.

Major George Bromhead

Major George Bromhead was one of three of the original seven column commanders still alive when research for this book began in 1995 (Calvert, Bromhead, Dunlop). He knew Wingate well.

I first knew Wingate in 1936 during the Palestine rebellion. I was an intelligence officer and as the rebellion continued and units were added to the brigade we began to look like a division. (In those days a Brigade Headquarters had four staff officers!) Eventually a Division HQ was sent from England to take over and Wingate was the intelligence staff officer.

The next time we met was in New Delhi six years later. I was doing a temporary staff job at GHQ. One day down a passage came a slightly untidy figure wearing a Wolseley helmet instead of the more normal topee. This I later knew was Wingate's trademark. The figure greeted me with 'Just the sort of chap I am looking for, I need a Brigade Major.' My temporary staff job was nearly complete, so my boss let me go and there I was. Wingate explained that he had been running guerrilla operations behind Italian lines in Ethiopia, now finished since the enemy had packed in. Wavell had sent for him to do a similar job behind Jap lines in the jungle. Thus was 77 Indian Infantry Brigade formed. A British battalion raised for defence in the United Kingdom and sent to India for peacekeeping and, on average, rather old for their new role. So we had the unenviable task of sorting out the older members. A Gurkha battalion rather too young. There are no birth certificates in Nepal! Lastly a Burmese battalion which had previous experience in the retreat through Burma. One of their majors, who was left out because of age, I met in a hotel in Delhi. 'What are you doing here?' I said. 'A bit of leave before I go back to Rangoon. Yes, I walk. You see I am working for intelligence and every few weeks I have to walk across Burma to report and I take a spot of leave in a comfortable hotel.' And we left him out for reason of age!

Two incidents stand out in my mind during jungle training. First, an early monsoon was drumming on my office tent and the flies were sagging.

Approaching through the mud came a pair of bare feet; as they came nearer a pair of naked knees appeared, and then some more naked body and finally Wingate crouched under the tent flies – wearing his Wolseley helmet and nothing else! Second, the river where the Gurkha unit was camped started to rise and we were out of touch. Nothing for it, I had to swim through the flooded water to make contact. It was a nightmare. Every animal which could swim was in the water with me. I could rest by holding the branches of trees which was what the snakes were doing. An alligator gave me a dirty look. But it ended happily. The Gurkhas had taken to the trees and were safe if not happy, and the water went down quite quickly.

Wingate had a convenient theory about official correspondence: if left in the pending tray, most of it answered itself. If really important a reminder would follow and that was the time to reply. Sponsored by Wavell, he had of course the ear of all the heads of department in Delhi. However, he didn't understand the Indian bureaucracy and didn't want to, so every time he visited Delhi I had to nip up next day to get the results in black and white and signed. I didn't mind, I knew the system and had a girlfriend there.

Perhaps the most important aspect during training was to work out supply by air. We had an RAF officer volunteer with each column, but there was no radio in those days to enable us to speak to the pilot from the ground. The method of marking the dropping zone was with fires in a recognisable pattern and the pilot had to rely on his fellows on the ground. Working out the rations caused many a headache. They had to be compact enough for each man to carry six days on his back and within the resources of India to produce, not to mention acceptable to the religions concerned.

Sergeant Tony Aubrey

Sergeant Tony Aubrey had only been in India for a week when he was sent from the Reinforcement Depot at Deolali to join the 13th Kings. They started the first of their long training marches on 19 September, when they left for a jungle village which was to be their centre for the next period of training. They had 52 miles to cover, ate their breakfast at 0415 hours and set off at 0500. They would abandon the usual three-abreast method of marching; from now on they would march in single file in a column 'snake' a mile and a quarter long. They marched for six hours with only two short halts and it was 1100 hours before they stopped for food and could experience the pleasant sensation known only to soldiers when they remove their heavy packs and stretch their shoulders. The hot stew was welcome, but for some there would be no water to wash it down with. Against orders they had emptied their water bottles and would now have to go without. They would learn that lesson the hard way.

One thing that did surprise the men was that the officers, including the Brigadier, marched on foot as well, even though there were chargers available.

Not only that but in addition to the same packs and equipment carried by the men, the officers carried field glasses, revolvers and rifles as well. The carrying of rifles was not done just to impress the men – enemy snipers are taught to seek out the officers first, but if they are carrying rifles just like the men it might aid their longevity.

The men resumed their march at 1600 hours, after the heat of the day had passed. The next two hours were the worst of the day, until dusk began to fall. It was still very warm, the sweat and the dust formed a sort of mud pack around their eyes, and the flies were everywhere. They halted at 1800 hours for ten minutes, then continued marching until 0500 hours the following morning, with a ten-minute rest period every two hours. All through the night trains of bullock carts passed them, loaded with sacks of beri-leaves, the Indian substitute for cigarette papers. Most of the drivers of the carts were asleep, confident that the bullocks knew where they were bound for.

The long march was the beginning of the toughening-up process for the troops. An ambulance followed the column, but only the very ill were picked up. If a man fell out because his feet were blistered, his blisters were dried and plastered, and he marched on. If he fell out because he was too tired, or if it was his nature to do so, then he was left to find his way either forward or back. Thereafter he would be returned to his unit and, as far as Wingate's expedition was concerned, that was the end of him. Eventually the men would manage 4 miles per hour, but it would take practice and more marches to toughen them up. As dawn broke they marched wearily into their allotted training areas, dropped their packs and removed the boots from their steaming feet. Then it was time for breakfast.

Wingate had a lot to teach the men and not enough time in which to do it. There would be no time for drinking beer or playing skittles and there would be no tents or beds either. Their life now would be modelled on what was likely to happen when they went into action. The ground would be their mattress, the sky their roof and their pillow was a kitbag.

Each column was divided up into four platoons, and they slept by platoons, with each one responsible for its own all-round defence of its segment of the entire bivouac area. There was no attempt at running a mess for the NCOs or officers – they all ate together, worked together and slept together. It bred respect between the officers and men, who were not used to such familiarity with the officer class.

Food was rather monotonous with biscuits and bully beef forming the staple diet. There were no restrictions on the use of rifles and ammunition, however, and any animals spotted were fair game for the pot. This included peacocks, goats and the occasional monkey. The men did their own cooking individually in their mess tins, with instruction from men of the Burma Rifles. They even learnt the gentle art of making the invaluable chupatti, which was easy to make and sustaining.

Wingate was a great believer in the common or garden onion and sacks of them were usually available. They could be eaten raw, added to stews in a mess tin or just boiled on their own.

A typical day began at 0600 hours with half an hour of strenuous bayonet training and a period of unarmed combat. Sergeant Aubrey was given the job of instructing the Burmese in his column and they were keen to learn. After breakfast there were lectures on jungle craft and the use of compass and map reading, a skill that most men would find useful before the expedition was over. During the heat of the day the men rested, then from 1500 to 1700 hours they carried out such fatigues as were necessary, mainly the construction of their sanitary arrangements. They also prepared lines for the mules, which some of the Gurkhas had gone to fetch. They were responsible for the protection of their own mule lines and this meant clearing an area of jungle in the middle of the column perimeter. They would drive in pegs in lines 9 feet apart, attach tether chains to them and open four clearance paths for them through the surrounding scrub, one leading to each point of the compass, so that no matter from which direction they were attacked, there would always be an escape route for the mules.

There were many schemes in which the men would be sent out laying ambushes, blowing bridges and attacking other columns, but there was one notable difference between the schemes designed by Wingate and the ordinary tactical exercises they were used to. The difference was that every single man knew before the start exactly what it was about. He knew as much about the strength and dispositions of the enemy as the Brigadier did, he knew the objective and what kind of country he would be operating in. Whereas in most units the Commanding Officer would brief the company commanders and the RSM, who in turn would brief the platoon commanders and they the NCOs, who in turn would give the orders to the men, Wingate's idea was that the main body of each column would be put in the picture the night before by the Column Commander himself.

The training was hard and occasionally dangerous. Each column had a platoon of commandos with them and they would demonstrate the art of blowing things up. One day a commando made the mistake of tamping a stick of gelignite into its hole with his bayonet. The explosive does not take kindly to such treatment and showed its displeasure by sending the offending commando into the hereafter and one of those watching lost a leg.

Sergeant Aubrey took to the training like a fish to water and soon became a fit and valuable member of 6 Column. Unfortunately many others could not stand the pace of the training or were weeded out as unfit for jungle warfare.

The column would eventually be broken up and the remnants sent to join one or other of the seven columns remaining. While that was going on Sergeant Aubrey had other things to attend to, for soon he was to leave the training area and take part in a reconnaissance patrol to see what would be waiting for them once they crossed the Chindwin River.

Arthur Willshaw RAF

Two of the most important innovations to be tried out by Wingate's men were the use of long-range radio communications and the dropping of supplies to the men in the field by the Royal Air Force. Wingate took the unusual but very sensible decision to take Royal Air Force personnel with him to co-ordinate the air drops. Who better to talk to a pilot in the air than a pilot on the ground? In April 1942, a message was received at Headquarters 222 Group, RAF in Colombo, Ceylon: 'Volunteers are required for a special mission – officers who have knowledge of Japanese aircraft and wireless operators who have a thorough knowledge of ground-to-air communication.' Arthur Willshaw, a wireless operator, received the message in code. An alleged friend in the Orderly Room told him the rumour was that a captured Japanese aircraft in India was wanted for examination in the UK – a pilot to fly it and a wireless operator to work signal stations on the route. 'This was just up my street,' Arthur recalled.

> I had been a wireless operator in Singapore from 1939 until it fell and I had worked every wireless and signals station from Singapore to the UK during this time. I wanted to fly and above all I wanted to get home to take an eagerly awaited chance at 'Aircrew'. After an interview with my Commanding Officer a signal was received from Headquarters at New Delhi instructing me to report for an interview with the AOC-in-C. It was on Colombo railway station that I met up with my first two compatriots, a Flight Lieutenant Longmore and a Sergeant Davies, who knew no more than I did – except a rumour. Their rumour very nicely agreed with mine – little did we know!
>
> During the journey from Ceylon, across India to Delhi, we got to know each other. Arthur Longmore was an ex-rubber planter from Malaya, the first man, he told me, ever to loop a glider. Cliff Davies was an Australian, quiet, studious, wanting anything except a nice secure desk job. And so to Headquarters, New Delhi. Marble staircases, a very ornate office and a personal interview with Air Vice-Marshal D'Albiac. His questions rather puzzled me. What were my teeth like? Could I live on hard biscuits for a few weeks? And finally, the truth! A senior Army officer was going behind the Japanese lines in Burma. We had to try to get on to a Japanese airfield where we would take some photographs, probably even throw a few grenades, and then a quick return to India. He assured us that this would be all over in a matter of weeks. The clinching argument came: 'How long have you been

overseas?' 'Two and a half years, sir.' 'H'm – well by the time you have done this job we should be able to see you home immediately afterwards.' Twelve months later, having walked some 1,500 miles over some of the most difficult country in the world, in the company of some of the world's finest soldiers, the Air Vice-Marshal kept his word!

In those twelve months I had enough adventures to last me a dozen lifetimes. We were ordered to report to a Long-Range Penetration Group, training in the central provinces at Jhansi in India. Our RAF element had now been joined by Flight Sergeant Allan Fidler and we arrived at Jhansi in best uniform – tailored gabardine – in the middle of the monsoon. Getting off our train we were told that the brigade we were to join was in camp at Malthone some ten miles away in the jungle. On asking for transport we were none too politely told there was none available and that orders were 'all personnel joining the brigade were to walk it'. Leaving our suitcases behind, walk we did, the first few miles along a reasonable road and then a plunge on to a jungle track which we followed to our destination. Most of the track was signposted with the odd Army notice board and for the last few miles it was completely under water. Wet, miserable, bedraggled we reached the Brigade Headquarters – just a few tents in a jungle clearing. All around, people seemed to be living in trees and the surrounding water was deep enough in places to swim in. Tired, weary and fed up with life in general, I found myself having to make a bed in the forks of a large tree and then, dreaming of wild animals, especially snakes, I dropped off to sleep.

And so began three months of hard and bitter experience. How I hated it – used to the comforts of barrack life, it became a fight for existence. We were paraded before daybreak, plunged into icy cold rivers, taught how to build bridges, how to cross lakes and fast-flowing rivers, how to shoot, how to handle explosives, how to be amateur Tarzans swinging on ropes from tree to tree, how to travel in the jungle and, above all, how to live off the jungle. The explosives tent was always open – take what you want and learn how to use it. Woe betide the careless! March, march, march ten, fifteen, twenty miles from camp along the only track in existence. We were then turned off the track into the jungle and told to find our way back to Headquarters. Added information was that the track we had come down was mined and anyone found on it was likely to be shot. It was – and they were! Soon we began to be exactly what Brigadier Wingate, the brigade commander, required – an efficient jungle warfare force.

We lived off the jungle, no food except biscuits – if we wanted food we foraged for it. We ate snakes, frogs, lizards, fish, roots, leaves, in fact we tried everything at least once! Pigeons were a great favourite, but there isn't much left of a pigeon that's been shot with a .303 from short range. Six pigeons just about made a meal. Stuffed with broken biscuit and served with young bamboo shoots – I can still taste them. But, of course, as we foraged, game became scarcer. Peacocks, which were plentiful to start with (they taste very much like sweet turkey), soon left the area and most of the other bigger game too. This meant foraging further and further afield into the jungle in order to get food, in order to live. We learned by experience which leaves, when dried, made tobacco substitute and which leaves to use for other vital necessities. One of my most painful recollections was the time when, somewhat in a hurry, I picked the largest leaf handy, only to find, too late, that it was covered with small hairs that, when crushed, caused a nasty itchy rash. I never made that mistake again! And so after three months of this type of living we had toughened up considerably. Flabby flesh had disappeared, chests had filled out, muscles developed where only outlines had existed before and we began to glory in a new feeling of self-reliance that was to be so important in the coming task.

I found myself allocated to the Headquarters column together with Flight Sergeant Allan Fidler and Squadron Leader (now promoted) Longmore. Our main job was to co-ordinate the requirements of all columns, the RAF element of each being an RAF officer and two NCOs. These teams would recce for a suitable area for an air supply drop, co-ordinate the requirements of all columns and pass the information to the Brigade HQ column via the RAF wireless set. They would then go out, light flare paths in a line with the dropping zone and supervise the drop from the ground. My job on HQ column was to keep wireless contact with all the columns and also with RAF HQ New Delhi who planned and put into execution the requirement for the air supply drops. We were to carry our wireless equipment on mules and learning how to look after and cope with these obstinate animals became part of our daily life. Together with these mules we marched many, many miles on exercises in the central provinces of India.

Our wireless equipment was the best then available, but still formed quite a cumbersome load which was carried in two leather panniers – one on each side of a mule's back. Ensuring that we had the best equipment caused quite a stir. I was instructed to proceed to Karachi to the Maintenance Unit at Drigh Road and to take what we needed from the shelves of the depot, then to bring the whole lot of equipment back by rail to Jhansi. I was assured that everything had been arranged and that I would be expected. I travelled by train from Jhansi to Gwalior, thence by BOAC Sunderland flying boat across India to Karachi. I was anything but expected, but put yourselves in their shoes; here was an NCO, with only an identification card, saying that he was authorised to take what he pleased of your scarce and important stocks. In next to no time I found myself in custody in the guardroom, and it was only when a disbelieving officer placed a telephone call directly to Air Headquarters, New Delhi and spoke to Air Vice-Marshal D'Albiac – who, on being given a situation report, requested the call be transferred to the

Commanding Officer of the depot – did things start to happen my way. I found myself walking around the radio spares section saying, 'Ten of those, twelve of these, all of those', while a very worried equipment officer was wondering how on earth he was to get replacements. All the items were packed on the spot and, together with a Corporal Stonelake, two truckloads of equipment were escorted across India by rail back to Jhansi. I will always remember the look on Corporal Stonelake's face, whom I am certain had been specially chosen to ensure that the precious equipment reached a service destination, when he saw our jungle home, and I know that an audible sigh of relief passed his lips when he escaped back to a normal RAF existence.

Another three months followed, getting prepared, getting fitter, experimenting, breaking down the myth that the Japanese were the world's finest jungle fighters. It was drummed into our heads that the jungle was like the sea – boundless – in which men could move around for weeks, even months on end, within rifle shot of the enemy but without ever encountering him. We were taught to regard the jungle as our environment, and as a friend.

Halfway through our training the sickness rate became very high and Wingate had to put his foot down. 'Everyone is to be taught to be doctor minded,' he said. 'Although it is all right in normal civilian life, where ample medical facilities are available, it will not apply to us in the jungle. You have to diagnose your own complaints and then cure yourselves. When we go into action and you are sick, it will be just too bad. We shall not stop for you, for our very lives may be jeopardised by waiting for stragglers. If you are sick you are of no use to us – you become an unwanted liability, we shall leave you to affect your own salvation.' Attending sick parades without good cause became a punishable offence and doctors only gave treatment to the seriously injured and really ill.

We were all given our own small dispensary – quinine and atebrin for malaria, sulfaguanadin for dysentery, and other sulphur drugs for infectious wounds. We learned lessons that were to prove invaluable during our months behind the Japanese lines.

Individual training progressed to platoon training, platoon to column, column to group, and group would exercise against group. Problems arose on all sides, signals, ciphers, transport, demolitions, all having to be solved and solved quickly. Exercises got stiffer, those that were considered unfit were weeded out. Soldiers were made NCOs and NCOs were made soldiers and had to prove themselves worthy of the leadership that would be required of them before either being ousted or re-admitted to the fold.

Lieutenant R. Allen Wilding

Lieutenant R. Allen Wilding was sent to India on an officers' draft in May 1942 and much against his will, he was sent on a cipher course the following

November. Determined to join a fighting unit, he was rewarded for coming second in his class with a posting to 77 Indian Infantry Brigade. He detrained at Lalitpur, dressed in immaculate bush shirt and slacks fairly creaking with starch, shoes brilliantly polished and revolver clean, bright and slightly oiled. A 3-tonner arrived and transported him to the brigade location.

> There I found a camp fire in the middle of the jungle with some rather scruffy officers sitting round it. Everyone was most welcoming and I was handed a soft drink. I later found out that Brigadier Wingate preferred us not to drink. Talk was resumed. It was about the terminal velocity of bombs of all things. When bedtime was upon us, the Brigade Major indicated a bush and said: 'Under that if you like.' So I slept there not at all disturbed by the information that this was splendid tiger country.
>
>   I got to know the other officers at Brigade Headquarters, with whom I was to work. The intelligence officer Captain Hosegood was a very nice chap who gave me lots of help. The signals officer Lieutenant Spurlock was quite brilliant at his job and a very good chap; we remain in touch. There were also two delightful Burmese officers named Major Po and Captain Aung Thin. Captain Sawba Pa was a Shan Prince and came to us as a replacement for Major Po; the Major being a bit old for the trip. We called him 'Pop'. He had a ferocious orderly whom we called 'Smiler', if he thought you were not being polite to his Officer he was inclined to whip out his Dah (a sort of knife). 'Pop' was a great lad and all ranks liked him. He tried to help out with my ciphers one day but everything came out as 'paraffin'. I think ciphers were just not his thing.
>
>   Major R. Ramsay from the Royal Army Medical Corps was our Senior Medical Officer. He was a very fine surgeon and an amusing companion. Although not yet 30 he gazed on our antics like an indulgent uncle.
>
>   Lieutenant L.W. Rose of the 6th Gurkhas had had a busy war. To France with the British Expeditionary Force, back via Dunkirk, commissioned in the Sherwood Foresters, posted to India, attached to the 6th Gurkhas, conducted a number of patrols on the east bank of the Chindwin and must have done pretty well because he was later promoted to Major and was awarded the Military Cross and that is a proper soldier's decoration.
>
>   The Brigadier found himself short of an Officer to command the Brigade HQ Defence Platoon when the officer detailed for the job came down with appendicitis. He commandeered Rose, but unfortunately forgot to tell anyone and I received an agitated signal in cipher asking if we had seen him because they were thinking of posting him as a deserter! I was able to reply that he was toiling away as Defence Platoon Commander and more than earning his pay.
>
>   Captain Moxham, Royal Indian Army Service Corps was posted to us as Brigade RASC Officer (BRASCO). I never go to know him very well but he

was the most organised chap I have ever known. No searching through his pockets for him! If you had been bitten by a snake, a razor blade and potassium permanganate crystals were THERE, not usually, but always – his jack-knife lurked in the dent in his bush hat –not usually, but always. Sadly he died, I am not sure whether it was just before or just after his party was put in the bag.

Flight Lieutenant Tooth, Royal Air Force, reached us at road head as 2i/c to Squadron Leader Longmore. He was usually a cheerful soul but on his first day's march he came upon me, during the mid-day break, beavering away at my ciphers and said mournfully, 'Twenty four hours ago I was drinking gin in New Delhi and now I find myself an infantryman and your Brigadier has put me in charge of those elephants! And they'll die! And the Army will stop their value out of my pay.' He needn't have bothered. We only took them as far as the Chindwin and they all survived. Anyway he was no more in charge than I was – the Elephants made it quite clear that they only took orders from their oozies (Mahouts) and the oozies were an independent lot.

I gathered that our task, briefly, was to march into Burma, create such havoc as we could and then return to India. The Brigadier's idea was that, as long as we had good signal communications and reasonable air superiority, we could do without conventional lines of communication. This may sound pretty obvious now – it wasn't then. The top brass, except for Wavell, were to put it mildly sceptical. It was up to us to prove them wrong. We expected to be seriously outnumbered and the Brigadier evolved the 'dispersal' procedure.

The whole brigade was split up into 'dispersal groups' each of approximately platoon strength. On 'First Dispersal' signalled by four Gs on the bugle, each dispersal group commander was to get his group into cover, arrange all-round defence, and await orders. The 'Second Dispersal' was signalled by the 'alarm' on the bugle. On hearing this, each dispersal group 'broke trail' and proceeded to an RV previously arranged. Everyone was supposed to know this and it was always a) forwards, rather than back the way we had come, and b) a line of some sort, i.e. a stream, so that if you missed the exact spot you could scout up and down until you found it. I got all this information from Graham Hosegood who added cheerfully that we should expect fifty per cent casualties.

Wingate was, most certainly, a great man. A lot of little men have done their best to denigrate him. They would have been better employed trying to help him. He had great physical and moral courage and possessed a will of iron. I have been fortunate in that I have spent most of my life in the company of very intelligent people, so I am some sort of judge of intelligence. His was a blazing intelligence. He was a great reader of the Old

Testament. I suppose he was possibly the last of the 'Sword and Bible Generals'. Of course he had his faults; he could or would not suffer fools gladly, he could be rather rude and he was ruthless. Ruthlessness is, I fear, something that all commanders must have. He never threw a life away, but you always felt that he realised that his life and the life of each of us was expendable if it was necessary. I remember, when things were very bad, sitting under a bush with my Sergeant trying to decipher a more than usually corrupt signal and hearing him ask the MO, 'How long can Wilding last?' The MO said, 'About a week I think.' The Brigadier's reply was, 'I only want him for another two days.' Of course neither of them knew I was within earshot and were taken aback by my not very respectful interjection, 'After that I suppose you will have me shot like the bloody mules.' But he was also very kind. One day I had developed a raging headache. The Brigadier was passing and stopped to ask how I was. When I explained that I had a cracking headache, he sat down and started to tell me some hilarious stories about the liberation of Abyssinia, in which he took a prominent part. His description of his entry into Addis Ababa on a most photogenic white horse sticks in my memory. When he had finished he put his hand on my head and went away. My headache had gone.

As the Brigade was formed, the size of the headquarters increased until it was nearly as large as a column, but with the exception of the Gurkha Defence Platoon, it was not a coherent fighting force. Apart from staff officers, their orderlies and grooms, there was an intelligence section, a small cipher section, an RAF signals section, the senior medical officer and his orderlies and a propaganda section, complete with loudspeakers. All these, with their respective mules, horses, bullocks and those animals' attendants, came to about 200 people. Allen Wilding was allocated half of a mule, to carry his cipher tables.

About ten days after I joined the brigade, we set out for Saugor. It was about 100 miles and we took four days to do it. We arrived on 4 December 1942 and set out for Jhansi on the ninth, my thirty-second birthday. The march, which was mainly at night, took nine days and the distance was between 150 and 160 miles. I used to go to sleep on the march, and, as my normal gait was quicker than that of the column, I often found myself marching alongside the Brigadier who was leading. At first he asked if there was anything wrong, but later he got used to me and merely said, 'Wake up Wilding.' Sleeping on the march is a useful knack, but should not be used in enemy country!

Chapter 4

First Across the River

One Sunday morning, six weeks after he had arrived in the jungle, Sergeant Tony Aubrey was summoned to see his Column Commander, Major Anderson. He was told to report the following morning to a certain map reference, to proceed on special duty. He was told to bring all his kit with him and the Quartermaster Sergeant gave him 50 rupees, which was indeed a lot of money. He was also sworn to secrecy.

The next morning he reported at the appointed place to find Lance Corporal Tommy Vann and Private Allnutt waiting for him. Vann was worth his weight in gold; he never complained and had a great sense of humour and the three of them discussed the various possibilities of what awaited them until a 3-ton truck rumbled into sight. On board the truck were a score of Burma Riflemen and their two officers, Lieutenant Bruce and Captain Herring, the latter known by his nickname of 'Fish'. They climbed aboard and suffered a long, dusty ride until they reached their destination.

The next morning they were issued with various extra items of kit, which convinced them that they were destined for a great adventure. They exchanged their pith helmets for felt terais and signed for mosquito ointment, water sterilizing kits, camouflage capes, mosquito veils for their faces, calf-high hockey boots, a Kashmir blanket and seven ration bags, containing tea, sugar, milk powder, rice, salt and dried fruits. Sergeant Aubrey takes up the story:

Next morning, Captain Herring gave me a railway warrant for myself and the two others and warned me that aboard the train we must have nothing to do with him or his Burmese, for security reasons. He also advised me not even to look at the destination on my ticket until we were aboard the train. When we looked we discovered that we were bound for Manipur Road. None of us knew where this was, but a European who was sharing our compartment had a railway guide which we borrowed. Then we knew the worst!

After six days in train and boat we arrived in Manipur, and from there had a hair-raising drive by lorry to Imphal. The road climbed steadily all the way, making a series of hairpin bends, and perching precariously on the edge of breath-taking drops. At intervals we saw wrecked vehicles, and I, for one, was scared stiff of sharing their fate.

We did not stop long in Imphal, and were soon on our way again in another truck to a post nearer the Burma frontier. This was manned by a Battalion of the Mahratta Regiment, with whom we spent the remainder of that day and the night, eating heartily of curry and rice, and dumping our heavy kit, such as army blankets, greatcoats and all our spare clothing, with the exception of one complete change. In the morning we set off on foot along the narrow dirt track leading to Burma. Countless gangs of coolies were working on widening this road, and we passed two or three bull-dozers at their gigantic shovelling.

Our numbers were now much smaller than the original party, as Lieutenant Bruce had left us to strike out on his own at Imphal, taking with him all the Burmese, except six. Our first halt was at Tamu, seventeen miles farther up the track. This had been, in the days of peace, an elephant station belonging to the company of which Captain Herring had been an employee. He was the ideal man for the sort of job we had in hand, for he had been in Burma for a good many years, spoke the language like a native, and knew intimately the country through which we would travel. Also, he had been a Territorial Officer in the Burma Rifles, and had fought against the Japanese in the retreat. He didn't like them at all, and he did love the Burmese. He was as pleased as a child with a new toy at having been given this chance of getting a bit of his own back. I don't actually know, of course, what orders he had been given about this reconnaissance, but I imagine they had simply said to him, 'Get across the Chindwin River and find out all you can. Oh, and by the way, back by the first of January, will you?'

At Tamu we collected an elephant and his mahout, Nandaw, and left on the final stage of our march to the Chindwin. The path was now very narrow, and passed through jungle denser than any I had ever seen before. Visibility was sometimes practically nil, and I was lost in amazement at the silent progress of the elephant, which manoeuvred its colossal bulk through the scrub with less fuss and commotion than that made by any of us.

Every now and again, along the edges of this ill-omened path, we came on traces of the retreat from Burma. Now it would be a single corpse, or two or three together in a melancholy huddle. Now it would be an old-fashioned motor bus, lonely and incongruous in its tropical surrounding; now a motor car or a lorry, overturned and defeated by the narrowness of the way, some heaps of bones around it showing that its occupants, too, had given up the unequal struggle.

The distance from Tamu to the Chindwin River is forty-seven miles as the crow flies and it took three days to cover it. We arrived at a spot three miles from the river on the evening of the third day, and here Captain Herring decided we should camp. Straight ahead of us on the river itself lay a large village, and he did not feel inclined to let our presence be known there until he had found out how the land lay.

As darkness fell that night, the surrounding trees and bushes, except those lighted up by the glow of our fire, disappeared from my sight and the jungle came to life. In an instant, where before it had been silent and dead, it was now full of flurries and scurries in the undergrowth, of the stealthy cracking of branches, and of squeaks and whimpers and cries. It was only then I realized that all through the days when we had been marching, the jungle about us had been absolutely silent, with an utter stillness you could almost have cut with a knife. All the birds and beasts are on the night-shift, but it is eerie and disconcerting until you are used to it.

Ever since they had crossed the frontier of Burma a day or two before, they were in country technically occupied by the Japanese. Although Japanese patrols sometimes crossed the river they did not expect to contact the enemy until they reached the far bank of the Chindwin River. It was reasonably certain that they would have posts along the river bank, due to its strategic value. To penetrate into Central Burma it is necessary to cross it and there is not a single bridge over it. The river itself presented a number of problems. The banks of sunbaked mud were steeply shelving and below water the current ran at 8 to 10 knots. Even then, when the level of the river was at its lowest it was 15 feet deep and at least 600 yards wide.

Back in the bivouac, Captain Herring outlined his plan. The first essential, he said, was secrecy. The local villagers must on no account be allowed to know that they were going to cross. They would make the crossing at night, using two boats belonging to the villagers that he had seen drawn up on the bank that morning. They were simple Burmese river boats, made out of the trunk of a tree, hollowed out and flattened on the sides and bottom. They would each hold three men and their kit, which meant that two journeys would have to be made. The plan was that Lance Corporal Vann would stay behind, together with the elephant and his mahout and would be on the lookout for their return in twenty-five days time.

At midnight they left their bivouac. Each man carried his ration bags, together with as many tins of bully beef as he could manage. He also carried 50 rupees in silver coins to pay for food or guides along the way. They also left behind their heavy Kashmir blankets, as the extra weight would not be compensated by the extra comfort. Sergeant Aubrey later recalled:

The night was pitch black and there was no moon. Captain Herring led the way, and I brought up the rear. We stole along as quietly as we knew how towards the village. The traverse of the main street held us up for twenty minutes but at last we made it, and made it in complete silence too. Not even one of the mangy pi-dogs had been awakened to give the alarm.

We were justifiably pleased with ourselves, and our pleasure was still further intensified when we reached the river bank and discovered that the two boats were still there. It had been arranged beforehand that Captain Herring should go in one boat with two Burmese, and myself in the other, with another two. I was to go first. I dumped my pack in one of the boats, slung my rifle and grabbed the bow. The two men who were to come with me seized the thwarts. 'Are you all ready?' Captain Herring asked softly. 'OK Sir' I answered. 'Off you go, then, and good luck. I'll be close behind you.' I gave my men the word and we took the boat into the water, stern-first, at a smart run. Into the water she went and not only into it, but straight under it, too, and we with her. The prudent Burmese had taken the precaution of removing a large plug from the bottom before leaving it for the night.

I don't think I've ever felt anything so cold as that water. For a minute or two, I was paralyzed. By the time I was able to draw breath I had been carried ten yards downstream, and, strong swimmer as I am, it was all I could do, burdened with my clothes and rifle, to make the shore. And no sooner had I made it than I had to plunge in again, because one of the Burmese was a poor swimmer, and I had to give him a hand. After we had got him safely back on dry land, the next half-hour was spent in diving for packs and for the two rifles of my companions, which had gone down with the boat.

At last everything was retrieved without loss, except for the damage done to the rations in our packs. I was shivering as uncontrollably as though I had a raging go of malaria, and Captain Herring made me strip to the skin and presented me with his only spare garment, a pullover. Gracefully clad in nothing but this and my soaking pair of hockey boots, I made my dreary way back in the file through the jungle. We would try again tomorrow, and this time we would make certain that whatever craft we were using didn't have a hole in the bottom of it.

As soon as it was light, Captain Herring sent Nandaw down to the village to buy what food he could and to pick up all available information. He was gone two or three hours, and when he came back his amiable face was wreathed in smiles. 'What are you finding so funny this morning?' Captain Herring asked him. He smiled more widely than ever. 'I have a message from the headman,' he said. 'Headman wants to know, why, if you want to cross the Chindwin, you don't ask him? He will be very pleased to row you across.' The village can't have been sleeping so soundly as we thought. I expect it was shaking with silent Burmese laughter.

The next night the headman produced a sampan and they were ferried over in no time. Now at last they would meet the real jungle, with the tracks surrounded by an impenetrable wall of green on both sides and a thick green roof over their heads, through which they would occasionally catch a glimpse of the sky. Two days later they came across their first village and found the villagers in a state of confusion and mourning. The Japanese had only left the night before, but they had taken all the food they managed to discover as well as some of the young men to use for slave labour. Two of the young men had refused to leave their wives and families and had been shot on the spot.

The same scenario presented itself in every village they visited. Eventually the villagers proved themselves smarter than the Japanese. They would hide the majority of their food and leave visible only enough to satisfy the capacity of the Japs. Captain Herring and his men were hospitably received and he bought enough rice and fowl to feed his men before they continued their march.

After they had marched east for fifteen days without seeing any sign of the enemy, Captain Herring decided that they had gathered enough information and that they should now return. They returned by a different and more circuitous route and, on 24 December 1942, stood on the opposite bank to their crossing point. They crossed over without difficulty to find a very happy Tommy Vann waiting for them. The next day they set off for Tamu and made camp late in the afternoon. Suddenly out of the trees appeared a British major. He was in charge of the bull-dozers and coolies improving the track, which was now a broad thoroughfare. He gave them a good meal and supplied transport to Tamu. There they spent Christmas Day and Boxing Day, relaxing with a bottle of gin and a bottle of rum donated by one of Captain Herring's old colleagues. They had done all that had been asked of them and had earned a couple of days off. Soon they would be returning to the Chindwin, although this time it would be not to reconnoitre, but to fight the elusive Japanese.

Chapter 5

Across the Threshold of Battle

By January 1943, the Brigade was finally ready for the great adventure. They could still have done with more time for training the latest arrivals, but the clock was ticking and the plans had been laid. At last they packed up and boarded a train from Jhansi to Dimapur where they met Wingate at Milestone 7 on the Manipur Road. Here the officers were given orders for the approach march, during which they were to iron out the many faults in march discipline that had become apparent during the command exercise carried out at the end of training. It was also a time for the new muleteers to get used to their cantankerous charges.

Ahead of the men lay a march of 133 miles to Imphal. They were to pass through the IV Corps area of responsibility and the well-run staging camps were much appreciated by the weary men. Wingate stood with the Corps Commander and watched the stragglers, mostly young Gurkhas, and commented that, although they were immature, they were worth a trial.

The Brigade arrived at Imphal during a rainy period and bivouacked 7 miles north of the township. Wingate kept them out of the town in order that they would not be softened by its pleasures, and the men rested while Wingate conferred with Field Marshal Wavell. Wingate already knew that he would receive no support from other troops as there would be no main force offensive in 1943.

The two men were in agreement that, just like the young Gurkhas, the Brigade and its new way of fighting would be worth a trial. The Brigade was as fit and ready as it could be and to delay would see it go off colour. There were also many staff officers who doubted that the theory of penetration was sound and it was therefore necessary to prove otherwise. There was also a profound ignorance of Japanese methods and reactions, and a distinct possibility that they may start to infiltrate across the Chindwin into India. A spoiling operation into Burma might also affect the Japanese operations against the Chinese in the North, particularly if their supply lines could be cut.

On 7 February 1943, the troops were visited by Field Marshal Wavell, who gave them great encouragement and assured them that they were about to play an important part in the war effort. As they marched away the Commander-in-Chief saluted them, an act which most impressed the men. The die was cast and clouds of dust began to rise as the 3,000 men and 1,000 animals marched off towards the Burmese border, the Chindwin and the supposedly invincible Japanese Army.

The move of 1 Column towards the Chindwin started badly for one of the officers as they crossed the India-Burma border on the night of 9 February. Lieutenant Watson, the Guerrilla Platoon leader, was riding his charger when some trucks came up the road. All the chargers were very jumpy and quite unsuited for the job ahead of them. Watson's charger took fright and threw him, his head striking a tree stump. He was taken away to hospital and his place was taken by Lieutenant Johnny Nealon, who had been recently commissioned after fifteen years in the ranks. He did not know it at the time, but Watson's mishap very likely saved his life.

The rest of the approach march to Auktaung, the crossing point on the Chindwin, was uneventful and Wingate took their salute as they crossed the Yeu River Bridge. His goodbye was short and to the point: 'I shall meet you at the Tagaung Taung. Good luck.'

The Burma Rifles and the RAF Liaison Officers from both columns had gone ahead to Auktaung to arrange the first and largest supply drop. It was to be carried out in daylight by Hudson bombers and was intended to draw the attention of the Japanese to the Auktaung area. The drop took place on 14 and 15 February and that night a company of Patialla Sikhs with some mountain artillery crossed the Chindwin on a large raft and a fleet of country boats. They then turned south to make a feint attack on Pantha where there was a Japanese post.

The reconnaissance platoon of each column sent over a section as well, to report by wireless on the track which led from Ta-Nga on the river to Maingnyaung. They were followed by 1 Column which crossed at sunset on the 15th, and 2 Column and Group Headquarters which crossed the next night. There would be no lines of communication to supply the columns on the expedition, so the supply drop at Auktaung was expected to last a week until they had cleared the hills and reached the Mu Valley. They had been told by the RAF that there must be no obstruction higher than 300 feet within one mile of the DZ, so there could be no supply drops while they were crossing the hills.

Once over the Chindwin 1 Column moved off southwards and bivouacked the first night at the Pabaing Chaung. It was during the second night that the Burma Rifles Reconnaissance Party arrived with news that there were 250 Japs around Maingnyaung and more at Pahe. Both columns were to cross the barrier of hills to the East of the Chindwin by the only track known to exist, by way of Ta-Nga, Maingnyaung, Pahe on the Nankamu Chaung, up that chaung and over the highest ridge, coming out on the plain south of Pinlebu. There was another route reportedly to the south-east of Maingnyaung, but it was basically a little-used elephant path. Both columns would then move south-east to Kyaikthin to destroy the railway station and a bridge 6 miles north of the station. Whichever way they went they were sure to meet the Japanese.

The column had just finished their midday halt when a Burma Rifleman came in to report that the enemy were coming their way. He said that he had run into them, had shot the first and managed to get away. Dunlop sent one platoon of Gurkhas forward to set an ambush on the track and he sent another forward in reserve. The third platoon, Support and Guerrilla Platoon, were too far back to deploy at this time.

At 1530 hours the Gurkhas opened fire on the leading Japs and the battle was joined. The fighting flared up and subsided, before flaring up again as it does in the jungle. Then the enemy opened up with mortars at the Gurkhas blocking the track. The Jemadar in command ordered his mules back out of the immediate danger area. Unfortunately the muleteers retreated in such a panic that the whole mule train took fright. The muleteers threw off their loads, as well as those of the spare chargers, including all the grain for the animals and galloped off towards India. Fowler the ATO followed in hot pursuit.

By this time the enemy had broken contact and withdrawn, leaving half a dozen dead including their Captain. It was two or three days before the animals finally caught up again. As the ATO, Fowler knew where the column was heading and because 2 Column was following behind them, Dunlop decided to press on.

In order to avoid the Japanese in Maingnyaung and Pahe, Dunlop decided to cross the hills to Ywaitha to the south of Maingnyaung and, rather than risk the known route, they would try the elephant path instead. On their journey over the hills they had met a party of Karens who were busy working timber with elephants. Their leader had been a school friend of Lieutenant Chet Kin, and was dressed in the college blazer and Burmese sarong. He told them he had brought some of his company's elephants up from Toungoo during the 1942 retreat, but had got stuck in the rains and had remained there in hiding ever since. He also confirmed the existence of the elephant path.

Dunlop sent his Reconnaissance Platoon ahead to mark out the elephant path and also said goodbye to Major Jefferies who went on his way to his adventures at Indaw, dressed in his brigadier's regalia. The rest of the column moved on up the Maingnyaung Chaung, following in the footsteps of some very nimble elephants.

The ensuing days were a tale of hunger and exhaustion, wading through streams for miles, manhandling loads and all on short rations. The loss of the grain was particularly telling on the mules and the large quantities of bamboo leaves that they ate contained very little nourishment. Some were badly galled and all were very thin. Eventually they reached the summit of the escarpment and saw the Mu Valley laid out in front of them.

The long-awaited supply drop finally arrived in the area of Thaiktaw, much to the glee of the British troops who were suffering from a lack of meat. At a conference the next day between Lieutenant Colonel Alexander, the Group Commander, Arthur Emmet, the commander of 2 Column, and Dunlop they decided to give the troops a day off to have a good feed and rest. That evening they parted company for the last time with 2 Column and moved off towards the railway. The men cheered Flight Lieutenant Edmunds as he rode away on his charger, reading a newspaper.

As the Southern Group moved away from the Chindwin and the diversion raid on Patha was underway, the main body of the Brigade prepared to cross the river. Just before the Brigade set off, a group of journalists arrived. Alec Wilding later recalled:

> They much appreciated the Brigadier who talked to them for three-quarters of an hour without losing their attention. When we set off they came with us, for about, I think, two days' march over the Chindwin. Then they went home. On the march to the Chindwin one of them gave his camera to one of the Burma Rifles to carry, which was a liberty. The Burrif (short for Burma Rifles) was wheeling a bicycle – heaven knows why – and he strapped the camera to the luggage grid. Clearly the path was unsuitable for cycles so the Burrif cast it down the khudside, camera and all. The journalist was not amused. I once described the crossing of the Chindwin as resembling a boat race between Colney Hatch and Bedlam, but we got away with it. Sadly one of the British muleteers was drowned – our first casualty. Over the next six weeks we covered about 600 miles. Our usual day's march must have been about twenty miles and this would have been a piece of cake had we received proper rations and if water had not been such a problem. The brigade's ration scale was designed for use by paratroops and for a trip of four to five days. We lived on them for ten weeks, and averaged, according to my reckoning, only one third of the proper ration per day.

Crossing the Chindwin was not as easy as it looked. Major Ken Gilkes and 7 Column arrived the previous afternoon and were told to cut down bamboo canes to make rafts ready for a dawn crossing. Before they began the Major read them Wingate's 'Order of the Day':

Today we stand on the threshold of battle. The time of preparation is over, and we are moving on the enemy to prove ourselves and our methods. At this moment we stand beside the soldiers of the United Nations in the front-line trenches throughout the world. It is always a minority that occupies the front-line. It is a still smaller minority that accepts with a good heart tasks like this that we have chosen to carry out. We need not, therefore, as we go forward into the conflict, suspect ourselves of selfish or interested motives. We have all had the opportunity of withdrawing and we are here because we have chosen to be here; that is, we have chosen to bear the burden and heat of the day. Men who make this choice are above the average in courage. We need therefore have no fear for the staunchness and guts of our comrades.

The motive which has led each and all of us to devote ourselves to what lies ahead cannot conceivably have been a bad motive. Comfort and security are not sacrificed voluntarily for the sake of others by ill-disposed people. Our motive, therefore, may be taken to be the desire to serve our day and generation in the way that seems nearest to our hand. The battle is not always to the strong nor the race to the swift. Victory in war cannot be counted upon, but what can be counted is that we shall go forward determined to do what we can to bring this war to an end, which we believe best for our friends and comrades in arms, without boastfulness or forgetting our duty, resolved to do the right so far as we can see the right.

Our aim is to make possible a government of the world in which all men can live at peace and with equal opportunity of service.

Finally, knowing the vanity of man's effort and the confusion of his purpose, let us pray that God may accept our services and direct our endeavours, so that when we shall have done all we shall see the fruit of our labours and be satisfied.

The men were then issued with Tommy cookers, small round tins filled with a substance that showed no flame. They immediately lit them and made some tea. Once the rafts were ready they settled down to sleep, resting their heads on their backpacks. No sooner were they asleep than they were wakened and told to get on to the rafts. Unfortunately the rafts sank as soon as they left the bank and the soaked men scrambled back to shore. Eventually canoes were found and the men climbed aboard. Private R.V. Hyner later recalled:

I was carrying my big pack, small pack, four grenades attached to my belt, 100 rounds of .303 bullets, four bren gun magazines containing 28 rounds each and the Bren gun itself. I carried a bayonet on my belt and a commando knife strapped to my wrist. In my pocket I carried a flick knife which I had bought in Bombay and also a flick dagger. Seven of us went into the first canoe which formed the Bren Gun Squad and we began to cross the river.

Nerves were on edge by now as we stared into the dark of the jungle, listening to the frightening noises within. We felt much better when we saw more men crossing to support us.

The crossing of the river took all day as the canoes plied back and forth bringing over the men. The rest of Wingate's 'circus' followed: mules, horses, bullocks and a couple of dogs. Captain Jealous led Hyner and the rest of 14 Platoon in single file, called 'column snake' as they made their way to their first supply dropping.

When Brigadier Wingate's first expedition crossed the Chindwin River into Burma on 13 February 1943, they were not to know that almost one third of them would never see India again. Wingate had forecast that their chances of survival were fifty-fifty and warned that any wounded who were unable to walk would have to be abandoned. The thoughts of the men, as they trod their first steps on Japanese-occupied soil, can be imagined.

At that time the Japanese Army had no reason to suspect that a force of raiders was about to enter their territory. After completing the conquest of Burma the previous summer, they had come to the conclusion that North Burma and the Burma-India border area to the west of the Zibyu mountain range was not suitable for large-scale operations. Their assessment was that the British would need to construct suitable lines of communication in the shape of roads, supply dumps, camps etc. before they could invade Burma, and that would take between two and three years. In addition, the complete defeat of the British Indian Army and the Chinese Army had caused the Japanese High Command to become overconfident.

The Japanese forces in Burma in early 1943 comprised Fifteenth Army with its headquarters in Rangoon and commanding the 18th, 33rd, 55th and 56th Divisions. Their defensive plan was for the 56th Division stationed in Yunnan west of the Salween River to prepare defences in anticipation of an offensive by Chinese forces. The 55th Division was in the Akyab area on the north-western coast of Burma where a British counter-attack was being planned. Between Yunnan and the Akyab area, the 18th and 33rd Divisions were deployed facing to the north and west. The plan for these two divisions was to hold the north Burma and Chindwin River front with a skeleton force of only one or two battalions, stationed on a line Myitkyina, Kamain and Kalewa, while the main force was assembled on the Shan Plateau for training and recuperation. If the British did decide to attack the defence line, the main force could swiftly counter-attack. No measures were taken at all to guard the direct approaches in front of the Zibyu mountain range, on the assumption that not even small units could cross that obstacle, save through one or two mountain passes.

Luck was with Wingate as he led his brigade into Burma. Japanese patrols had been positioned at several important points on trails crossing the Zibyu Taungdan Escarpment. In addition, two companies of Japanese infantry had been despatched to reconnoitre the situation along the Chindwin River and were in fact still on their way when Wingate crossed over. Whether by luck or design, 77 Brigade was advancing along the operational boundary between the 18th and 33rd Japanese Divisions. The Japanese plan at that time was purely defensive as far as India was concerned, while they reorganized and tightened their grip on Burma. However, Wingate's expedition would change all that – he would well and truly put the cat amongst the pigeons.

Each of the five columns in the main Northern Group was given specific tasks as they advanced into Burma. 3 Column under the command of Major Mike Calvert, and 5 Column led by Major Bernard Fergusson, a volunteer from the Black Watch, would head for the railway with the aim of cutting the line in as many places as possible. While those two columns made for the railway line, laden with explosives and demolition equipment, the other three columns would seek out and engage the enemy. Lance Corporal George Bell, a section commander in 13th King's, was with Northern Group Headquarters, under Colonel Sam Cooke. He recalled the start of the great adventure, in particular the approach march from the railhead to the Chindwin:

> All regimental and battalion flashes were removed, and we walked only by night in silence; secrecy was the order of the day. I do, however, remember the glorious sunrises. Finally down to the plains and Imphal. The mules arrived a few days later, but there were insufficient Gurkhas to act as muleteers. By the usual Army style of volunteering, 'You, you and you', I was given a mule to look after. As a townie, I hadn't a clue, but after a few errors of judgement initially, I really enjoyed the experience. The mules were obstinate, awkward, occasionally playful, but I soon found that, as with most animals, if you were kind to them they reciprocated. I was rather sorry to lose 'Daisy Bell' when the remaining Gurkhas arrived. We stayed at Imphal for a while, and on 7 February we were inspected by General Wavell. My mule did not appreciate the occasion and was very awkward as he approached.
>
> All the columns set off, the first hazard being the crossing of the Chindwin. On the way we crossed the Burmese border, which is to the west of the river. We were told to throw away any unnecessary articles to reduce the load we had to carry. My first error of judgement was discarding one half of my mess tin. It caused me great inconvenience during the next few months. I threw away all my shaving kit and eventually sported quite a beard – Victorian style with 'mutton chop' whiskers. An officer had thrown away a copy of For Whom the Bell Tolls and I read it in the next few days in the periodic breaks, then slung it.

Our last-minute instructions were, 'Do not stray away from the main party. You are in Nagaland and some of the natives were recently head-hunters!' Actually, they were very friendly people. The order of the day was 'The River Chindwin is your river of Jordan. Once over, there is no return except via Rangoon.' I wonder if Wingate really meant that – it seemed a long way to walk!

Most of the lads had no idea what was the purpose of our expedition, other than vague ideas. 'To overcome the fallacies that British troops are inferior to the Japs in jungle fighting.' We were excited about where we were going, but what would happen when we arrived there was a mystery. Did the top brass know? Nevertheless, we plodded on until we finally reached the Chindwin and the columns crossed at different places. I crossed late in the afternoon on a large raft with about ten others. There were no problems generally, apart from some awkward mules who insisted on going back.

On guard that night I was concerned that the Japs might attack and realised how noisy the jungle was. As we pushed on, we reached the first village. There had been a supply drop before we got there, enough for five days' ration per man. Our mail had, however, gone astray – rumour had it that it had fallen into Jap hands and despite all our secrecy they knew almost everyone in our columns. One day's rations consisted of three packets of hard biscuits, four in each pack; one tin of cheese for two days; milk powder; nuts and raisins; three tea bags; one bar of chocolate or acid drops; sugar; twenty cigarettes and one box of matches. Our menu for the next few weeks consisted of one packet of biscuits for each meal, broken up and boiled in the mess tin, mixed with cheese, chocolate or nuts and raisins. As we had a limited time to prepare these delicacies, my loss of half a mess tin mentioned earlier, meant that at times I had to forgo the tea. If the Japs were around, fires were not allowed and the biscuits had to be eaten cold. They were almost as hard as dog biscuits. In retrospect, this was a serious error of judgement by Wingate. Those rations I felt were only suitable for a short raid, e.g. Dieppe, and not for a campaign of a few months. The problem became even worse when at times we received five days' rations every eight or ten days, and as we proceeded further east no droppings were possible on some occasions. We relied then on rice from the villages. Bearing in mind that on most days we were walking twenty miles or more, with a temperature of over 100 degrees, the conditions of some of the men, especially those about thirty years of age, deteriorated quicker than expected. This obviously affected their fighting abilities.

In the first village, a girl complained about the behaviour of one of our lads and we were given a strict warning direct from the top that if anyone interfered with a Burmese girl, Wingate would personally shoot him in front of the assembled villagers. As he pointed out, our lives were dependent on these villagers being on our side.

Reports came in that there were Jap troops at Sinlamaung and a party under Colonel Cooke and Major Scott, the commander of 8 Column, including myself, marched all day and night only to find the Japs had fled. For the first time I thought we were going to see action and was apprehensive, but not frightened. We went deeper into Burma and had a further supply drop at Tonmakeng. Apart from rations, I received eight letters from home. One air letter card had only taken about two weeks. Surely this was air mail at its best!

We then crossed the Zibyu Taungdan Range by a little known path which had been used by British troops and civilians the previous year, during the retreat to India. Quite a few skeletons at the side of the track of those who did not make it. Occasionally met lads of other columns who had had several skirmishes with the Japs. The position at that time was one of aggression in that orders were given to attack Japs wherever possible or feasible. Much different to the orders given later when we were coming out

On 19 February, probably as a result of translating the mail that had been inadvertently dropped near to a Japanese outpost on 15 February, the enemy began drawing in its patrols and by the 24th had evacuated all posts between the Chindwin and the Mu Valley, including Sinlamaung. It was later discovered that one of the pilots taking part in the supply drop had arrived over the DZ just as a thunderstorm began and he failed to find the flare path. Not wishing to attempt the return flight over high mountains with icing occurring with a full load, he jettisoned the load on a sandbank within a mile or two of a Japanese outpost. The Japanese immediately collected the supplies, including the mail, and were soon aware of the British Order of Battle. However, it may have been providential that this occurred, because if the enemy had not pulled back and battle had been joined at Tonmakeng and Sinlamaung, the force would not have been able to reach the railway.

On 1 March, the main group dropped down the Zibyu Taungdan Escarpment into the Chaunggyi Valley and bivouacked not far from Pinbon. Wingate sent 3 and 5 Columns ahead towards the railway and directed 7 and 8 Columns towards Pinlebu and Pinbon, while 4 Column moved towards Indaw. Early reports of British troops east of the Chindwin were not taken too seriously by the generals commanding the 18th and 33rd Japanese Divisions and the commander of Fifteenth Army, Lieutenant General Renya Mutaguchi (after 26 March). They judged them as small intelligence units and left countermeasures in the hands of local regimental or battalion commanders. It was not until 1 Column started bridge demolitions between Kawlin and Kyaikthin around 20 February that they revised their estimates of the British strength and plans. Clearly greater steps had to be taken to counter them. Both 18th and 33rd Divisions were ordered to cut the enemy ground lines of communication, not knowing at the time that the Chindits were being supplied by air. General Sakurai, 33rd Division commander, sent his 215th Infantry Regiment to Kyaikthin to mop up the enemy there. However, they were ambushed by 1 Column and Major Nasu, the commander of their 2nd Battalion, was killed. The manoeuvring of 4, 7 and 8 Columns caused the Japanese to move troops up from the area of the railway to counter the threat in the Mu Valley, allowing Calvert's and Fergusson's columns to slip through unobserved to the railway.

Chapter 6

The First Casualties

U nfortunately, 4 Column's days were numbered. It would be the first of the seven to break up and return to India. It had been led from the start by Major Conron of 3/2nd Gurkhas and had reached the brigade rendezvous at Tonmakeng on 24 February. Thereafter it was tasked to protect a brigade supply dropping and then to reconnoitre and improve Castens Trail, the secret track of the Zibyu Taungdan Escarpment. It was hard work clearing the route, but necessary to avoid the Japanese. As the columns descended they saw a deep valley, in reality the headwaters of two: the Chaunggyi or Great Stream, which went northward for a few miles before turning abruptly to the west to break through the Zibyu Taungdan in a deep gorge; and the Mu Valley proper. Across the valley rose the hills of the Mangin range, running up to 3,700 feet of the Kalat Taung opposite. Beyond the hills was the Meza Valley and beyond that, the railway and the important communications centre of Indaw.

On 1 March, after a relatively easy march through the mountains, Brigade Headquarters and accompanying columns dropped down the escarpment into the Chaunggyi Valley, crossed the Namkasa and Namkadin and bivouacked not far from Pinbon. When Wingate discovered that Pinbon and neighbourhood were strongly held and patrolled, he ordered 4 Column to ambush the Mansi motor road and try to bypass Pinbon through the mountains, while the rest of the columns marched down the Mu Valley on Pinlebu. 3 Column had already entered the Mu Valley from Sinlamaung and Major Fergusson's 5 Column were ordered to proceed to the Bon Chaung railway gorge via Mankat, destroy the bridges and bring down the cliff.

As the columns reached the valley floor, Fergusson noted that: 'Wingate was not in the best of tempers. He was annoyed with 4 Column for some sin of omission.' That day, 1 March, Wingate relieved Major Conron of his command and replaced him with Major Bromhead, his Brigade Major. The official reason for such a drastic step is hard to fathom. The change of command was not mentioned in Wingate's after-action report. However, Bromhead himself told the author: 'We were halfway across Burma when 4 Column's commander lost his nerve. He could not stand the sound of a battery charging engine and so his radios failed. Wingate withdrew him to Brigade HQ and I took his place. We managed after a day or two to get the main radio working and set off to follow Brigade HQ, now way ahead.' Conron was never able to tell his side of the story. After Wingate later ordered the dispersal of the columns he was last seen near the Shweli River in command of a group of Gurkha muleteers from Brigade Headquarters. According to an eyewitness account he was drowned through the treachery of Burmese boatmen while attempting to cross the river.

On 2 March, the day after Bromhead took over command, the Burrif reconnaissance detachment bumped a group of Japanese soldiers near Pinbon and one man was lost. A fighting patrol out searching for the missing man encountered another Japanese patrol and shot dead an NCO. In the meantime Wingate had decided to shift his attack on the railway from the Indaw area to the Wuntho-Bonchaung area, 35 miles further south. He took the unusual step of marching his whole force less 4 Column down the Pinbon-Pinlebu motor road before dispersing into forest bivouacs near Didauk. From dawn on 2 March until dawn on the 3rd, in pouring rain, 3, 5 and 7 Columns and Brigade Headquarters boldly marched along in the open, with little fear of interference from enemy as the road by then was impassable by truck. He wanted to put the Mu Valley behind him and to prevent the enemy catching him, Wingate ordered 7 Column to blow all bridges behind them.

On reaching their bivouac 10 miles north-east of Pinlebu, Wingate reviewed his options. Number 1 Group was at that moment reaching the railway at Kyaikthin, with George Dunlop's 1 Column a bit ahead of Emmett's 2 Column. They would soon be in position to launch their attack on the railway. In the meantime, the Japanese were under the impression that Pinbon was about to be attacked by 4 Column and Pinlebu by 8 Column. Number 3 and 5 Columns were three days' march from the railway, heading for Wuntho and Bon Chaung respectively.

After Wingate decided to make Wuntho his objective rather than Indaw, he instructed 4 Column to rejoin the main group without delay. However, during the morning of 4 March, while the column was marching south-east along the base of the mountains in the neighbourhood of Nyaungwun, all hell broke loose. The column was in the usual single-file 'snake' formation and strung out over 1,000 yards, when the undergrowth came alive with enemy small-arms fire. Half of the formation had already crossed a small stream, when a shower of enemy mortar bombs began to fall on the ford, preventing the rest from crossing. The column had walked into a trap. While a rearguard platoon held the enemy at the stream, Lieutenants Stewart-Jones and Green, and Subedar Tikajit, led 135 men and thirty mules away to the north. The remainder of the column who had already crossed the stream dispersed in small groups and headed for the pre-arranged Operational Rendezvous 20 miles to the south. Bromhead's dispersal group comprised about fifteen souls, including Captain Ray Scott of the Burma Rifles, whose knowledge of the countryside would help to get them home. But their radios were finished. Bromhead recalled:

> We met a Jap patrol and although we beat them off our only radio got a bullet. Since the Japs used soft-nosed bullets it was the end of that radio. The column was split by the encounter, but all reached the RV that evening and we sat down to consider our situation. No communications, little food and no way of getting more except courtesy of the locals, and the British officers of the Gurkha column reported very poor morale. What to do?
>
> We could not influence the war, so I decided to turn back. At this point our luck changed a bit. A villager told me that at the top of a steep hill behind the village there started a forest boundary trail, going, roughly, the right way. The hill was certainly steep, but the Gurkhas with their kukris cut steps for the mules and we all reached the top. And there was a well marked trail and I could recognise the forest blazes. We managed to buy enough rice and had an uneventful march back to the Chindwin. I mapped the route and by coincidence a battalion of my regiment used most of it later when Burma was invaded. On the way back my main worry was that we might be mistaken for the enemy by our own forces. Fortunately we spotted a British patrol east of the Chindwin before they saw us and made contact. We crossed the river where a battalion of a state force held the front. Jaipur I think. Memorable because the CO said, 'I expect you could do with a bath,' and his men dug a hole, lined it with ground sheets and filled it with hot water. The best bath I can remember.
>
> I had written a series of non-committal 'air grams' before we went into Burma and left them back at air base to be posted weekly. Thus is was that my mother got a brief letter saying that all was quite routine at the same time as she opened her morning paper to see my ugly mug spread across the front page.
>
> I went back to Imphal and set up shop at the Army HQ. My tummy rebelled in a big way at the rich food and I realised that when the brigade got back some hospital checks would be necessary. Eventually Wingate and the columns returned but, alas, with many a gap. The Gurkhas to their own centres and the British to Bombay. Wingate and I visited Simla, the summer capital, to report. Finally he started raising the next year's force. At that moment the Army sent me to Staff College at Quetta, presumably to learn how it should be done. Next year I was in New Guinea with the Aussies.

As for Lieutenant Stewart-Jones, his troubles were only just beginning. On the evening of the ambush he led his men north in an effort to contact the other columns. After two days he handed over command to Captain Findlay of the commando detachment and went ahead with eight others. Six days later, out of food and near collapse, they made contact with 8 Column. In the meantime Captain Findlay and his party had turned back for India, menaced by starvation. Weeks later, Stewart-Jones and his four faithful Gurkha riflemen reached safety in Fort Hertz, a British outpost on the border with China.

Wingate had no adverse comment to pass on Bromhead's actions. He had lost much indispensable equipment, was without supplies or the means of obtaining them. He was also separated from the Brigade Group by strong enemy forces and rightly decided to march back to the Chindwin.

After Lieutenant Colonel Alexander's Southern Group crossed the Chindwin 50 miles south of the main body, Group Headquarters and 1 Column pressed ahead. 2 Column, under Major Emmett, followed at a distance and on 20 February, while passing the village of Ywaitha, it was learned that a Japanese unit which had recently bumped into 1 Column had just passed through, carrying a number of wounded. Over the next seven days the column climbed the escarpment and slowly descended to the plain below. Alexander gave 2 Column the task of destroying Kyaikthin railway station, 40 miles to the east. The period of concealment was over. The group would now move openly in order to attract enemy forces away from the area to which Wingate's group was heading. Scouts halted in villages to convey misleading information that might reach the ears of the Japanese, while Major John B. Jefferies, in his brigadier's uniform and accompanied by his deception group, held court in various villages before hurrying to catch up with Major Emmett's column. They finally joined them on 2 March, 3 miles from Kyaikthin. That night the column was scheduled to blow up the railway station.

The two columns were supposed to contact each other each midday and evening to coordinate the attack, 2 Column from the east and 1 Column from the west. The arrangement worked well enough until the evening of the attack when Dunlop found that he could not raise 2 Column or Group Headquarters. Both columns had to make speed to get into position for the attack and 1 Column only just made its bivouac west of the railway by nightfall. It seems likely that Major Emmett was trying to make up for lost time and may have been a trifle careless. While 2 Column bivouacked in the Wild Life Sanctuary Forest a couple of miles west of the station, Burma Rifle scouts reported that two trains had arrived during the afternoon. Unbeknown to Emmett, they were full of Japanese soldiers from the 215th Infantry Regiment. At this time alarm bells should have been ringing.

At 2200 hours, Major Emmett formed up his column and marched down the line of the narrow-gauge railway. Young Lieutenant Ian MacHorton was near the rear of the column as the 250 men and twenty mules made their way along the top of the railway embankment. They had been walking for two hours in the darkness, their silhouettes bathed in the silver light of the moon. They were taking a big risk – the sound made by steel-shod boots can travel a long way down the steel of the railway line and with 20 yards of cleared jungle either side of the embankment there was little cover for them. Scouts had been trying unsuccessfully to find a trail into the jungle to give them cover as they made their final approach to the railway station. Unknown to them, oriental eyes followed the progress of the column. In the black of the jungle, Japanese soldiers took up the slack in their belts of machine-gun ammunition and prepared to drop the first bombs into their light mortar tubes. MacHorton later recalled:

> There came the sound of just one bang up at the front somewhere beyond my vision. But only for a split second, then an inferno of noise engulfed the world around me! Then came the high-pitched staccato scream of a machine-gun. Instantly my battle training told me it was a Japanese light automatic. Then overwhelmingly many more machine-guns joined in an ear-splitting chorus. The crash – ping of rifles and banging of grenades, joined in to swell the noise of sudden battle to a fearful crescendo. Somewhere ahead there was an uncertain scuffling. A hoarse voice cried: 'Take cover!' and another screamed 'Christ Almighty!' and was silenced.

They had walked into an ambush. Men dived to the ground as salvoes of mortar bombs began to land among the laden mules, causing them to buck and rear as their handlers tried to control them. British Bren guns began to rattle out their reply as the screaming enemy ran towards them, their bayonets fixed. The Gurkhas hurriedly drew their kukris as the British soldiers clicked their own bayonets into place and were soon in close combat with the enemy. Swarms of tracer swept over the embankment as MacHorton and the Gurkhas near to him watched the line of screaming Jap soldiers charge towards them. He grasped the hand grenade hanging from his belt and pulled it free with the drill-book downward jerk that left the pin still fastened to the webbing. He lobbed it over the embankment and saw the red and black fire as it exploded in front of the line of advancing men. Tommy guns and rifles joined in and the line of advancing shadows twitched and fell as the bullets found their mark. As suddenly as it had begun, the battle died away with just isolated shots echoing through the jungle.

MacHorton looked to his left and saw Rifleman Lal Bahadur Thapa lying dead beside him. The bodies of mules and men lay in grotesque positions along the railway track and down the embankment. Amongst them lay men of the Nippon Army and piles of mule loads wrenched from the animals' backs as they stampeded from the scene. As another Japanese machine-gun began to spew .280

calibre bullets from behind them, MacHorton shouted, 'Follow me!' and ran for the cover of the jungle, seven Gurkhas hot on his heels. They crashed blindly through the undergrowth, seeking the cover of the thick jungle as dark shadows turned their heads towards the noise and began to follow the fleeing men.

MacHorton heard the sounds behind them and turned at right angles to try to shake off the pursuers. They found a track and followed it towards some high ground where British Bren guns were exchanging fire with Japanese machine-guns and rifles. Ordering his men to stack their heavy packs at the edge of the track, the young officer lead his men forward and into a dry chaung which led towards the British positions. Suddenly one of his Gurkhas cried out: 'Japun Ayo!' and began to fire back down the chaung at the shadowy figures with their smooth-domed steel helmets reflecting the moonlight. The darkness was lit by red and yellow flashes as both sides opened fire on each other. Japanese bayonets and Gurkha kukris flashed in the darkness as the men scuffled and fought to the death. When the guns fell silent the Japanese lay dead at their feet, but there had been casualties on both sides. Naik Premsingh Gurung lay groaning on the ground, his thigh bone smashed by a bullet fired at close range. He had given a good account of himself though – on the ground nearby lay a Jap with Premsingh's kukri buried in his neck. The wounded man was given a shot of morphine while his wound was dressed and bamboo splints were tied to his shattered leg. MacHorton and his men were then joined by Havildar Lalbahadur Thapa and five more Gurkhas who, like MacHorton had neither seen nor heard of the rest of the column since the ambush. The exhausted men slumped to the ground to await the coming of dawn.

An hour before dawn the men 'stood to' in the time honoured tradition of the British Army, for experience has shown that the first signs of dawn often presage an enemy attack. It was clear that Wingate's deception plan had been successful and it was very likely that the area would soon be crawling with Japs. But where were they? Were they lying in the jungle waiting for MacHorton and his small band to break from cover, or were they already pursuing the larger elements of the column as they withdrew from the ambush? MacHorton assumed that the 'dispersal' had been sounded, but they did not hear it at the rear of the column. It was very likely that the bulk of the column would even now be marching forward to the rendezvous in the hills which formed the western watershed of the Irrawaddy River. MacHorton decided that he would follow, but what was to be done with the wounded Premsingh? He was a tough and competent soldier and had returned from his machine-gun course with the two stripes of a naik. His father had also fought for the British Raj, but with a wound like that he clearly could not march and the men could not carry him for days through the jungle.

MacHorton moved over to Premsingh and knelt on the ground next to him. Their eyes met as he squeezed his arm, but no words were necessary. If he was lucky he could attract the attention of a passing Burmese, who might be able to hide him in a village until the broken bone had knit and he was strong enough to make his way back to British lines. He held out his tommy gun for Kulbahadur to take. 'Give me your rifle and you take this. It will be more useful to you.' Then Premsingh looked up at MacHorton and held out his hand. 'Goodbye Sahib,' he said. The men clasped their hands firmly and then the officer turned away and led his men through the undergrowth. As they made their way down the hillside they heard the sound of a single shot. Naik Premsingh Gurung had been the bravest of the brave.

MacHorton and his men stealthily retraced their steps back towards the scene of the ambush. As they peered through the bamboo thicket at the edge of the forest, the wreckage of the previous evening's disaster lay before them. Heavy packs lay everywhere, just as they had been shrugged from the shoulders of the men diving into cover from the hail of bullets and grenades. Every type of mule load lay scattered on and around the railway embankment. The bodies of three British soldiers lay sprawled on their faces across the railway line. It was clear that the Japs had been waiting on both sides of the railway embankment as the column advanced in the moonlight. From the enemy point of view it had been a successful ambush.

A sudden movement 50 yards away caught Kulbahadur's eye. Three shadowy figures were creeping amongst the bodies, one of them carrying a knife in his hand. As they came closer MacHorton recognized Arthur Best and they burst out of the jungle waving their arms and shouting greetings as they ran. Arthur told him that he had returned with three Gurkhas to collect the identity discs of the fallen and to collect what supplies they could recover. His experience had been similar to MacHorton's, ducking for cover accompanied by a handful of Gurkhas. He later met Flight Lieutenant Eddie Edmunds and Lieutenant John Griffiths of the 3/2nd Gurkhas, and a few others.

The group found two mules and loaded them with ammunition and supplies, and Arthur Best led them through the jungle to join up with Edmunds and the others. Flight Lieutenant Edmunds was just the sort of man to have with you in the jungle. A big-game hunter by profession, he had joined the Royal New Guinea Air Force on the outbreak of war. When the Japs overran the country they murdered both of his parents and Edmunds was now out to kill as many of them as possible.

They set off south-east, heading for the pre-planned rendezvous and came across it later that evening. As they walked around a bend in the track they found themselves at the mouth of a little valley where, sat next to a stream, was Doc Lusk, their Irish medical officer. 'Aha! Flight Lieutenant Edmunds, I presume?' he laughed as they shook hands with delight.

Doc Lusk confirmed that he had heard the column bugler sound the dispersal and broke away with his section before making for the chosen rendezvous. He had been there for a day and a half and had seen nobody else. It would be two days before they discovered what had happened that fateful evening. On the evening of the second day George Dunlop and his column marched into their bivouac area and put them in the picture.

As the ambush had developed and, hard pressed by what was later estimated as a full battalion of 800 Japanese, Major Emmett had ordered his men to try to break through, but it was impossible. As individual firefights continued along the length of the column, the dispersal call was sounded. Those who were able broke away from the railway line and into the jungle. Jemadar Manbahadur Gurung covered the withdrawal with his platoon, accounting for many Japanese. Wingate's decoy uniform was discovered by the Japanese at the site of the ambush so that for a while they thought they had destroyed the main force and announced this fact in a printed broadsheet which they took the trouble to drop on 5 Column as it crossed the Irrawaddy at Tigyaing, a week later. Major Emmett and other groups marched through the darkness towards the rendezvous. Half of the column eventually joined him there and took stock of their situation. They were without signal equipment, medical stores or reserve ammunition and could neither contact Wingate nor ask for resupply by air. Harassed by the enemy, Emmett turned his men around and headed back towards the Chindwin and India. A large body of Japs were right behind them, so the Chindits dropped their heavy equipment and marched light, fighting a rearguard action all the way. Wingate was later damning in his comments on 2 Column's lack of success. He charged that their movement had been too slow, the bivouac near Kyaikthin too obvious. In addition, during the fighting, Emmett had changed the rendezvous point to one in the rear, replacing the original rendezvous at Taunguan, 12 miles east of Kyaikthin and 15 miles from the scene of the ambush. As a result the column split in different directions. Whether or not Wingate's comments were justified, the result was to be expected. The column had been ordered to lay a plain trail and attract the enemy to them, and they did just that.

It was unfortunate that 1 Column could not come to the aid of 2 Column on the night of the ambush, but they were 10 miles away, settling into their bivouac. They did hear the sound of the fighting though and guessed wrongly that the Japs were at the receiving end. Dunlop decided not to blow his bridge until the following day, after a reconnaissance patrol checked out the area. In the meantime two of his Guerrilla Platoon broke standing orders and went off in search of water. They got lost and found themselves near the railway line. A Burmese railway official met them and passed on the information that the Japanese had inflicted a crushing defeat on the British at Kyaikthin, had captured many of them and dispersed the remainder.

When the errant pair finally found their way back to the bivouac they passed the news on to Dunlop, who decided to go ahead with his part of the plan regardless. That night, as the column crossed the open paddy land to approach the bridge they saw what they took to be lightning to the north, followed by the low rumble of an explosion. It was Mike Calvert and his men at work. At 0200 hours the demolition party let their charges go on the bridge. Nealon's men had used a lifting and cutting charge which deposited the bridge on the river bed. The column formed up again and moved off towards the east.

One puzzling aspect of the ambush at Kyaikthin is the whereabouts of Lieutenant Colonel Alexander, the Southern Group commander, when 2 Column was ambushed. Wingate's report on the expedition states that he was with Emmett and 2 Column at Kyaikthin, and George Dunlop confirmed to the author that he was not travelling with 1 Column at that time. However, the few published reports of the ambush and dispersal of this column do not mention Alexander at all. As the senior officer present and the group commander, surely the responsibility for 2 Column and its fate was his, rather than Emmett's? At any rate the column commander and group commander went off in opposite directions.

Many of the dispersed groups continued towards the east and the rendezvous at Taunguan. Subedar Major Siblal Thapa spent the night in the area of the ambush, collecting men and equipment. He arrived at the RV together with four young British officers, seventy Gurkha other ranks, sixty-five mules, four machine-guns and a quantity of ammunition. He had also found the bodies of seven Gurkhas and delivered two seriously wounded riflemen into the safety of the nearest village.

It is not quite clear when Lieutenant Colonel Alexander and Southern Group HQ joined forces with MacHorton, Best and the others. Dunlop recorded that around 7 March, as he approached the range overlooking the Irrawaddy River, his scouts found Alexander outside Hinthaw. When he went over with Weatherall, Chet Kin and Subedar Kulbir he found the Colonel, De La Rue, Edmunds, MacHorton and around 100 others, comprising all Group HQ plus stragglers, as well as thirty mules. Because all the ciphers of Southern Group and 2 Column had been lost in the ambush, Alexander decided not to use 1 Column's radio to contact Wingate. He was mistaken in this, because they were using one-time cipher pads and in fact no ciphers were carried which could have compromised others if they fell into enemy hands. However, for four days the remains of Southern Group struggled through dense jungle to throw the enemy off their trail, while Wingate waited for word from them. When MacHorton wrote about his experiences years later he did not mention Alexander's party joining them at the rendezvous and the author assumes that they arrived just before 1 Column came across them. At any rate, the survivors of the ambush joined Dunlop's column and by 9 March, they stood on the bank of the Irrawaddy. Major Dunlop told the author:

Jefferies, Edmunds, Weatherall and I were on the bank looking across this vast river. Someone, Jefferies I think, remarked, 'And how do we get over that?' Edmunds retorted at once, 'Call up the old man. He'll tell you how Jesus Christ did it!' This comment was not without its bit of irony. Wingate's HQ had constantly refused to take our radio calls. Perhaps he thought that the Japs were putting out bogus calls, using ciphers captured from 2 Column at Kyaikthin. In the whole operation I received only two messages after reporting the success of our first encounter. These were both the two biblical ones telling us to take to the mountains and not turn back the way we had come.

Dunlop's reconnaissance platoon crossed over the next day and the rest of the column followed slowly, having commandeered three large country boats. The crossing took almost twenty-four hours but eventually all 500 men and 130 animals were over on the east side of the river. A Japanese Army reconnaissance plane came over at midday and showered them with propaganda leaflets informing them that Wingate and the bulk of his force had been destroyed at Kyaikthin. As the column formed up and moved away to arrange a supply drop, the radios at Fifteenth Army Headquarters crackled out orders to 18th Division to send troops to the area.

Chapter 7

Attacking the Railway

While Southern Group remained out of contact, Mike Calvert's 3 Column reached the area around Nankan railway station on 6 March. As they moved into bivouac he sent out a Burma Rifle patrol under Lieutenant Gourlay to reconnoitre the area. His target was some bridges over chaungs (streams) with 45-foot banks, together with the railway line itself. Calvert divided his column into two demolition parties, three covering sections and a transport and headquarters group, the latter to remain hidden in the jungle. With Lieutenant Harold James and his platoon of Gurkhas as escort, Calvert advanced along the railway line dropping off some of his commandos to start cutting the line at 100-yard intervals with 1-lb slabs of guncotton. At Milestone 555 they came to a box girder bridge with a 100-foot span and a long drop to the chaung below. Calvert, Sergeant Major Blain and his party set to work fixing the charges and connecting the fuses. Calvert was almost ready when the distant boom of an explosion reached his ears. Lieutenant Jeffrey Lockett of the commandos had brought down his bridge, a three-span steel girder bridge with stone abutments stretching 120 feet over a deep chaung. Harold James later recalled:

> The next moment Calvert was running towards me, shouting for everyone to take cover behind a bank. We scrambled over and not long afterwards there was a great roar as the bridge went up, pieces of metal flew in all directions, and a large section passed low over our heads like a fighter aircraft, screaming past to embed itself in a tree-trunk with the noise of a large drum.

Lieutenant Gourlay and his reconnaissance party had returned with the news that, while there were no Japs at Nankan, there were 200 of them at Wuntho, 10 miles to the south-east. A road led straight from Wuntho through Nankan village to the station, and Captain Griffiths of the Burma Rifles and his men were sent to ambush anyone coming to join the party. While Calvert and his men were preparing to blow their bridge, Gurkha Subedar Kumba Sing

Gurung was crouched behind a Boyes anti-tank rifle, squinting through the sights at the first of two Japanese trucks which had come into view on the road to the north of the station. He slowly squeezed the trigger and the truck burst into flames before veering out of control into the jungle. His Bren gunner opened fire on the Japanese leaping from the second truck, and the riflemen of his small section joined in too. They were outnumbered three to one and a brisk fight ensued. Captain Taffy Griffiths and his Karens ran over from the east of the station to join in, as more trucks appeared with Japanese reinforcements. A runner was sent to Calvert at the bridge. Leaving Blain and his commandos to continue cutting the railway line, Calvert, with Harold James and his platoon ran towards the firing. Suddenly a bearded face appeared in their path. It was Captain Erik Petersen, a free Dane, and two platoons who had been separated from 7 Column during the fighting at Pinlebu and were following the tracks of 3 Column in the hope of catching up.

'You are just in time for a bit of action, if you wish,' said Calvert.

'I think we would like that,' replied the Dane, and Calvert led them forward.

The King's men from 7 Column soon dealt with an armoured truck which came into view and the Gurkhas' mortars blew another truck to pieces. Other enemy soldiers were shot down as they tried to cross open ground to outflank the Chindits. As the firing petered out and darkness approached, Calvert and his men withdrew to their rendezvous. Without losing a man, Calvert's column had accounted for over fifty of the enemy.

Willy Borge Erik Petersen looked like a Viking of old and fought like one as well. He had left his native Copenhagen at the age of twenty-five and sailed away to manage a rubber plantation in Malaya. He joined the Malayan Volunteer Forces and in May 1940, when the Germans invaded Denmark, he joined the British Army. Just three days before the Japanese attacked Singapore he was sent to Burma to join the Scandinavian Commando School at Lashio. Two months later he followed the Burma Road into China and continued his training at Kunming. Despairing of ever coming to terms with the enemy he volunteered at the British Embassy for service in Burma, but the Japanese occupied Lashio before he could return there. He travelled back to India where he met Wingate, a man after his own heart and was quickly conscripted into 7 Column, under the quiet-spoken, scholarly Ken Gilkes. Now at last he was happy.

That night Calvert sat beside a fire in the jungle, surrounded by sleeping Gurkhas, and produced a bar of chocolate, half of which he gave to Second Lieutenant Harold James.

'It's my birthday and I have reached the ripe old age of thirty.'

'If I had known I would have brought you a present,' James replied.

Calvert grinned. 'I had my present today. How many people can say they celebrated their birthday by blowing up a bridge!'

It had been a good day. Apart from destroying the bridges, they had cut the railway line in seventy places and left numerous booby traps in their wake. Taffy Griffiths was later awarded the Military Cross for this action and others during the expedition. Kumba Sing received the Indian Distinguished Service Medal. And Petersen the Dane? He rejoined 7 Column, but was later wounded in the head. After Wingate dispersed the columns his men tied him to a horse and brought him out with them to China.

The same day that 3 Column carried out their attack on the railway at Nankan, Major Fergusson's 5 Column reached their target a few miles away. Together with his adjutant, Duncan Menzies, the Major reviewed his plans. Captain Fraser and a patrol of Burma riflemen were to cross the railway and search for a good place to cross the Irrawaddy, where the rest of the column would meet them three days later. Captain Tommy Roberts with forty men were to deal with an enemy post to the south. Lieutenant Harmon, with one rifle platoon and some commandos, was ordered to mine both sides of the Bonchaung Gorge and blow it down onto the railway line. Column Headquarters led by Major Fergusson, together with a rifle platoon and a commando section, would attack Bonchaung Station and blow the railway bridge. The rest of the column under Captain MacDonald were to cross the railway and make for a rendezvous 4 miles away, where the others would join them eventually.

Lieutenant Whitehead was given the job of blowing the 250-feet-wide railway bridge. Large concrete buttresses lifted the bridge 100 feet above a dried stream bed and supported a 100-foot span at each end, and a 50-foot span in the middle. His men began unloading the mules and crawling along the girders with their charges and reels of fuse. In the distance they could hear the sound of firing and assumed that Tommy Roberts and his men were in action.

Sadly, there had been casualties. Captain Roberts and his men had bumped a truck full of Japanese in the village of Kyaukin. Within a quarter of an hour fifteen of the enemy had been killed and, assuming they had accounted for all of them, Roberts gave orders to return to the column. As Lieutenant Kerr formed up his platoon, an enemy machine-gun opened fire, killing four of the men and wounding six others, including the Lieutenant. By the time Fergusson reached the scene, there was little he could do. Lieutenant Kerr and four other wounded were left in the deserted village with some food and water, in the hope that friendly Burmese might find and take care of them. Sadly it was not to be. Two of the men died on the spot, another was found and murdered by Burmese, while the fourth died after capture on the way to Rangoon. Kerr himself was tortured by the Japanese to divulge Fergusson's plans, but managed to hold out until it no longer mattered.

The railway bridge at Bonchaung was blown at 2100 hours and the centre span dropped into the river. Two spans and all the buttresses had been irreparably damaged. In the meantime Harmon and his men were having a hard time at the gorge. They intended to blast a 200-yard section of high rocky cliff from both sides down onto the line and were working from improvised rope ladders while quarrying at the rock face. It was midnight before the fuses were lit and with a tremendous explosion a landslide of hundreds of tons of rock tumbled down onto the railway line.

Fergusson was soon aware that the Japanese were rushing reinforcements to the general area and even drawing troops away from their operations in the Fort Hertz area. He hurried his column on towards the Irrawaddy.

During this time, 6 to 11 March, Wingate reconsidered his options. 4 Column had returned to India and there was no sign of, or sound from, the Southern Group. He debated whether the four remaining columns could take to the impassable mountains west of Wuntho, form a permanent rendezvous for the columns where they could be supplied by air, and launch them forth to attack the roads and railway. The Japanese had never followed a column into dense jungle and would therefore avoid a mountain stronghold. Once established the columns could do the job they had been trained for, laying ambushes rather than avoiding them and carrying out hit and run raids. The problem with this idea was that the columns were then operating over an area of 10,000 square miles and it might have proven difficult for 3 and 5 Columns to rejoin 7 and 8 and Brigade Headquarters.

Finally, Wingate received news that in compliance with his orders, Southern Group had crossed the Irrawaddy. It had not been an easy task.

Calvert and Fergusson now requested permission to cross the river and this was given. Wingate decided to follow suit and take the rest of his brigade across the wide river. The decision was not made lightly. To those who suggest that Wingate should have remained on the west side of the river, to form a bridgehead if the other columns should need to return, I quote his reasons for crossing, direct from his post-expedition report:

Had I not crossed the Irrawaddy I should have learned nothing real about crossing wide and swift streams, nor about opposed crossings. It is this want of real as opposed to second-hand, book-derived or related experience that leads to so many mistakes by commanders in war. Further, although it is easy to be wise after the event, I had at this time every reason to believe that we would find conditions far easier on the east bank. I did not know the difficulty of the country between the Irrawaddy and the Shweli from our point of view at that time of the year. It is true to say that had I throughout known all that I know now, I could have done almost anything, including the generous use of Emergency Landing Grounds and irruption into China. But I did not know one tenth part of what I know now. Neither did anyone else.

Wingate signalled Calvert to take command of both 3 Column and Fergusson's 5 Column and move towards the Gokteik Gorge on the Maymyo–Lashio road. During the 1942 retreat to India, Calvert had spent a week at Gokteik awaiting orders to destroy the huge viaduct that straddled the gorge. The order never came, but when Calvert later reported to General Alexander, the first thing the General asked was, 'Did you blow up the viaduct?' When Calvert replied that he asked for permission half a dozen times, but was told to leave it alone, Alexander looked rather put out. He explained that the order could not be given for political reasons, but he had sent Calvert there because he had been told that he was the most likely person to disobey orders! Now, a year later, he would do the job properly. Wingate directed Southern Group to move towards Mongmit for a rendezvous at the end of March with Captain 'Fish' Herring of the Burma Rifles and his Kachin guerrilla platoon. Herring had been despatched in advance of the Brigade to cross the Irrawaddy with the intention of raising the hill tribes in revolt against the Japanese. He found many supporters of the British cause but was hampered by Wingate's refusal to give him a long-range radio with which to report his success. The only way Herring could signal Wingate would be after a planned rendezvous with 7 Column at the end of March. However, Southern Group was despatched to the area instead, and by the time they arrived the area was crawling with Japanese troops.

PART 2 – March or Die

Chapter 8

A River Too Far

On 18 March, Wingate and his Northern Group Headquarters reached the Irrawaddy near the village of Hlwebo and crossed over. Here the river was between seven and eight hundred yards wide and swift flowing. Wingate discovered that given country boats with skilled native paddlers, the process of loading, crossing, unloading and returning occupied one hour. The RAF circular dinghies holding 1,500 lb net weight could be towed across by a country boat, but were quite unmanoeuvrable alone. He made a note for the future that each column would need at least forty men skilled in handling boats and at least 80 per cent of the men should be able to swim. At that time the great majority could hardly swim at all.

The crossing began during the afternoon and was completed by daylight. Fortunately the Japanese kept away, as did the local members of the enemy sponsored Burma Defence Army based at Inywa on the east bank. The village itself was raided by the Headquarters Defence Platoon, and a number of boats and a large junk were commandeered to assist in the crossing. Meanwhile 5 Column had crossed at Tigyaing with the cheerful assistance of the villagers. The Japanese arrived just as Major Fergusson made the crossing in the last boat. He was the last man into the overloaded boat and had to kneel on the stern with his head under the canopy and his rear in the air. Fortunately the Japanese were poor shots and Fergusson later remarked, 'I am the first British officer to have crossed the Irrawaddy on all fours.' Calvert's column played a game of hide and seek with the Japanese on the way to the river, leaving booby traps behind them as they moved. A Japanese force caught up with them as they prepared to cross over just south of Tigyaing, but a rearguard held the enemy at bay while the bulk of the column got across. There were a few casualties and many animals had to be abandoned, but disaster was avoided.

After 4 and then 2 Column suffered their reverses in early March, Headquarters Fifteenth Japanese Army believed the main force of the enemy had been destroyed and some staff officers estimated that the enemy had already retreated to the west. However, troops from the 55th Infantry Regiment reported that the enemy was in fact crossing the Irrawaddy and soon after realized that they were being supplied by air. It was troops from this regiment that had attacked 3 Column as it crossed the river. Consequently 18th and 56th Divisions were ordered to locate and destroy the enemy, which was easier said than done. Lance Corporal George Bell, still with the Northern Group Headquarters, takes up the story:

> We had several skirmishes as we eventually crossed the railway and reached the Irrawaddy River. We hid in the hills overlooking Wuntho for five days as Wingate contemplated attacking the garrison there, but he decided against it. We crossed the Irrawaddy by boat late in the afternoon with the CO, Lieutenant Colonel Cooke. At the time, several of the officers still had bedding rolls carried on their chargers. Most of the lads by then had nothing, we kipped down on the ground. The CO was one of those officers and it annoyed some of the lads; to me it was typical of Army life. When we arrived at the far side of the river the CO's bedding roll had disappeared. He was very annoyed and asked his batman and me to find it. The lads told me that it had been thrown into the Irrawaddy by some disillusioned soldiers who didn't see why the CO should have such privileges. I daren't tell the CO.
>
> For some time I had been what can only be described as the CO's bodyguard. On occasions either Wingate or the column commander wished to rendezvous with the CO. I would walk ahead of him down the tracks towards the agreed RV with rifle cocked, on the assumption that if the Japs pounced on us, I would be expendable rather than the CO. Luckily that never happened. Remarkably it never crossed my mind either then or later that I would be killed. Others might, but me, never!
>
> We continued marching further eastwards. Our casualties up to this stage were not too bad, but were increasing. Two further major problems were arising. The supply drops were becoming less frequent, but infinitely worse was how to deal with the wounded. Initially we tried to carry them on improvised stretchers, but soon realised in the thick jungle it was not possible. I recall leaving about ten of our lads in a deserted village. We shook hands with them as we left, with everyone trying to keep a stiff upper lip. We knew that they hadn't a cat in hell's chance of surviving and what made it more painful, was that they also knew. Terrible decisions to make! Most of our lads thought it better to be killed outright than be badly wounded. 'Still marching eastwards. Would we reach China? If not, where? No one seemed to have any idea.'

Major Dunlop and 1 Column, together with the remnants of 2 Column and Southern Group Headquarters spent the first couple of days after crossing the river replenishing their supplies by air. One Gurkha was unlucky enough to be struck by a free falling sack of grain and was carried on a stretcher for a day until he recovered enough to walk unaided.

All the time there had been great difficulty in contacting Brigade 'on the air'. They had not heard from them since the night before Kyaikthin and the only news they had was from villagers. From them they learnt that several other columns had also crossed the Irrawaddy.

Around 15 March they met up with Mike Calvert's 3 Column near Pegon. They exchanged information and learned that Brigade HQ was moving to Baw, while Calvert was on the way to the Gokteik viaduct. In the absence of other orders Dunlop decided to head for Mongmit, whose Sawba (princess) was married to an Englishman, and see what was to be done. Dunlop considered marching to the Shweli suspension bridge near Namhkam on the frontier with China. Several of his demolition men had been with him the previous year when they blew a fine suspension bridge over the Namtu River east of Gokteik.

The next day they set off, keeping to the south-west of Baw. They found that the area was rather short of water and were glad to come across the Inbale Chaung where they could clean themselves and refill their water bottles. One man had discovered lice in his clothing and within a week everyone had them. Removing the loathsome creatures and their eggs proved practically impossible while on the move and combined with thirst and hunger it had a depressing effect on morale. It was around here that they met Major Fergusson and 5 Column on 20 March. The Japs had been hard on their heels and they advised Fergusson not to linger too long.

The following night they had their largest supply drop yet and managed to re-equip a large part of the column. Unfortunately their benefactors had included sizable quantities of tinned butter and white bread – the ensuing feast was too much for most stomachs and nearly all the British were sick. Dunlop decided to rest his men for a day to recover. He did however send a patrol to look at the Shweli River at Pinlon. They found a few Japanese asleep in a house and threw in a grenade to keep them company.

One of the Burma Riflemen was killed by a free-dropped sack during the supply drop and he was buried by the 'Pastor' – one of the men who was a Baptist lay preacher. On the plus side a Gurkha turned up who had been lost at the previous supply drop. He was carrying a full untouched supply pannier and no other food. He claimed that a 'small hairy man' had taken him away into the hills to a cave, and put him in a trance. After a long time he was released and told how to find the column. Dunlop never discovered what lay behind the tale, although there is a Burmese legend about 'small hairy men' and he may have heard it. But why had he not fed himself from his pannier?

They finally managed to contact Brigade that day, but they were in a deal of trouble and the only instructions they could get were 'Jesus remembers His little children'. After that Dunlop decided to make for Mongmit.

They marched southwards crossing the Mongmit–Male road and made their way along the foot hills of the Shweu-daung Range below Bernardmyo. They decided to bivouac and then received their last message from Brigade: 'Remember Lot's wife. Return not whence ye came. Seek thy salvation in the mountains. Genesis.' This gave Dunlop food for thought as they had no Bibles with them. He later recalled:

> Here I was with 500 men and 130 animals, to raise rebellion in a town which we had now learned usually held more than a thousand Japanese. The previous night we had heard their MT on the road below and the Reconnaissance Platoon had reported armoured cars. The idea that we might have to abandon the animals and turn 'guerilla' came into my mind, but I said nothing except to Weatherall. He was not quite sure of the idea.

During the research for this book a number of discrepancies were unearthed that will probably never be explained. One of them was exactly who was supposed to meet up with Captain Herring. In a letter written in 1951 to Colonel Barton, the official narrator in the Cabinet Office who was tasked with writing the story of the expedition, Herring states:

> When I left Gilkes of 7 Column I arranged with him to meet *him* on the RV and have no knowledge of any change of instructions. I waited on the RV for four long, weary, dreary days and when I left I arranged with the headman of the nearby Kachin village to keep an eye open for any of our chaps, but I never heard a thing. It was damnably disappointing as if only Wingate could have known of the situation in the Kachin Hills he could have found asylum there for the whole brigade and in comparative safety and we could then have made an orderly withdrawal although Wingate had spoken of making a stronghold to weather out the monsoon.
>
> As far as my force is concerned we had several near misses with superior Japanese forces who were out looking for us. We had our fair share of ambushes and skirmishes but I think on the whole we managed to fill our bellies better than many of the others. Remember that in the hills we were amidst friendly folk – and many of them paid for the help they gave us afterwards. Perhaps enough said on this point as I get very bitter when I think of how the Kachins have been treated since by us – a lack of treatment might be more descriptive.

Perhaps, if Wingate had allowed Herring to take a radio with him, the story might have had a different ending, with more men alive at the end to tell it.

Chapter 9

Disperse – Get Back to India!

W hen Wingate crossed the Irrawaddy he had good reason to be optimistic about the future. The attack on the north-south railway had been successful and he still had 2,200 men and 1,000 animals under his command. The ciphers and radio system were working adequately and supply dropping had proved an unqualified success. He was still under the impression that Herring was continuing with his mission of raising rebellion in the Kachin Hills. Unfortunately, what Wingate did not know was that between the Brigade and those hypothetical friends in the east lay a dry, hot belt of waterless forest, intersected by motorable tracks and heavily patrolled by the Japanese.

While the Brigade Group was crossing the Irrawaddy near the junction with the Shweli River, the Southern Group, comprising 1 Column, Lieutenant Colonel Alexander's Group Headquarters and parts of 2 Column, was slowly moving south towards the Nam Mit. Wingate is rather critical of them in his after-action report, stating:

> The correct course for this Group was to have carried out the original intention which had never been changed, to proceed to the Mong Mit area where Herring was due to be met and his information passed to Brigade. For reasons which have not yet been explained, the Group did not attempt to carry out this plan until yet again ordered to do so. Eventually on 25 March the Mongmit-Shwebo motor road was crossed, 16 days after crossing the Irrawaddy, at a point only 50 miles to the northwest. This long delay had the effect of concertinaing the Brigade and making clear to the enemy both numbers and probable intentions. The R.V. with Herring was reached on 8 April. He had left on 29 March having waited for five days.

While Southern Group was approaching the Mongmit motor road, 3 and 5 columns were also having trouble finding safe bivouacs. The numbers of Japanese troops in the area had greatly increased – a battalion had arrived at

Myitson and numerous patrols, usually of one officer and twenty men, sought to pinpoint the columns prior to attack by stronger forces.

The columns hit back though, with Fergusson reporting the presence of the enemy at Myitson to the RAF, who promptly bombed the place. Mike Calvert's 3 Column took on a force of Japanese on 23 March and inflicted heavy casualties on them, concluding afterwards that the British 3-inch mortars and type 36 and 68 grenades were superior to those used by the enemy. After the battle Wingate was advised that 3 and 5 columns and Southern Group were losing their effectiveness due to the heat, lack of water and the constant pressure of their pursuers.

At the same time Wingate was asked by IV Corps whether or not further operations were possible. He replied that further operations were indeed possible and he proposed marching into the Chin Hills for subsequent attack on the Lashio-Bhamo line. To this IV Corps replied that supply drops much further east would become increasingly difficult. The transport aircraft had the range, but the fighter escorts did not. They instructed Wingate to consider a withdrawal.

It was easier said than done. However, on 23 March, the day that Mike Calvert's column carried off a masterful ambush and destroyed a full company of Japanese troops, Wingate cancelled his operation against the Gokteik viaduct and ordered Calvert to return to India by any route. Fergusson was ordered to bring 5 Column to rejoin the Brigade Group and participate in a supply dropping at Baw, before attempting to recross the Irrawaddy. Until then his column would go hungry as Wingate had cancelled their own planned supply drop on the grounds that the fewer supply droppings at that time the better. Not long afterwards a fierce fight in a village would split Fergusson's force and lead to the loss of two-thirds of his men over the coming weeks. Lieutenant Colonel Alexander, Major Dunlop and Southern Group were ordered to continue on to Herring's rendezvous while Wingate pondered the options for the rest of the Brigade Group.

As the columns had moved deeper into enemy territory they found themselves in a great bag formed by the Irrawaddy and Shweli Rivers, and across the mouth of the bag ran a motor road. By now the Japanese hornets' nest had been well and truly aroused and substantial reinforcements were being moved into the area. In addition, the rivers were being patrolled and eventually the Japanese confiscated all the boats they could find. They were aware that the villages would attract the Chindits in search of food and guides, so they occupied them.

The fighting capabilities of the men was now being eroded by the heat, shortage of water and the fatigue caused by the long marches. Wingate decided that a good supply drop was needed and ordered one for 24 March in the paddy fields near the village at Baw. He did not know whether the Japanese were occupying the village, though, and decided to block the approaches during the hours of darkness. He gave strict orders that no one was to approach the village until first light when the Chindits would advance in force. Wingate later complained:

Had these orders been obeyed a satisfactory little coup would have resulted. A Japanese Company would have been surprised at its ease and a motor convoy coming from the Shweli to remove rice collected by the company at Baw would have walked into a sufficient ambush. Some local produce would have fallen to the hungry Column's hands and the supply dropping would have taken place as arranged. The foresight was made of no avail and the plan spoiled by one officer failing to realise the importance of getting into position before it was light, while another blundered into Baw itself with his small road block party which was not strong enough to avail itself of the surprise its appearance caused. The consequence was that the Japanese had time to man their defensive posts around the perimeter of the village. The road block party never reached its allotted post and the enemy was able in the course of the day to evacuate his wounded. By the time Number Two Group had arrived a dog fight of the usual type had developed. I reached the scene shortly before the supply dropping was due to start. It could not take place in the paddy fields and efforts were hastily being made to light a flare path in jungle. This flare path was out of necessity within a few hundred yards of the Japanese. I judged it necessary to clear the village and ordered Cooke to do this. There followed a number of attacks by platoons of 7 and 8 Columns. Great difficulty was experienced in penetrating the thick jungle and the fact that we did not know the situation of the enemy dug-in posts made these attacks costly.

Major Scott and his men got into the village and found the No. 68 hand grenades very useful for driving the enemy out of a number of houses. In the meantime the parachutes began to fall and about one and a half days of supplies arrived before the planes became suspicious and went home before completing the supply drop. Later in the day they returned, but the quantity delivered was only enough to supply each man of the Group for two days. In addition two wireless operators parachuted in with the supplies, although they were unfortunate to lose their lives later on.

In the course of the fight at Baw, Captain Petersen was wounded in the head. He was greatly respected by his men and they were determined not to abandon him, so he was tied to a horse and remained with Major Gilkes and 7 Column until they reached safety weeks later.

One good thing about the experience was that Wingate realized that supply drops could take place just as well in the jungle as in open paddy fields, and

Squadron Leader Longmore arranged a similar drop two days later, near the Salin Chaung, when four more days rations arrived. In the meantime Wingate had come to a decision: 'News of 3 Column's difficulties added to no news from Herring decided me to withdraw. 5 Column rejoined us at the Hehtin Chaung and Major Jefferies with his Headquarters of 142 Company arrived from Number One Group at the same time.'

On 26 March, Wingate held a conference of column commanders at the Hehtin Chaung. He outlined the options open to them as well as the Corps Commander's instructions to consider withdrawal. He told them that they were returning to India at all speed and would try to recross the Irrawaddy at Inywa, the same place they crossed on their outward journey. Wingate reasoned that it was the last place the Japanese would expect them to try. In order to reach the river without alerting the enemy to their intention, Wingate proposed a 50-mile forced march followed by a swift crossing of the river. If they could get the minimum number of mules and W/T sets across they would have a good chance of making their way home again. The majority of the mules and the heavy equipment would be abandoned. The mules were too tired to make it back to India and the 6 tons of equipment that would be rendered useless was a drop in the ocean in view of the fact that a million tons of war material was being sunk in the space of a month at sea.

Major Scott asked whether his column could attack the railway again on the way back. Wingate replied that he was considering the destruction of the Meza bridge and a possible attack on Indaw, and that they would keep enough mules to carry the W/Ts, mortars and machine-guns, but demolition stores could be dropped from the air.

Colonel Wheeler reminded Wingate that it was agreed before entering Burma that, when the time came for them to withdraw, permission would be given for some of his Burma Riflemen to stay behind, especially those who found themselves near their villages. Wingate, in order to prevent the withdrawal being regarded as a retreat, ordered his commanders to tell the men that they were marching north to cooperate with parachute troops in an attack on Bhamo and Indaw. In order to maintain morale, he considered such subterfuge as justified.

It was a bit too late for 5 Column, though, because they had already picked up the news of the decision to return home from men of 8 Column. Major Fergusson was very unhappy that the news had reached the men and later wrote:

This was the most unfortunate thing which could have happened. As long as the men knew that they were staying in and carrying on with the campaign, they were perfectly alright; but as soon as the news got round that we were homeward bound, one's first reaction was to think, 'Splendid! Now it would be too bad if I got pipped on the way home. I must start taking care of myself.' And that is a disastrous frame of mind for soldiers whose whole safety depends on prompt, resolute and unhesitating action. I shall always wish that we had told them instead that we were going to another area to operate.

Fergusson was convinced that he could fight his way home with his column in one piece and initially Mike Calvert was of the same opinion. For his part, Wingate was leaning towards dispersal of the columns.

Fergusson would be taking an extra man home with him, the officer previously mentioned, who had been sent prior to the supply drop at Baw to seal off part of the area from possible enemy interference. Having failed to reach his allotted position by nightfall he had bivouacked short of it. When he moved on at dawn, he found the Japs already in the village between him and the supply dropping area. He was judged guilty of having failed to carry out his orders through negligence and was summarily reduced to the ranks by the Brigadier. It would have been impossible to stay in his own column, where he had been a captain, so he went to Fergusson as a private soldier. Within a few days Fergusson had elevated him to the rank of Sergeant and after his return to India and on Fergusson's recommendation his rank would be restored.

On 27 March, at 0100 hours, the columns set off across country, avoiding the tracks and the paths. Fergusson's column was at the rear, followed by the Burma Rifles whose job was to try to eliminate all traces of their passing. As they made their way across the chaungs and hill-tops, handfuls of mules would be lead off the track and shot. When the noise of the pistol shots began to worry the Brigadier he gave orders that the animals were to be killed silently, using knives. It was a very sad state of affairs, especially for Bill Smyly who had looked after them from the very beginning.

Wingate's plan was to reach Inywa by 1800 hours on the 28th and to begin crossing the Irrawaddy that night. They marched for twelve hours and then halted for an hour to rest and eat some of their meagre rations. Suddenly shots rang out from a hill near the rear of the column. Apparently a Burma rifleman had wandered a couple of hundred yards from the bivouac to attend to the course of nature and had been fired upon by a Jap patrol. Wingate later reported:

Owing to the carelessness of a Burma rifleman our tail was attacked by an enemy patrol about 1400 hours. I sent a verbal order to Major Fergusson, the commander of the rear column, to ambush our tracks to prevent the enemy following up, and continued to march north. Fergusson decided to leave the main body and make a false bivouac and generally to engage whatever enemy might be about. This was not my intention. However, he was successful in making the enemy attack his dummy bivouac. But at 0300 hours on the twenty-eighth, he endeavoured to pass the village of Hintha. This village was at the junction of several tracks frequently patrolled by Japanese and probably held a company.

Finding the jungle impassable, Fergusson decided to advance through the village. He walked into a hornet's nest. The sound of 5 Column's fight at Hintha echoed through the night as the rest of the Brigade Group marched for Inywa. At 1600 hours on the 28th, the exhausted men arrived 4 miles short of Inywa and lay down for a three-hour rest before moving down to the Irrawaddy. When they reached the river at 0300 hours on 29 March, they expected to meet Colonel Wheeler and his Burma Rifles Headquarters party, who had been covering their tracks when the columns crossed vehicle roads. However, they had missed the rear column and gone on to the operational rendezvous at Debin.

Wingate was depending on the Burma Rifles to obtain boats and men to paddle them, and it took until 0600 hours to gather about twenty country boats of various sizes, with paddles for only half of them. Eventually some native rowers were rounded up, ten RAF dinghies were inflated and the crossing began. A platoon of 7 Column had just begun to land on the west bank when firing began. Apparently a force of Japanese were living in the village one mile upstream and Wingate could see twenty or thirty of them running along the river bank. Soon mortar and automatic fire began to sweep the river. Snipers began to fire aimed shots at the men on the east bank, one of which went through Major Scott's map as he stood on the bank. When the first boat was sunk, the native oarsmen began to scurry for safety. Wingate estimated that the remaining six boats would require two and a half days to transport the Brigade Group of just under a thousand men, already exhausted after marching 50 miles in forty-eight hours. The mantle of responsibility rested heavily upon Wingate's shoulders that morning. Allen Wilding was one of the men who came under fire during the attempted crossing:

As soon as we arrived at the river, I was told to take my ciphers, my Sergeant and a transmitter across the river and be ready to encipher and send a message to the RAF for help if our crossing was interrupted. As the only canoe immediately available held but three plus the paddlers, we decided to take one of the bomber dinghies which I had acquired at Argatala and tow it. I put the transmitter in the dinghy. To my horror we were fired on from the west bank. I much regretted the dinghy which was bright yellow! It is a very odd feeling when you, personally, are fired at, especially for the first time. Also the noise made by bullets ricocheting off the water is a bit intimidating! The paddlers, who were locals, knew that the Japs would kill them, but were pretty sure that in spite of my lurid threats, I would not, so they turned back and we regained the east bank. Very sadly, Sergeant Crawford of the Royal Signals was killed. It was rotten luck, he was hit by a bullet which had ricocheted off the water and, going sideways, hit him in the throat, killing him instantly. I reported to the Brigadier who, fortunately, had seen it all. We withdrew from the bank and rested. Thinking about it all these years later we should, of course, have forced a crossing. It would have been costly, but not as costly as the alternative. But this is with hindsight.

Private Charles Aves was one of the men from 7 Column who reached the west bank:

As quietly as possible, we made our way to the small boats at the bank of the river where boatmen had been paid to ferry us across. I think I was in the second or third boat. We proceeded across the river and it seemed ages getting across. I suppose there were eight or ten of us in the boat. Just as we and a couple of other boats reached the bank, the Japs opened up with mortar and automatic fire from a point some few hundred yards north of our landing. We couldn't see them, for they were well concealed in a copse. We scrambled ashore to find Lieutenant W and a few men from the first boat standing around. I shall never forget the Lieutenant; he was eating cheese from a tin with a penknife quite unconcerned about the firing which was directed on to the boats trying to get over, also at the troops on the other side.

Contrary to what has been written before, we were not under fire on the west bank. The Japs did not have control of this area. I firmly believe that it must have been only a patrol of Japs with a mortar unit and automatic fire. Perhaps also with a sniper. I can vouch for the fact that we were not fired at on the bank. For some reason Lieutenant W decided that I would attack the enemy position. Yes, ME. He told me to make my way across an open paddy field to a point some two hundred yards away and direct some grenades on to the Japs wherever they were. I looked at him in disbelief. I couldn't see the enemy, I had never used a grenade launcher, I only had two grenades and no launcher attachment. I told him this but he found a launcher and told me to just fix it on the end of the rifle. I was completely in the open as I crossed this paddy field; had there been any Japs looking they could have mown me down easily. I made myself as small as possible and safely reached this point. [Charles Aves told the author that there was a reason why he might have been singled out for such a foolhardy exploit. Some time previously the men had been told by Lieutenant W and a Sergeant that there was no chocolate being dropped with their meagre rations. However, one night Charles came across the Sergeant eating chocolate and challenged the officer about his claims that none had been dropped. He did not reply, merely turned his charger around and rode off.] What was I to attack? I couldn't see anything. There was no firing at this time. Just a small forest of trees. I decided to return and ask for further instructions. When I got back to the main group I found them forming up to move off. Had the Japs been any stronger I am sure they could have attacked us. The total number of men that formed up was sixty-five. One Captain O, one Lieutenant J, one second Lieutenant W, two or three Sergeants and some Corporals and about fifty other ranks. I asked about Captain Hastings, who had been my platoon officer until he was promoted to column adjutant. I was told that the boat he was in had been hit and he was flung into the river and swept away.

Another member of 7 Column to survive the crossing was Private R.V. Hyner of 14 Platoon. He later recalled:

15 Platoon began the crossing first. It was beginning to get light. One or two of the villagers began to show themselves. Two more natives with trays were selling sweet balls which tasted of toffee. Those of us who had any annas paid; the rest of the men just took them. 15 Platoon continued to cross, one man bringing back the boat each time. We could see this way of crossing was going to take far too long. I was glad when my lot, the 14th, were ordered into the boats. There were seven men in my boat and we were sitting in each other's legs. I was the last man in with only enough room to rest my gun in front of me. Two Gurkhas were doing the paddling with oars. We were further down the left hand side of the river to the rest of the boats. I said to Bill, 'It's just like being at Southend.' The sun was shining, it was a beautiful day. Suddenly a sound like church bells ringing came from over the river. Machine guns and mortars began opening up. Boats were being hit, columns on the far shore were scattering and my illusion of Southend vanished. Johnny Gurkha lost his paddle and the boat was momentarily out of control, heading down the river being taken by the current. This turned out to be lucky as the boat, with the help of one paddle, drifted into the bank which gave us plenty of cover from the Japs.

Protruding over the river was a tree which we somehow had to get past. Our boat by now had turned round, making me the first man. I managed to get out and tried to swing around the branch of the tree. I found this very awkward with my bren gun strapped to me, and the bank was very slippery. Another small boat had got behind us by now and I was still struggling to get round this big tree which was about ten feet wide, with its branches sticking out all over the place. I heard Captain Jealous's voice telling me to jump in the 'bloody water'. I didn't think this was a very good idea as I was making quite good progress round the tree and up the bank.

Once up the bank I found a large ditch where I immediately took up a firing position. By this time two or three more men were with me. We heard a noise of something coming towards us. Coming round the bend were two natives with a Gurkha soldier whose hands were tied behind his back. One native had the soldier's rifle and the other had his pack. We made signs to the men behind us to keep quiet. The four of us kept out of sight and we allowed them to approach us until they were so close I was able to poke my bren gun in the belly of the one carrying the rifle. The other one, who was carrying the pack, was covered by the three riflemen who were with me. We ordered the two Burmese to untie Johnny Gurkha. They said they had thought he was a Jap and were taking him to the British, which we knew was a lie. Captain Jealous had by now arrived on the scene. We wanted to know what he wanted us to do with the two Burmese. We wanted to shoot them, but he said no, as the noise would give our position away. So we suggested either drowning them or using a knife. He said no and made us let them go. I am sure he made the wrong decision even up to this day.

There was a sunken ferry boat on the shore and we could hear firing coming from it. We joined up with 15 Platoon and put the ferry boat out of action with a few grenades. We continued to engage the Japs along the river bank, realising that we could not do this for much longer because the columns seemed to be dispersing and making no more attempts to cross and we were this side running out of ammunition. Our officers decided we could do no more good staying where we were so the long trek began back to India. Unfortunately we now knew there would be no more food or ammunition as we had no wireless communication with anybody.

We left the river bank and returned to the jungle until we came upon a village. We cautiously entered and found no Japs were there. One native man came out carrying a large enamel washing bowl full of cooked rice. We shared this amongst the platoon. Other men were getting rice in banana leaves. We were all foraging. After a short stay in this village we began moving again up the hill. We tried to get some sleep as we had been marching since the night before. We just laid down and rested our heads on our packs. Firing could still be heard practically all night. The Japs seemed to be firing across the river.

Charles Aves remembered:

In retrospect we could say that had we attacked the Jap unit it is possible that the rest of Wingate's force could have crossed reasonably safely, but I don't know what orders our senior officers had. I believe we had no means of signalling across the river and at this time most of the men were ill and short of food. The sixty-five of us who had crossed the river moved quickly away and a few miles later made camp in dense jungle. This was the rendezvous point for those who had crossed the river, but by the morning no one else had turned up. We waited another day and then our officers led us off towards the Chindwin. Captain O, our senior officer, had maps so we knew where we were going, but we were very short of food. It was decided to make for a village where we hoped to obtain some rice and a little rock salt.

After a couple of days we came to a village, a friendly one we hoped, without any Jap troops nearby. We each obtained a wedge of cooked rice within a large banana leaf envelope. The rice was delicious. The Burmese have a way of presenting boiled rice like I have never tasted since. We ate half of this and went on our way.

A number of men were feeling pretty bad by now and a particular friend of mine, Freddy Raffo, said to me, 'I'm not going to make it, I can't go on any more.' I knew Fred wasn't married, but he had an elderly mother who lived alone in a small house in Salford. I said, 'You can't give up, it's all right for you, but what about your mother, all on her own waiting for you, you've got to make it for her sake.' We split up all his equipment and took his rifle and carried it all for him. I am glad to say Fred did get out and he thanked me later for saying what I did at the time.

We made our way slowly for another day and at about one p.m. the officers decided we would have a rest and a brew-up. We flung our weary limbs down in the dried bed of a river. Two men were posted as sentries and we took off our packs, laid down our rifles and made some tea. I was with Corporal Stan Hickman; I did not know him very well, but he was a good chap, who came from South London. We were relaxing and completely off guard when suddenly we heard the sound of footsteps running through the trees. Looking up we saw the two sentries running for their lives past us. They didn't say anything, but at the same time we heard shots being fired and shouts from some twenty yards away. I went to run, for everyone else had gone, but Corporal Hickman said 'No, don't go.' I stayed with him and then we saw them, about fifteen yards away, coming at us. We moved like lightning, carrying only our rifles. We ran up the nullah and as we did so we both grabbed a pack each left by someone else. We broke the speed record and managed to climb up behind some rocks; there were a few of our party there and we poured rifle fire on where the Japs were coming from. After a while we ceased fire. We couldn't see the Japs but we could hear them shouting to each other. I think they must have been looting the packs left behind. We withdrew up the hill and then sorted ourselves out. There was Lieutenant J, two sergeants, Corporal Hickman and seven other men. Corporal Hickman and I looked into the two packs we had picked up; mine was Captain O's and contained all the maps on the way to the Chindwin. In the other that belonged to Lieutenant W was a quantity of silver rupees. We then found that we only had two water bottles between us. We went back to the site of the attack, but the Japs were still there, so we took off west as fast as we could without a stop for two hours.

Private Hyner also recalled the chaos as the Japs came across their bivouac:

We decided to have a brew up and I ate the last of my rice wrapped in a banana skin. Sentries had already been posted on guard, so some men went outside the perimeter area to go to the toilet. When some noises were heard the guards did not challenge or open fire as they thought it was our own men coming back. The first noise I heard was someone saying 'Ah English'. He sounded to me like an educated Japanese officer speaking perfect English. He was shouting to his men to fire. At that time I had been speaking to my mate Bill about his future wedding and his inviting our little gang and wives.

I was in possession of two rifles because I had given my bren gun to one of the guards. As I went to stand up a small Irishman caught me off balance by rushing past me. My pack slipped down my right arm on to the ground leaving me with what I thought was more important, my two rifles. There was no time to pick up my pack as things were getting hot and I began running to the mountain. In front of me first was a wide precipice with about a 30 foot drop. I had not time to go round it so, to my surprise, I jumped it zig-zagging all the way up the mountain, feeling imaginary bullets in my back all the time. Three-quarters of the way up I met an officer, who for the moment, seemed to be at a loss as to what to do. All he kept repeating was, 'Where is Captain Jealous?' At this time there were four of us and we decided to go to the top of the mountain and blow three blasts on the whistle to signal whatever men we could to join us.

About 34 men got together here but my mate Bill was not one of them, so two or three of us went back to the hill overlooking the nullah. All we could hear were Jap voices coming from underneath where we were standing, so we slung a few grenades down and scarpered back to the men at the top of the hill. We had not come across Captain Jealous or any of the men on guard, although we heard later they had gone in another direction. So the only officer, Lieutenant Oaks, decided we would now continue back towards India down the other side of the hill. Sergeant Jarvis and another Sergeant decided to go on their own and we later found out that they didn't make it out of Burma.

Following the surprise attack at the bivouac our two correspondents, Private Hyner and Private Charles Aves, went off in different directions with their respective parties to find their own way back to India. Aves remembered:

As night fell, we took stock. We all had rifles, ammunition and grenades, but no food and little water. The Lieutenant was a good officer who decided to involve us all in decisions if needed. We had another bonus, me, as I was the only one who could speak any Burmese, thanks to Stan Allnutt. Anyone can make themselves understood in their quest for food, but I was able to ask the villagers for the headman and for the position of the nearest Japanese.

In the morning we decided to make for the nearest village. Most of us really found ourselves during this period. We enjoyed being in the jungle, the thicker the better, and we felt safe. We could find paths among the undergrowth, however indistinct and we knew that they would eventually lead to water or a village. The first village was quite near and I went in first with Lieutenant J, while the others kept a look out. They were very friendly and helpful, all smiles and generosity. In fact our experience showed all the Burmese to be very helpful, with one exception; I can't recall the name of the village, but shall call it Maungde.

We had travelled quite a few miles, probably about twenty each day, when we reached Maungde. We knew this village was different to all the others, we could tell straight away there was something wrong. The headman was uneasy; we always watched out to see whether anyone disappeared when we entered a village and it seemed to us one or two shifty characters moved out of sight. We didn't hesitate, let's get out now, no messing. We didn't give them a chance to call on any Japs, we shot through like lightning, and disappeared over the horizon with no casualties.

It transpired that some others of our original group were betrayed when they went through the same village and a number of them were killed by crossfire and mortar fire when they left. On arriving safely at Imphal the survivors of that group reported the behaviour of those villagers and HQ arranged to send a plane over and a couple of days after we left, the village was bombed.

Major Scott's 8 Column arrived at the Irrawaddy just before the attempted crossing began; 7 Column and Brigade Headquarters were already there. Nick Neill, a young subaltern from 3/2nd Gurkhas attached to 8 Column as an animal transport officer, recalled the scene as the boats carrying the bridgehead platoon came under enemy fire:

This was the first time I had heard the sound of Jap medium machine-guns. They had a much slower rate of fire than our Vickers MMGs and their distinctive tok-tok-tok-tok noise was imprinted in my memory from that moment on. British troops eventually christened them 'Woodpeckers'. The area we were in on the eastern bank of the Irrawaddy was a vast stretch of open paddy fields and I had a clear view of the far bank of the river, some two miles away. I could not see any sign of our men, but I could see the bursting Jap mortar bombs from time to time. A group of men were approaching me across the paddy and when they came closer I realised that they were a group from Brigade HQ, led by Wingate himself. He was still wearing his sola topee, but now had a beard like the rest of us. I remember thinking that he looked just like a figure straight out of the Bible. As he passed by he was almost trotting, and his speed was causing his pack to bump up and down on his back. His eyes were wide and very staring; he called out to me and the others of my column standing nearby, 'Disperse, disperse, get back to India.' I recall thinking to myself, 'My God, the man's gone mad. Here we are, a force of some 700 men, we have a platoon already across the Irrawaddy and he's not prepared to carry on with the crossing. This is too improbable to be true. There must be some other explanation to his behaviour.'

As Charles Aves and the sixty-four other men from 7 Column tramped westwards away from the river, Wingate led the remains of his force east, back into the jungle. Perhaps if the bridgehead party had attacked the Japs firing on the boats, while the remainder of the troops forced a crossing, the story would have had a different ending. One can only speculate. As Nick Neill and 8 Column made camp that night, Major Scott told him that all mules and chargers were to be released during the next day's march and driven away from the column as they could become a hindrance when the time came to head for India. Nick was aware of the cruelty that the Japanese often showed to animals and as his own charger, Rate, nuzzled his face with his soft nose, he stared up at the stars and cried. He continues:

The next morning we hid the saddles and other equipment as best we could. Johnny Carroll made the mortars and MMGs as unserviceable as possible and hid them. Only the big radio-carrying mules were to be retained until the following day, when we were due to receive our final air drop, after which they would be released as well. From this day on, each man would carry his own pack, rations and bedding.

The following day we received our air drop and then, for the first time, I was invited to join Scotty's 'O' (orders) Group. It was indeed true that all columns of the brigade were to be split up into much smaller groups and were to find their own way back to India, or China, the latter country being nearest to us now. Our one radio in the column would go with Scotty's group after we had dispersed – lucky for some!

Wingate had now played his final ace card. He had taken us deep into enemy-held territory and now we were required to return to safety in penny-packets, on our own and without any communications, thus condemning us to receive no further administrative or tactical support. In my judgement, we should have forced a crossing of the Irrawaddy when we had the chance and when we were in considerable strength. We would of course have taken casualties during the crossing, but these, I believe, would have been far fewer than those ultimately suffered by the brigade as a whole during the retreat we were about to carry out in small groups, without any inter-linking support of any kind.

Chapter 10

A Long Way from Home – 1 Column

On the evening of 29 March, when Wingate ordered his columns to withdraw to India, 1 Column was the furthest from home, bivouacked 6 miles west of Mongmit. In the morning Lieutenant Colonel Alexander ordered all but seven mules to be released and all heavy equipment, including mortars and machine-guns, to be dumped. Three days earlier Wingate had sent a message to Southern Group: 'Remember Lot's wife. Return not whence you came. Seek thy salvation in the mountains. Genesis XIX.' However, there was no salvation to be found in that direction. Herring had waited in vain for them to arrive and had finally left the area, and although the Kachins provided food for the hungry Chindits, the Japanese were everywhere. George Dunlop was far from pleased about being left out on a limb. In later years he wrote to the author: 'Wingate should have known that he was sending 1 Column and Southern Group HQ into a death trap. It was the area in which the Japs were confronting the Chinese Yunnan Armies.'

The Japanese were indeed everywhere and they soon found the rear of the column as they climbed the mountain on the way to the Mogok-Mongmit road. They had left booby traps behind them though and this slowed their pursuers during the day of 31 March. That evening they reached a long spur about 4,500 feet high, overlooking Mongmit and the road to Mogok. As it grew dark they could see fires burning at intervals along the length of the road and fires were burning below them too. It was clear that a fight was on the cards.

Early in the morning of 1 April, sentries below the spur reported enemy coming up the path that they had made the previous day. Soon their 81mm mortars came into play and a bombardment lasting two hours began. The Chindits had no picks or shovels to use to dig in, so all they could do was sit close to tree trunks and hope for the best. In the meantime Weatherall, with one of the Gurkha platoons, held the perimeter at the end of the spur and kept the Japanese troops at bay.

As the fight developed Dunlop could see a long column of lorries winding its way out of Mongmit and along the Mogok road which wound its way behind their position. They radioed Agartalla for fighter support and soon five Mohawks appeared and began to strafe the enemy on the road. The Japanese troops below the spur were becoming more cautious now and Dunlop decided to pull out while the going was good. The climb would be too steep for the surviving mules though, so they radioed final instructions to Agartalla for future supply drops and destroyed the wireless sets.

Casualties had been very light, but they included young Lieutenant Ian MacHorton who had been hurled from the cover of a boulder by a great blast of air as a mortar bomb burst behind him. He tried to scramble back to his position but found that he could not walk. There was a jagged tear in his trousers at his right hip and a dark blood stain was spreading ominously. Suddenly Kulbahadur, his Gurkha orderly and Havildar Lalbahadur, the Gurkha sergeant who was his second in command, risked the hail of bullets to scramble over the boulder and drag their officer back into cover. They pulled MacHorton's trousers down to expose his hip and thigh, and discovered an ugly wound where a long thin mortar splinter had cut into his flesh and muscle a few inches below the hip joint. By now Captain Stocks, the Column Medical Officer, had scrambled over the bullet-swept hillside and was pulling out a phial of morphine. He jabbed the needle into the officer's arm and MacHorton lapsed into unconsciousness.

When MacHorton came to, it was quite dark. His orderly Kulbahadur leaned over him with a water bottle as Lieutenant Arthur Best appeared. He quietly informed him that they were about to pull out before more Japanese reinforcements appeared from Mongmit. They were joined by George Dunlop and Lieutenant Colonel Alexander, the latter now sporting a ragged black beard and straggling moustache. 'Do you think you can possibly keep up?' he asked. When MacHorton replied that he could not, the Colonel told him that they would carry him down to the motor road and assured him that he would have a good chance if he gave himself up unarmed. Major Dunlop squeezed his hand and wished him 'Good luck, old boy.' Arthur and Kulbahadur helped MacHorton to his feet and supported him as the column threaded its way down to the road.

The trio were the last to cross the wide, dusty road and they struggled up a steep slope overlooking it as the rear party tried to cover their tracks. They settled MacHorton against a tree, surrounded by undergrowth and bamboo and made him comfortable. His wound had been tightly bandaged and his pack was set down beside him as his friends made their farewells and disappeared into the darkness. As MacHorton lay still, gathering his strength, he heard the distant sound of lorry engines on the road below. He was now on his own.

Their last mules gone and the wireless set destroyed, 1 Column and Southern Group Headquarters continued eastwards. Dunlop later recorded that the road crossing had an adverse effect on morale and this phenomenon was to be repeated, worse each time, on every similar occasion. Another setback occurred on 6 April when they expected to be in the vicinity of Man Ton for a pre-arranged supply dropping, but were still a long way off when they saw the plane circling and then departing without dropping any supplies. Morale went right down and never recovered. Dunlop spent the evening burning out lice with his last cigarette.

The grim-faced officers held a conference that evening to decide what to do next. They only had a few maps so they would try to take the column out in one piece, but which way to go? They considered heading for China, via the route they were on, but they knew that at least one Japanese division sat between them and safety. They could turn west for India and although it would be a journey through enemy territory, things should have quietened down a bit. The last option was to turn north for Fort Hertz. It was even further away than India and their only maps were silk escape handkerchiefs. They would also have to cross the Shweli Gorge which would be difficult as it would be a mountain torrent a hundred yards wide. Dunlop voted for India, but Alexander, supported by Weatherall and Flight Lieutenant Edmunds, voted for Fort Hertz, so he found himself outvoted.

On 10 April, they reached the Shweli River and attempted to wade it with the help of a rope made of rifle slings. This broke, so they made small rafts of bamboo and the following morning started to ferry over half a dozen men at a time. At the same time the Guerrilla Platoon sent a party over to an island downstream and had just reached it when the enemy opened fire from the far bank. They had lingered too long and allowed the enemy patrols time to catch them in the process of crossing of the river.

At the sight of the Japanese on the opposite bank, panic set in amongst the column and Subedar Kulbir had to work hard to quieten the men down before withdrawing the bulk of them to a hill further along the bank. Dunlop and Weatherall remained on the bank with a few others to cover a lance naik and a rifleman of the Burma Rifles who twice crossed the river to recover the score of men who had got across before the enemy arrived. They managed to get a dozen back and the remainder disappeared up the opposite hill.

Eventually only the platoon stationed on the hill above the crossing place remained in contact with the enemy across the river. Weatherall announced that he was going to get them back. Dunlop ordered him to stay with him and told him that the experienced Jemadar in charge would know what to do. He was an old hand at mountain warfare and would bring his men along to rejoin the rest eventually. Dunlop later recorded:

However Weatherall for the first and last time disobeyed me and started to double off down the way we had come. He had just reached the first turn in the path when there were two long bursts of fire from the opposite bank. He was hit badly in the chest and died almost immediately. Many men wept quite unashamedly when they found out. With Weatherall's death we lost the best officer we had, and the only one who really knew the Gurkhas of the 3/2. Morale became non-existent and never again recovered until our last battle as a column near the Chindwin.

It was clear that crossing the Shweli River was no longer an option, so the decision was made to head for the Irrawaddy. The route from the Shweli to the Irrawaddy was governed by the need to go as straight as possible, via any available source of water on the way. It was imperative to avoid all clashes with the enemy who were now patrolling the roads in their path. By the time they reached Sinhnyat on the banks of the great river everyone was exhausted. The column had become a nervous mob which panicked at every loud or sudden noise. It was the jungle fire season and on several occasions burning trees and bamboo caused wholesale flight. The lack of food and water, infestation with lice and the desire to get home had done its work. The problem now was how to get 480 men across the river in safety. The villagers produced some food for the ravenous men, but they were so desperate that proper distribution broke down. When the chaos subsided Dunlop managed to lay in some stocks for the next stage of the journey.

Lieutenant Chet Kin of the Burma Rifles located two native boats that could carry about thirty men between them. A patrol under Lieutenant Wormald was sent across in the smaller boat and half an hour passed while they scouted the far bank. Suddenly firing broke out and for five minutes they could hear the sound of enemy weapons before silence descended. Later the boat returned, empty except for the native boatman.

At dusk on 20 April, they tried again and all night long the boats plied back and forth. During the evening Subedar Padanbahadur Rai with fifty-nine men joined the queue on the riverbank. Attached to Wingate's Headquarters as Defence Platoon, they had been left behind when Brigade Headquarters recrossed the river and continued westwards on their own. The crossing continued throughout the night and as the men reached the west bank they quickly took cover and moved on in their dispersal groups. As dawn broke, the covering platoon under Naik Devsur Ale began to cross.

As the last men began to climb into the two boats who should appear but Ian MacHorton, who had been left behind at Mongmit. He had avoided capture by the Japanese and, limping badly, had set off towards the west. He had been assisted on the way by friendly natives who fed him and tended his wound. Doc Lusk, the Irish doctor of 2 Column, slapped him on the back and propelled him towards the waiting boats. There were eleven men in the leaky craft already, but they made room for him and pushed off. Doc Lusk and the rest of the rearguard followed 30 yards astern.

The first boat was a hundred yards from the safety of the far bank when the Japanese arrived. Running along the west bank, they opened fire on the boats – some of the men in MacHorton's boat were hit and collapsed against their comrades. Then the boat capsized, the water swirling around the desperate men. MacHorton clung to the upturned boat as it floated downstream and struggled ashore. He could hear the sound of British and Japanese weapons in the distance, and saw that Doc Lusk's boat had turned around and was making its way back to the relative safety of the far shore. The occupants of the boat, including Second Lieutenant Harvey, Redman of the RAF and Doc Lusk were later captured by the Japanese. The genial Irishman would die in captivity.

When the firing began on the far shore, a general stampede ensued and the officers were hard pressed to restore control. Dunlop discovered that around a hundred of the men had disappeared, most of whom were collected by Subedar Major Siblal Thapa of 3/2 Gurkhas and led by him back to India. As Dunlop moved away from the sound of firing he gathered the remains of the column around him. Now reduced to around 350 men, they continued on their journey, travelling by night and lying up during the day.

In a clearing not far from the river crossing, Ian MacHorton came across a dozen wounded men, gathered together by a brave, but also wounded Sergeant Hayes of the RAF. He had found them scattered around the area and carried them away from the fighting. All of them had various wounds and three of them died in the clearing. The rest struggled to their feet and followed the officer and the Sergeant in the wake of the column.

On the morning of 26 April, the men of the column carefully broke their trail and went into bivouac in teak jungle. Dunlop and Johnny Nealon of the commandos took their clothes off to get some relief from the ever-present lice and lay down in the sunshine to sleep. Around 1100 hours Dunlop was informed that there were villagers nearby and a patrol was sent out to collect them. However the natives took to their heels and presumably went off to report the presence of the Chindits to the Japanese. Soon afterwards reports came in that Japanese were coming up the hill. There had been so many false alarms that at first Dunlop did not take it seriously, but he sent a platoon down anyway to investigate. Ten minutes later firing broke out below and the panic-stricken platoon rushed by the startled officers. Within seconds the whole column had bolted, leaving Dunlop and Nealon searching frantically for their clothes.

A handful of Japs came along the path, firing at the fast-disappearing Chindits. They saw Nealon and gave chase as he took to his heels, completely naked. Dunlop, in the meantime, finished dressing and went off in the direction that the column had taken. He found them, exhausted and lying along a ridge. He was furious and harangued the men in his best but rather inadequate Gurkhali. When a count was taken he found that eighty men were still missing, along with John Fowler and Nealon.

The officers of 13th King's, taken on the *Oronsay* on the way to India in 1942. Rear row, left to right: Cowper, Freddie Jones, Tuck, Coughlan, Scott-Farnie, Williams, Pickering, Holland, MacDonald, Summerfield, Neville Randall, Foulds, Brian Horncastle. Centre row, left to right: the Doctor, Scott, Gilkes, 2 i/c Lockhart, CO Lieutenant Colonel Robinson, Adjutant David Hastings, Anderson, Waugh, Cotton. Front row, left to right: Saffer, Carroll, Roberts, Bill Edge, Leslie Cotterell, Graham Hosegood, Thorpe, Walker, Blackburne. (Courtesy the family of Graham Hosegood)

The 13th King's Regimental Band at Secunderbad in 1942. (Courtesy Mrs Georgina Livingstone)

A group photograph of the officers and NCOs of Headquarters 13th King's before the expedition. The author would like to hear from anyone who can put names to the faces. (Courtesy Mrs Georgina Livingstone)

CQMS Duncan Bett of 8 Column was with Major Scott for most of the journey back home to India. As this book goes to print he is possibly the last living member of that column. (Author's collection)

Crossing swift-flowing rivers in RAF dinghies was a very difficult undertaking. Very little was known about the art of crossing wide rivers before the expedition began. (Author's collection)

General Wavell visiting 77 Brigade just before they set off on their journey into Burma. Brigadier Wingate is on the extreme right and Major Fergusson is nearest the camera wearing the rucksack. Note the censor has obliterated the Black Watch badge on his hat. (Author's collection)

It was very often difficult to persuade the mules to swim the rivers. Here two are tied to a boat and towed across. Note the bayonet and Lee Enfield rifle carried by the Gurkha holding the reins of the first mule.
(Author's collection)

A Chindit column crossing the Meza River. Note the heavily laden mules.
(Author's collection)

As the Green Light comes on, three despatchers struggle to push a load of supplies through the door of the Dakota to the Chindits waiting below. (Author's collection)

Brigadier Wingate (right) and Major George Bromhead, his Brigade Major, plan 77 Brigade's expedition into Burma in early 1943. Bromhead later took over command of 4 Column a day or so before it was scattered by a Jap ambush. (Author's collection)

Canvas bags clipped to the supply parachutes contained four ration tins. In each tin can be seen, left to right: biscuits, dates, cheese, sugar, salt, tea, matches, chocolate, powdered milk, cigarettes enough for two days' rations. (Author's collection)

Chindits brewing tea in their bivouac. This type of ubiquitous aluminium mess tin, issued in pairs, and clearly seen being used by the trio on the right, was still standard issue when the author joined the Army thirty years later.
(Author's collection)

A Chindit column fords a river while Burmese construct rafts in the foreground.
(Author's collection)

Without mules to carry weapons, radios and supplies, the expedition would have failed. The muleteers had their work cut out manhandling the mules and their cargo up and down the steep terrain.
(Author's collection)

Signallers operating a wireless transmitter in the jungle. The men worked long hours, setting up their equipment at the end of the day's march, while the other members of the column caught up on their sleep in the bivouac. (Author's collection)

Chindits preparing a bridge for demolition. This photograph was taken during the Second Chindit operation in 1944, but Mike Calvert's 3 Column would have used the same methods a year earlier.
(Author's collection)

Blowing the railway line, a speciality of Major Mike Calvert's 3 Column.
(Author's collection)

Lieutenant Duncan Campbell Menzies of the Black Watch. The Adjutant of 5 Column, and Major Fergusson's right-hand man, he was killed after capture on 4 April 1943. (Author's collection)

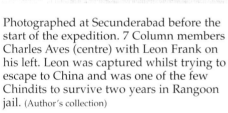

Photographed at Secunderabad before the start of the expedition. 7 Column members Charles Aves (centre) with Leon Frank on his left. Leon was captured whilst trying to escape to China and was one of the few Chindits to survive two years in Rangoon jail. (Author's collection)

Japanese jungle troops disembarking from lorries. (Author's collection)

The message hurriedly put out by Major Scott's men when they realized the size of the clearing. 'PLANE LAND HERE NOW' as seen from the supply plane.
(Author's collection)

Regimental Sergeant Major Livingstone, left, and Company Sergeant Major Cheevers with his faithful tommy gun.
(Author's collection)

This is the landing area discovered by Major Scott and 8 Column as they trekked back towards India. They marked out a landing strip running from the finger of jungle at top left, towards the clear area in the top right of the picture. The area was known as 'Piccadilly' in the 1944 campaign.
(Author's collection)

The crew of the rescue plane jump down to be greeted by a smiling Major Scott and the men of 8 Column. (Author's collection)

Private Jim Suddery of Islington was shot in the back by a Japanese rifleman. He survived and shows the bullet removed from his abdomen. (Author's collection)

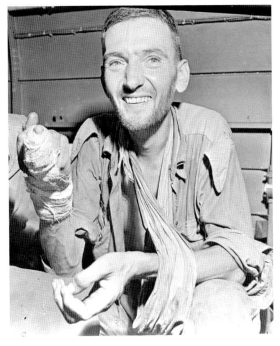

One of the lucky ones to be flown home, Private John Yates of Manchester, still smiles despite his wounds and jungle sores. (Author's collection)

On their way home at last. Private William Crowhurst, a Londoner from South Norwood, sits next to Sergeant Tony Aubrey and displays a Japanese bank note that they picked up in a Burmese village. (Author's collection)

Sergeant Tony Aubrey, left, discusses their experiences with Private Robert Hulse who is suffering from a bad rupture. Aubrey was one of the first men into Burma, accompanying Captain Herring of the Burma Rifles on a reconnaissance patrol before the expedition set off. (Author's collection)

On board the rescue plane, Lance Corporal Fred Nightingale from Lancaster is wearing a piece of parachute silk around his neck. Worn down by ulcers he almost gave up the day before the men reached the clearing. (Author's collection)

Lieutenant Colonel Sam Cooke was evacuated with boils and jungle sores on his back, and is sick with intestinal trouble. He is reading a copy of *Punch*, dropped to him two days earlier. He would later reach the rank of Major General. (Author's collection)

Two men of the 13th King's and a Gurkha comrade show their relief at being rescued after they marked out 'PLANE LAND HERE NOW' in a clearing in the jungle. Note the deep jungle sores on the left arm of the man on the right. (Author's collection)

Water is passed around inside the rescue plane as seventeen of Major Scott's men head for safety. The party comprised one Gurkha, one Burma Rifleman and fifteen men of 13th King's including Lieutenant Colonel Sam Cooke. Burma Rifleman Tun Tin sits on the right. (Author's collection)

This Chindit has lost his hat and is using his small pack to shield his head from the strong midday sun. Most of their large packs containing the bulk of their supplies were abandoned during the various river crossings and ambushes on the way back to India.
(Author's collection)

Lieutenant Albert Tooth was also left behind with Signaller Eric Hutchins when Wingate crossed the Irrawaddy. When his boat capsized Tooth saved the life of Lance Corporal 'Paddy' Dermody, one of the muleteers. Sadly Squadron Leader Longmore was swept away and lost. Tooth eventually brought the survivors of the party safely back to India.
(Author's collection)

Lieutenant Nick Neill, twelve months after successfully reaching India with Lieutenant T.A.G. Sprague and their party. He still has the tommy gun that he acquired on the way out and used it to good effect a few days after this picture was taken. His patrol ambushed and killed thirty Japanese without loss. (Author's collection)

Signaller Eric Hutchins was in the seventh and last boat of Wingate's party when they attempted to recross the Irrawaddy. Left behind by the others, only four of the seven in the boat made it back to India.
(Author's collection)

Wingate on the eve of his second expedition with Brigadier Scott on his immediate left, and his aide Captain George Borrow and Brigadier Mike Calvert on his right. (Author's collection)

Some of the prisoners still living in Rangoon Jail when their liberators arrived. Sitting third from left is Lieutenant 'Willie' Wilding and fifth from left Lieutenant Rose with a cloth around his neck. On the roof of the jail in the back ground is written 'JAPS GONE'. (Author's collection)

Five Gongs. Left to Right: RSM Livingstone, Major Pickering, CSM Richard Cheevers, RSM Jackie Cairns and an unknown Sergeant wearing their newly awarded medals. (Courtesy Mrs Georgina Livingstone)

Sixty-six years after Wingate took his leave of Ken Spurlock at the side of the track in Burma, his granddaughters, Emily and Alice, and their mother Holly meet Ken at the Chindit Annual Reunion in June 2009. (Courtesy Stephen Evans Photography)

The author with the late Brigadier Mike Calvert DSO in London, 1995. (Author's collection)

Mr Denis Gudgeon holding a copy of his Japanese prisoner-of-war record card, photographed by the author in his house in Farnham in January 2009. (Author's collection)

There was nothing more to do but carry on and the depleted column eventually reached the Mu River. Amazingly, Ian MacHorton, Sergeant Hayes and their half dozen walking wounded caught up with them there. They were on their last legs and gratefully accepted the mess tins full of rice that Ian's fellow officer Arthur Best produced for them. As they ate Major Dunlop sent Burma Rifles patrols up and down the river to check for the enemy and when they reported the area clear, the column began wading across the 200-yard-wide swift-flowing but shallow river and moved into the cover of the thick jungle beyond. The ground was covered with very thick scrub growing beneath large trees and the column was moving slowly to allow the rearmost members to close up when suddenly firing broke out to their rear. A party of Japanese had come up the river just in time to see the last men enter the jungle. They opened up with a random, but very heavy fire and mortar bombs began to explode around the men as they hurried to move out of range. One mortar bomb exploded near enough to Dunlop for him to feel the blast and hear the splinters as they flew by.

The jungle opened out and the men extended by platoons and ran across to the forest on the far side of the clearing. They carried on a bit further until they were well under cover and then halted to take stock. A distraught Lieutenant Clarke appeared and informed Dunlop that the last mortar bomb had blown away most of Lieutenant Colonel Alexander's and De La Rue's legs. Flight Lieutenant Edmunds and the officers' orderlies had carried them off into the jungle and no one had seen them since. Dunlop's old friend Sergeant Hill of the Middlesex Regiment, who had been platoon sergeant of the Guerrilla Platoon, had also disappeared. He had been just in front of Dunlop when the last mortar bomb went off and had been hit under the right shoulder. Lieutenant Arthur Best was also amongst the missing. He would turn up at Rangoon Jail along with other survivors. It was their worst day so far, with five officers and eighty men missing. On the plus side, Johnny Nealon had turned up, now wearing one of Dunlop's rabbit wool pullovers.

The column pushed on to the escarpment, but could not find the elephant path they had used on the way in to Burma. They were, however, joined by Fowler and the eighty missing men which brought their numbers up to around 350 again. Food was their most serious problem now, and although they had been throwing hand grenades into the chaungs to obtain a steady supply of fish, there was always the risk of alerting the Japanese to their presence.

The days that followed were a nightmare of mountains, rivers and hunger. Dunlop considered heading for Ywatha in the hope of obtaining food there, but when he spoke to Subedar Kulbir about the prospect of getting the men to fight for food, if necessary, he replied frankly, 'No, Sahib, they would rather chance reaching the Chindwin without fighting.' It would be easier said than done.

They were following a river one day when Fowler asked if they might take a short cut over the hill to avoid a big bend in the river. Chet Kin advised against it and Dunlop was not keen on the idea either as he had torn off a toenail and was walking without boots on. However, he allowed the bulk of the men to go with Fowler as they were aware of the location of the next RV where their chaung joined the Kaung Baung Chaung.

As Dunlop and his small group approached the RV through the elephant grass at the side of the river they notice Japanese boot prints. Soon a party of Burmese appeared, but bolted when they saw the Chindits. It was pretty clear that enemy search parties were near and Dunlop and his men took up defensive positions on a low hill above the chaung to wait for Fowler and the men to arrive. They had found a dead buck, presumably killed by a tiger and delayed their journey to cook and eat the unexpected rations. When they finally arrived at the RV Dunlop held an orders group to decide how to proceed.

It was highly likely that the enemy were about and a fight might well be on the cards. They therefore decided to send two platoons ahead up the track, followed by HQ and the remainder of the column. If they met the enemy they were to disperse and the platoon commanders would be expected to push on to the Chindwin as best they could. They had only moved a hundred yards when firing broke out on the left and mortar bombs began to drop through the trees. After an initial panic the men deployed into their dispersal parties and moved on through an area of thick, fallen bamboo. As the firing petered out Major Dunlop found himself with his HQ staff, the Guerrilla Platoon and about forty Gurkhas under the mule jemadar. Most of the latter were muleteers and in Dunlop's opinion, of little value as fighters.

Dunlop's group rested for a while and then suddenly Subedar Kulbir, the senior Gurkha officer, leapt to his feet, drew his kukri and rushed off towards the chaung, slashing at everything as he went. Dunlop later recorded:

So this was how Gurkha's ran amok! His orderly dutifully followed and I sent mine, Pithm Bahadur, to get them back. Kulbir, followed by the other two splashed across the river and into the jungle at the other side. Soon all hell broke loose over there; shouting and shooting. It died down and then there was silence. I questioned the man who had been sentry by the river as to why he had not seen the enemy. He said he had, both Japs and Burmans. However he had been so excited he had forgotten to tell anyone! We continued our journey. We were very hungry. Villages were few and far between and held unhusked rice and very little else for immediate use. Food gathering was strictly controlled and was done by the Burma Rifles. John Fowler did the issuing of what little there was. Private foraging was an offence. However, at this time we had virtually nothing to eat for a week and Lieutenant Nealon commanding the British demolition platoon asked permission to try for food in Maingnyaung as his British troops could not go on without it.

Dunlop gave his permission and he set off with his party. An hour later they heard sounds of a fight at the village, very short and sharp, then silence. They did not return. It later transpired that the men had been feasted by the villagers and then the Japs arrived. After a short fight, they decided to surrender and were eventually taken to Rangoon Jail from which only Nealon and four of his men would survive.

There followed days of more hunger and more hills until one night the mule jemadar and his party of Gurkhas disappeared, presumably to try to find their own way home. This left Dunlop with the MO, Doc Stocks, Dicky Clarke, John Fowler, the 2 Column Guerrilla Platoon officer, two signallers and three or four Gurkhas.

When Lieutenant MacHorton came across the party again they were resting on a sandbank with an air of lethargy about them, as if they had reached the end of their tether. They were all terribly weak due to lack of food, but there were a few smiles as they turned to watch the young officer approach along the chaung. John Griffiths was sitting by the prostrate form of Sergeant Hayes who was suffering from beri-beri and was close to death. 'They can't kill you, can they, sir?' Exhausted, MacHorton lay down on the other side of the Sergeant as the party prepared to spend the night on the sandbank. By the morning the Sergeant had passed away. They buried him at first light and moved on.

They had not gone far when a water buffalo lumbered into sight. One shot was all it took and the starving men fell upon it with knives, kukris and bare fingernails. While they were cutting it up they were approached by a party of Burmans armed with rifles and war dahs. They said that the Japanese were in the area and gave them three minutes to surrender. Dunlop suddenly turned and ran towards the far bank, shouting 'Follow me!' and the others followed, as bullets whipped around them. They regained the safety of the jungle and were not pursued.

When Dunlop and his men finally reached the Chindwin they had travelled 300 miles in a month, surviving on what food they could find on their journey. They now had 800 yards of warm, muddy water to cross, before they finally reached safety. John Fowler and four of the soldiers were unable to swim such a distance. They preferred to follow the path to Auktaung in the hope of finding a boat there. Dunlop gave them a map and compass and bade them farewell. In the early hours of the morning he took to the water, followed by Clarke and MacHorton. They became separated but eventually reached safety on the far bank of the river. A company of Mahrattas was at the confluence of the Yu and Chindwin Rivers and helped them on their way. It was about 10 May.

Dunlop learned that Chet Kin had already passed through with 250 of the column and had seized boats to enable them to cross in relative comfort. Doc Stocks and the other British officer had also arrived, having been ferried over by a friendly villager. On arrival at Imphal, Dunlop found that he weighed only just half of his normal weight.

When I got back to Tamu in the middle of May, I was ordered to report to IV Corps commander, Lieutenant General Scoones, as soon as possible. This I did. At the time I knew nothing of the fate of anyone in the 'Northern Group'. General Scoones told me to give him a written report as soon as possible, and sent me to hospital in Imphal, where I found a lot of survivors from other columns and learned that Wingate was alive. A 77 Brigade HQ had been established in Imphal and I asked the chief clerk to have my report typed for General Scoones. That is the last I saw of it and I don't know if he even got it. A lack of information about our group became apparent when the books started to come out. I later met Wingate out walking before breakfast one day at Imphal. His actual words to me were, 'I ought to have you court-martialled!' and he then turned about and stomped off. I don't know if it was to do with my report, or indeed if he was serious. I didn't see him again for many months and no mention was made at any time of the misadventures of number one group. I suspect that he was conscious of the fact that in sending us east when the rest turned for India, he had treated us as expendable. Getting back, with the very good help of Chet Khin and his Karens, rather upset all the glowing reports which had been rushed out for propaganda purposes.

Despite everything, Major Dunlop was later chosen by Wingate to head an aborted project to teach the ways of the Chindits to Chinese Army officers.

Chapter 11

First Man Home – 3 Column

When Major Mike Calvert received the message to return to India he was only 100 miles from the Burma Road. He initially decided to head for China or Fort Hertz in the north, but to do that they had to cross the Shweli River. Although they discovered that enemy pickets were in every village, they tried to cross at night on 27 March, using sapper rafts of bamboo encased in waterproof ground sheets. A Japanese patrol arrived on their side of the river just as the crossing began and two men were marooned on the far side when Calvert called off the attempt. Calvert was prepared as usual, and Sergeant Major Blain and his men ambushed the advance section, killing the lot. They made good their escape and moved back into the jungle to rethink their plans. Calvert sent out scouts who discovered that there were large enemy forces in all of the larger villages and a force of 700 had just arrived at Myitson. Squadron Leader Robert Thompson radioed the news to India and the village was bombed, causing 200 casualties. Calvert realized that forcing a crossing of the Shweli in the face of enemy opposition would lead to heavy casualties, so he abandoned his idea of heading for China or Fort Hertz. He preferred to try to take the column back to India in one piece, but his officers declared their preference for dispersal in small groups. Calvert decided to go for dispersal and wasted no time in organizing one last supply drop. When their packs were full Calvert divided his column into nine groups: Major Calvert, Lieutenant Jeffery Lockett and his commandos; Squadron Leader Robert Thompson and Doctor Rao with the RAF detachment and 15 Platoon; Lieutenant Harold James and Captain Taffy Griffiths, Burma Rifles with 13 Platoon; Captain George Silcock (Column 2i/c) and Second Lieutenant Denis Gudgeon with 14 Platoon; Lieutenant George Worte and Captain Roy 'Mac' McKenzie, each with a platoon of muleteers; and Subedar Siribhagta with Jemedar Cameron and support group personnel. The last two groups contained Headquarters men and Karens, one led by Lieutenants Ken Gourlay and Alec Gibson, and the other by Subedar Kumba Sing Gurung and Subedar Donny of the Burma Rifles.

The parties led by Calvert, Griffiths, Thompson and Worte chose to move off to the south-west, thus avoiding the area recently traversed. Silcock decided to return directly west across the Thabeikyin mountains and the other leaders elected to retrace their steps along the route of entry.

On the afternoon of 30 March, Calvert gathered all his officers together and drank a toast of rum. 'Good luck to you. We have been a great team and I thank you for your efforts. I hope that we will all meet again on the other side of the Chindwin.' Wingate later remarked that the groups that used routes south of Indaw-Banmauk had the hardest time, with the exception of 3 Column. It passed by routes south of Wuntho, some days before anyone else, and reached the Chindwin in good spirits and condition. This he attributed to the excellent orders of Calvert and the early adoption of dispersal.

Harold James, Taffy Griffiths and 15 Platoon marched to the Irrawaddy, found a large sampan with a Burmese family on board and paid them to carry their party across. No sooner had the first boatload got across than Bobby Thompson and his men arrived. He sent a runner back to Calvert with the message 'Ventre a terre to the river '. Once across the river Calvert wanted to join forces and attack the railway on the way back. The others demurred, deciding discretion was the better part of valour. Undeterred, Calvert and his commandos decided to go out with a bang. At the dead of night they laid their charges and Calvert felt in his pocket for his time pencils, which would set the explosives off after they had left the scene. To his horror he realized that he had failed to follow his own rules and nick the pencils with a penknife so many nicks to each colour, so that they would be easy to pick out at night. There was a Japanese working party nearby, so striking a match would be very risky. 'Lift up that kilt of yours,' said Calvert to Lockett. The young, bearded, toothless Scot watched warily as Calvert struck a match under his improvised black-out curtains and sorted out his pencils, as Lockett muttered darkly about suing Calvert for damages. Later, the other groups heard the distant sound of explosions as Calvert's charges cut the railway line in five places again. As the Japanese flocked to the area, Calvert and his party went to ground in a thick clump of bamboo.

'What the hell do we do now?' one officer asked.

'Let's have a cup of tea,' suggested Lockett. And they did.

Bobby Thompson and Taffy Griffiths combined their parties and travelled onwards together, finally meeting a Sikh patrol on the east bank of the Chindwin at 1400 hours on 14 April. They were the first of the brigade dispersal groups to reach home. The following day Calvert and his party crossed over. Subedar Kumba Sing Gurung's group escaped into China, but Alec Gibson, Denis Gudgeon, Ken Gourlay and Subedar Siribhagta were taken prisoner. The other groups made it safely back to India.

George Silcock took half of his party across the Irrawaddy on Sapper sampans, made out of bamboo and groundsheets, but when Denis Gudgeon tried to follow with the rest of the men, their rafts began to sink and they had to return to the bank. Denis later recalled:

I was left with a party of 11 Gurkhas and a Burma Rifleman, 13 in all including myself. I eventually managed to locate a craft and bribe the boatman to take us across the Irrawaddy. I had no maps of the area, other than those for the River Chindwin. I did have a prismatic compass and set a course of 300 degrees. Navigation was not easy as we were walking against the grain of the country and the odd mountain range intervened.

I got within a short distance of the Chindwin with my party when to quote the letter from the Under Secretary of State, The War Office, to my parents: 'Your son, who was in an exhausted condition, ordered the party to carry on while he rested. Two riflemen were detailed to wait for Lieutenant Gudgeon, and about one and a half hours later they joined the forward party which had bivouacked for the night some 860 yards away and reported that your son was following. Lieutenant Gudgeon did not however arrive and the darkness precluded an immediate search. Next day a search party returned to the spot but could find no trace of your son.' The rest of my party made it to safety.

I was now on my own with only my compass for guide and I realised that I must get some food urgently. Shortly afterwards I hit a track and hid beside it. I let several people pass and then selected what I thought might be a reliable person. He turned out to be a fishmonger selling dried fish up country. I asked him how far I was from the Chindwin and he said ten miles and that he could get me a boat across.

I was in an extremely exhausted state by this time and we eventually made it to a place called Tanga on the east bank of the Chindwin where he gave me a cup of tea in his house. I was drinking tea from a bone china tea cup and beginning to feel rather apprehensive, when there was a commotion and I looked up to find myself staring down the muzzles of a dozen Jap rifles. I thought to myself 'so this is what it feels like to be shot at dawn'. I had been betrayed!

I was taken to Mawlaik on the west bank where I saw a poster offering 50 rupees, dead or alive, for any member of our force.

I was then taken to the HQ of the local Jap garrison and given a Penguin book to read. A gentleman in a Kimono came in to the room but I went on reading my book. He exploded and left the room in a high dudgeon. Shortly afterwards an interpreter arrived to say 'Japanese officer very angry, you insult Emperor'.

The officer returned shortly and interrogated me for four hours with a double edged Samurai sword held at my throat. My hair stood on end and I found myself in an 'Alice in Wonderland' situation expecting at any moment to hear the command 'Off with his head'. The whole interrogation was held through an interpreter although the Jap officer could speak and understand English perfectly well. That was 'face' saving.

I was then taken to another basha where they tried a different technique. I was plied with Saki and sweetmeats and promised this, that and the other, but I did not fall for it. The only intelligence that the Jap gleaned from me was a lot of 'duff' gen. Subsequently I was taken by road – where I was shot at by a Beaufighter – and by Burma Railways, from Mandalay to Rangoon. I made a request to travel First Class in accordance with the Geneva Convention, but this fell on stony ground.

Out of the 360 men in 3 Column, 205 eventually recrossed the Chindwin. For his courageous leadership Major Calvert was awarded the Distinguished Service Order. Whether or not Calvert should have bowed to pressure from his officers to disperse the column rather than trying to bring it out in one piece is a matter of opinion. From the very beginning they had fought well together and if anyone could have taken their column home Calvert could, and probably with less losses than were eventually suffered.

Chapter 12

Nightmare at the River – 5 Column

When Wingate led his Brigade Group back towards Inywa on the Irrawaddy River, 5 Column was given the job of rearguard. However, they were in a worse shape than the other columns, having missed some supply drops, and had stopped to slaughter a mule in a dry stream bed. Unfortunately, one of Lieutenant Colonel Wheeler's Burma Riflemen left their bivouac area to answer the call of nature and stumbled into a Japanese patrol. Wingate heard the firing and forged ahead with 7 and 8 Columns, sending a message back to 5 Column to ambush their tracks. However, it was not possible to set up an ambush without having some idea of the direction from which the enemy would be coming. Instead Fergusson decided to draw the enemy away in an easterly direction, away from the main body which was heading roughly north-west. They blazed a wide trail along a dried-up river bed for the enemy to follow, then established a dummy bivouac complete with burning fires and scattered with booby traps. Stealthily they crept away and moved into another bivouac half a mile downstream. The jungle on either side of the river bed proved to be very thick and full of thorns, so they formed a cramped 'square' in the river bed and tried to get some sleep.

Around 0300 hours the column moved off again, towards the village of Hintha. They could not find a way around the village through the thick jungle, so Fergusson decided to lead his men down the track which led to the village itself. There seemed no way through the impenetrable barrier of thorns on either side of the track and in no time at all they found themselves standing at a T-junction at the entrance to the village. The Major was in the lead with Philip Stibbe's platoon, with the Commando Platoon right behind them. A fire was burning on the far side of the third house on the left and Stibbe whispered to the Major, 'It look's peaceful enough.' He nodded and told Stibbe to stay where he was while he went towards the fire with two of the Burrifs. As they rounded the corner of the house they saw four men sitting around the fire and thought they were Burmans, but as they got closer Fergusson realized that the men were in fact Japanese and immediately pitched a hand grenade into the middle of the fire. There was a loud explosion and Fergusson later recounted that all four fell over onto their backs with perfect symmetry. The explosion heralded the start of a pitched battle in the dark.

A Japanese machine-gun opened fire from the left-hand track leading away from the junction and Fergusson ordered Stibbe to take his platoon in with the bayonet. With Corporal Litherland's section on the left, Corporal Handley's and Corporal Berry's on the right, and Corporal Dunn's section right behind him, Stibbe led his men forward towards the firing.

It was difficult to see anything in the darkness but the stabs of flame from several Japanese machine-guns ahead of them on the track. Stibbe later remembered throwing a hand grenade at one of them and falling flat on the ground while it exploded. However, as he stood up again he was shot in the shoulder and the Platoon rushed on past. There was a confused medley of shots, shouts, explosions and screams as Stibbe fell to the ground again. Next to him lay a badly wounded NCO who passed his hand grenade to him, saying, 'Will you take this grenade, sir. The pin's out, but I stopped one before I could throw it.' Stibbe took the grenade with his right hand as the unfortunate man fell unconscious.

The firing was still continuing and Fergusson called out to Stibbe to see if he knew where it was coming from. Stibbe shouted back that it was coming from both sides of the track and that he had been wounded himself.

Fergusson replied 'Hard luck, Philip. You'd better get your platoon back now if you can.' Stibbe raised himself on his elbow and shouted 'Come back, 7 Platoon' into the darkness and a few moments later they started to reappear.

Someone helped Stibbe to his feet and he staggered back to the T-junction, his shirt soaked with blood. He handed over the Platoon to Sergeant Thornburrow and lay down at the side of the track while Private Roche put a field dressing on his wound. The bullet had caused a small entry wound under his collar bone, but a larger exit hole near his left shoulder blade. As his pack was removed he had the presence of mind to remove his last biscuits and a tin of bully beef, and push them down the front of his shirt.

In the meantime, Fergusson had sent the Commando Platoon down a little track off to the left to deal with some Japs who were getting closer to them. Captain Alec MacDonald, the Administrative Officer, went with them, but was shot and killed with Private Fuller. Lieutenant Jim Harman, the Platoon Commander, was also hit in the head and arm, but he went on with his men and cleared the track.

Fergusson himself had a narrow escape when he bent down to talk to Stibbe and the wounded Corporal Litherland. A Jap grenade landed beside him and he threw himself to the ground as it exploded, sending a splinter of metal into his hip. Touching the bone, there was no way to remove it in the field and he had to put up with the pain until he finally got back to India.

Doc Aird and one of his orderlies arrived and proceeded to dress Stibbe's wound and that of Litherland, who had been hit in the head and arm. Nearby a private soldier who had a terrible head wound begged Stibbe to shoot him. The young subaltern did not learn until later that Corporals Handley and Berry, Lance Corporal Dunn and Private Cobb had all been killed and a few others wounded.

Shortly after Fergusson had disturbed the four Japanese sitting around their campfire, another Jap soldier ran past them and the Major took a shot at him. Fearing that he had gone to rouse the enemy at the other end of the village, Fergusson sent Corporal Peter Dorans and some of the men from Column Headquarters down the track to head them off. The men returned shortly afterwards on the instructions of Dorans who had taken their hand grenades and was lying in wait at the side of the track. As shadowy figures in conical helmets rushed along the track the brave Corporal rolled his grenades into the midst of them.

By now it was starting to get light and news finally arrived that a way had been found through the dense jungle at the side of the track, so Fergusson ordered Brookes to blow the second 'Dispersal' call on his bugle. Duncan Menzies led Stibbe to a waiting horse and Private Joe Boyle helped him climb up into the saddle. Duncan told Boyle to follow one of the dispersal groups and wished Stibbe 'Good luck'. They would never meet again.

As the column broke up into dispersal groups to head for the RV at Inywa, a wounded Philip Stibbe realized that he was holding up his party and ordered them to continue without him. A mile and a half outside Hintha he sank to the ground and passed his maps to Lieutenant Bill Williamson of the Support Platoon. He was ravenously hungry and produced a packet of blood-stained biscuits from his shirt and ate them while he gave Bill a message to pass on to his parents. A brave Burma Rifleman, Maung Tun, volunteered to stay with him, and they moved off the track and into shelter as it began to rain.

Maung Tun could not speak much English, but he told Stibbe that he was a Karen and his home was in the Bassein district. He looked after the English officer as carefully as a mother looks after a sick child, boiling water to bathe his wound and helping him to eat and drink. He told Stibbe that he should try to sleep so he took a couple of morphia tablets and settled down for a couple of hours of welcome oblivion.

It was nearly dark when Stibbe woke up again and discovered that Maung Tun was not there. Eventually he heard a whistle and the rifleman pushed his way through the brush. He had donned his civilian 'lungi' and returned to Hintha where one of the villagers had told him that the Japs were still there, but would be moving on soon. He arranged to return in the morning and meet the friendly villager who would give him food and the latest news of the Japs.

The following morning Maung Tun dressed Stibbe's wound again and left around 1000 hours for his rendezvous with the villager. He was wearing his brightly coloured 'lungi' and a khaki shirt, and had slung his tommy gun over his shoulder. When Stibbe shouted after him to be careful he turned his head and grinned. He never returned.

Stibbe waited in vain for two days, hoping that his benefactor would return. He considered all sorts of scenarios in his head but kept on returning to the obvious answer: he must have been captured. Stibbe was now out of water and finally had to admit that he was on his own. Weak and exhausted, he dragged himself to his feet and staggered off down the track. He found himself approaching the village again, along the same route that the column had used three days previously. It was not until he got closer that he saw three or four men sitting in the shadow of a tree. They were Japs and they sprang up and dragged Stibbe to his knees. He was now 'in the bag', a prisoner of the Japs.

It was not until he met other prisoners later on that he found out what had happened to the loyal Burma Rifleman. The villager had betrayed him to the Japs who were waiting for him at the rendezvous. They knew there was a wounded English officer in the vicinity and tried to beat him to discover his whereabouts. Eventually, when they realized that torture would not get them the answer they shot the loyal rifleman.

The day after the dispersal of his column at Hintha, Fergusson and his party tried to rejoin Wingate at Inywa, but they were too late. The brigade bivouac area was deserted, although one of the missing sergeants and six men rejoined them at the edge of the jungle. The column radio was lost during the battle at Hintha when the mule carrying it was shot and fell into a gully. They were now unable to call for a much-needed supply drop. Fergusson decided not to try to cross the Irrawaddy, but to cross the Shweli instead and get into the Kachin Hills where food and friends could be found. Other members of the column joined forces with 7 Column, who were contemplating a trek home via China. Bill Aird, the column doctor, found himself in charge of some sick and sorry men from both columns and amazingly saw them all the way back to the Chindwin, where they were captured. Aird and most of the men would die in captivity.

Fergusson found himself with nine officers and 109 Other Ranks, of which five were wounded – Fergusson with a grenade splinter in his hip, Lieutenant Harman and three of the men. All were weak and hungry and desperate measures would be required to guide them all home. Fergusson told them, 'Only absolute discipline would get us out. I would shoot anybody who pilfered comrades or villages, or who grumbled. Anyone who lost his rifle or equipment I would expel from the party, unless I was satisfied with his excuse. The only chance was absolute trust and implicit obedience and there was to be no stragglers.'

Two days later they reached the Shweli River and persuaded two Burmese boatmen to carry them across in their three-man dugouts. They were ferried across during the night, but then discovered that they had been deposited on a large sandbank in the middle of the river, with 80 yards of water still between them and the far bank. Fergusson later recalled:

> There is no word for it but 'nightmare'. The roaring of the waters, the blackness of the night, the occasional sucking of a quicksand were bad enough, but the current was devilish and must have been four to five knots. It sought to scoop the feet from under you and at the same time thrust powerfully at your chest. It was about four feet six or more deep and if you lost your vertical position, you knew as a black certainty that you would disappear down the stream for ever.

Some who tried to wade across were swept away, their cries echoing through the darkness. Many men lost their nerve and remained on the sandbank. Signaller Byron White was one of those who gritted his teeth, clenched his rifle tightly above his head and walked slowly into the chest-deep water. He told the author:

> It was soon up to shoulder height and so fast flowing that it was difficult to keep one's feet on the bottom. Just in front of me was one of our younger lads and we were trying to keep as quiet as possible, but he was shouting 'Mother, Mother help me.' I got close to him and in no uncertain terms told him to shut up. Afterwards I was sorry for what I said. I never saw him again. He didn't make the crossing. We moved on slowly against the fast-flowing water, expecting to walk out on the far bank on dry land. Instead, to our dismay the bank rose sheer out of the water, about ten to twelve feet above the water level. Somehow some of the lads managed to get out on to the top of the bank and were able to reach our outstretched arms and assist us up the slippery bank.

Many men made it across, including all of the wounded and some of the Gurkhas, the smallest men of all. The rest refused to follow. Fergusson could not remain and jeopardize the safety of the men who had put their faith in providence and made the crossing. It was an hour before dawn and Japanese patrols could be expected at any time. He later explained, 'I made the decision to come away. I have it on my conscience for as long as I live; but I stand by that decision and believe it to have been the correct one.'

Fergusson was now down to nine officers and sixty-three men. Forty-six others had either drowned or remained behind on the sandbank. At daylight the Japanese arrived and took them all prisoner. A couple of days later the depleted column reached the village of Zibyugin and obtained some food. News reached them that the Japanese were on the way and they quickly withdrew to the outskirts of the village. One of their sentries did not return to the bivouac and there was still a need for more food and information on enemy dispositions, so Lieutenant Duncan Menzies volunteered to take a small patrol back to the village. The four men walked into a Japanese patrol and after a brief fight, Menzies and Lance Corporal Gilmartin were captured. Fergusson and the rest of the party waited until the next morning before continuing their journey to the north-west. Later that day, the Burma Rifle Headquarters, about 100 strong, reached Zibyugin and attacked it. The small number of Japanese in the village withdrew and the Burrifs discovered Menzies and Gilmartin. They were dressed in Japanese uniforms, their beards had been shaved, and they had been tied to trees and used for bayonet practice by the Japanese. Gilmartin was dead and Menzies was dying when Lieutenant Colonel Wheeler, the Battalion Commander, arrived on the scene. Menzies asked for a lethal dose of morphia and gave Wheeler his watch, to be sent to his parents if Wheeler reached India safely. It was not to be. One minute after Wheeler gave Menzies the morphia the Colonel was shot through the head by a sniper and killed. The two friends were buried together.

As the weak began to fall by the wayside, Fergusson decided to split his seventy men into three equal groups. Captain Tommy Roberts, the Commando Platoon commander, took one together with Lieutenant Bill Edge and Support Group; Flight Lieutenant Denny Sharp and Lieutenant Roberts with 7 Platoon another. The third was led by Fergusson and included Lieutenant Jim Harman, who had been wounded twice at Hintha, Lieutenant Blow and Captain Fraser of the Burma Rifles, the commandos and Column Headquarters.

Fergusson's party finally crossed the Irrawaddy on 9 April courtesy of two boys of thirteen or fourteen who thought the whole thing a great lark. Fergusson suspected they had borrowed the boat, unknown to its owner. They were paid 300 silver rupees for their trouble.

Fifteen days later on 24 April they crossed the Chindwin. Denny Sharp's party reached safety the same day, but Tommy Roberts was not so successful. Bill Edge and four others had crossed the Irrawaddy when the Japanese attacked the remainder, forcing them to withdraw. Edge and the others caught up with Fergusson's party four days later. Two weeks later and 50 miles further upstream the nine survivors crossed over and marched for four more days before they bumped a thirty-man Japanese patrol. Although they killed seven of the enemy, they had to surrender after two of their party were killed and five wounded. Roberts was the only member of the expedition to be flown to Singapore for interrogation. He was put to work on the notorious Siam Railway, but survived until the war's end. Out of the 318 members of 5 Column who marched into Burma, only ninety-five got out. Twenty-eight more survived Rangoon jail, but many others had died in captivity. Fergusson later described the story of 5 Column's part in the expedition in his book, Beyond the Chindwin.

Another officer of 5 Column lived through his own nightmare on the river, after becoming separated from the main body. This continued for some weeks and the fact that he finally reached safety speaks volumes for his spirit and determination. Bill Smyly was a Second Lieutenant with the 3/2nd Gurkhas and had the dubious honour of being the youngest officer on the expedition. He was given the unenviable job of Animal Transport Officer, in charge of the mules and the Gurkha muleteers. He described his nightmare to the author:

For some reason that I never learned, then or since, Wingate had crossed the Irrawaddy and boxed himself into a triangle with the great river to the west, a lethally fast tributary called the Shweli to the east, and a Japanese-infested road joining the two. When he realized his position he gave the order for all units to disperse in small groups and find their own way back to India. Emergency supply drops were ordered all over the place to furnish food for the journey. I don't know if our commander, Bernard Fergusson, had the map references but I certainly didn't. I think with hindsight a better officer than I was might have asked him, but he had just given me the order to slaughter all my mules – silently! I had 50 mules and apart from a pistol shot to the head I had no idea how to kill a mule. In the end we unsaddled them and tied them loosely to bamboo or weak branches and wished them luck. Some of them tried to follow us, poor animals. It was heartbreaking shooing the horses away. Without our mules we marched most of the day and well into the night, and around midnight we walked into a Japanese ambush in which Philip Stibbe was hit. In this action there were Japanese all around yelling in the dark. 'Hello Johnny', 'Hello Tommy', 'Yaa Ha Ha Ha'. The cries sounded as if they were all around us and in fact were a tactic like beating the heather for grouse. I had a notion the noise came from the platoon idiot. It was impressive but not very dangerous, unless like Philip you had to stand up in the dark and fight back. I was stuck in the middle of a track where I managed to get a few minutes sleep and that was the only sleep I had for the next 30 hours. At 3 am the column trumpeter blew a splendid call for the Column to disperse and we all took off in small groups in every direction. This was fine except that in practice we were supposed to know where we were going to regroup, and on this occasion we obviously weren't regrouping. So – go where? If we were to walk to India it was absolutely necessary that we got to one of the supply drops and collected food for the journey. At about 8 am I saw planes coming over and headed for the drop. We even helped collect some of the tins of food and bring them to a gathering point, but then I was told that my group was not on the list of units to be supplied from this store. Someone had counted the tins, worked out the strength of various units on his list, and pronounced an issue of one tin between eight men. I had 28 men not on his list and rather than argue the point I formed up an official looking working party – six riflemen, three to carry the tins and three to carry two rifles each on our return and picked up three tins and left. Three tins between 28 men was less than the stated ration but more than they would have given us for the asking, which was nothing, so those tins were hacked open and distributed and stowed in seconds. You never saw kukris work so fast. I felt OK about what I had done. We had taken less than the proper ration, but obviously some other unit had to go short because we hadn't been on the manifest. Then I was told to join Number Seven Column and we set off into the jungle with them. It was open teak forest and not the best cover. By nightfall we were standing in a queue on a sandbank all night, moving forward bit by bit, wondering what was happening at the front. The men were half asleep on their feet. So, unfortunately, was I! What was happening was that engineers had fired a line across the Shweli at the narrowest point and secured it on the other side. How the first man got across I have no idea because this was also the fastest point of a lethally fast stream. Apparently work was very slow and frustrating. The ferry party worked all night and got just a small party across under Lieutenant George Astell of 5 Column's Burma Rifles Platoon. As dawn began to break all the rest, about 200 men, started back into the jungle. As we were going back I was called up to speak to the commander of the Column who told me that there was a line across the river and an inflatable boat. They were mine! There would be an air drop that side in two days time. Would I take over and get my men to the other side. Lieutenant Astell was in charge on the other side and he would give me the map reference for the drop. Why didn't I go forward earlier that night to find out what was happening? Why didn't I speak to one of the engineers and ask him to help me organize the crossing and come with us? A bit late to ask why now. I had never seen an inflatable boat before, but now I had one, a rope across the water race, and 28 men this side. There was a real chance Number Seven Column would be wiped out or taken prisoner in the Shweli Pocket during the day. Had I asked an engineer he would surely have come with me. There were a group of them in bare feet in the sand holding the rope. The rope was tied to a tree root, high on the far bank, but hand held this side by a sort of tug-o-war team standing on a wide flat stretch of sand – a perfect target if any enemy should see them and the sun was coming up. Lieutenant Astell on the other side called across that he couldn't wait any longer and was heading off. I said I was coming right over. For some reason his map reference seemed top priority and I wanted to see it on the paper, not just in numbers. We were off my map and I wasn't sure where we were or which map we were on. Eight of my men, swimmers, took off their boots, packs and rifles and loaded them into the boat. They took over as the holding party. This was at my order and was a very bad mistake. Two men were supposed to man the boat, staying in the boat and holding the rope at all times. As passengers another six men and me bundled in. A group with rifles were ready for the second run, but as Seven Column left they spread out and took up a defensive position on the sandbank facing the trees. I take no credit for this. We had a good corporal. When we reached the other side I saw the six men landed with the gear, sent the boat back and raced up the hill to find Astell and get his map reference. The sun was up and everyone was very scared. I wasn't scared. I was even worse – I was flustered and Astell was crazy to get moving. I am not sure his instructions to me made much sense but he set off and I went back down the bank. When I got there, there was the rope across the racing water, high on this side, sloping down to the holding party. My holding party stood the other side with the riflemen spread out protecting them and watching the forest edge. But the boat was not there. On our way over the eight men in the boat had held the rope. Only two had been allotted to take it back. Maybe one had slipped and the other had let go? The force of the water was terrific. While I was up the hill our inflatable had been carried away and the two men with it. And my holding party was on one side in bare feet and their boots, rifles and packs were on the other. While I was standing on the bank Astell's batman, a Burma Rifleman, shouted to us and then came over holding onto the rope, hand over hand. As he got to midstream he was in very great danger. He had to keep his feet right up clear of the water. It could have torn the rope out of his hands, but he made it and there was a cheer.

'Does anyone else want to come over?' My men were silent, and then they began to curse. And they couldn't have cursed me more than I cursed myself. It was like the first minute after a traffic accident – 'Please God this didn't happen!' Then they turned and went back over the sand to track Number Seven Column who had already vanished into the trees. The holding team were now without their boots, without their rifles, and without their packs and their food, and all their own possessions were gone. In theory it might have worked. There were 8 swimmers to hold the rope, two to man the boat (with hindsight it should have been three with the Havildar in charge), six passengers and myself in the first party, and 12 standing by. Six on the east bank and 22 to come. If a second trip had reduced this to 12 or 14 we could have made it – ten in the boat and the swimmers hanging on. The current could have carried us all over to the west bank like a pendulum. The inflatable had a ring of rope right around the outside. If four of us had held onto this and slowly launched her out into the stream, pushing her out until the water carried our legs away from under us, and we had then held on for our lives, and those inside had held firmly to the rope across the stream, the current would have carried us over if it didn't carry us away. I keep playing that scene over in hindsight. Seven Column eventually got across the river and headed east for the Burma Road, crossing into China and ending up in Kunming from which they were flown back to India 'over the Hump'. I and my six men marched north towards a place called Fort Hertz in the Golden Triangle where Burma, China, Thailand and Tibet are all so close one can't tell the one from the other. We were without a map but caught up with the group of about 60 led by Lieutenant Astell. I think we spun out 8 days rations for 28 days. In the end I lost my central vision with beri beri and had swollen ankles that slowed me down going uphill. I refused to let my men hang back at my pace and drove them on, climbing the hills sideways or backwards and running down the other side. This worked well for several days till one evening I was running too fast, missed the path, and ran off into the forest. Lost, and with night coming on, I sat down by a stream, boiled some water, and then slept. In the morning I was covered with leeches. I undressed and shaved these off with my kukri. They fell off like grapes and swam away. The stream was the worst possible place I could have spent the night. In the morning, with my sight restored, I retraced my steps and found the track. To my surprise it was the greatest relief to be on my own and not have to keep up with the others, but I now went very slowly. Ahead was an enormous climb. Halfway up there was one place where I looked out over the surrounding forest canopy, wave after wave of it, and felt that I had only to press the ground with my toes and I would rise into the air and soar over hill and dale all the way back to India. Later on, up the hill the tribesmen had driven a hollow bamboo into a rivulet and clear water poured from this onto bright stones at the side of the path. Beside this was a mossy bank and I don't think any chair has ever been more comfortable or any water sweeter. I was sitting there half in heaven when an old mother and her pretty daughter climbed up the road. They found me totally exhausted and idiotically happy; and they were there again in the village at the top of the hill with a brew of rice wine for me, before they brought me on to the house of the headman of the village.

From then I was looked after in Kachin villages for nearly three months. Whenever I reached a village and took off my boots my ankles blew up like balloons and I would sit there till I could get my boots on again, maybe two days, and then press on. The swelling must have been unpleasant for others. A girl wrapped my legs in a poultice of leaves which brought out a viscous liquid with a sickly odour. I didn't like myself but my hosts never complained. They never mentioned it. I had no way of paying and they seemed to expect no return. For three months they looked after me in one village after another – always the same welcome and what they ate they gave to me. In all those months I never slept again in the open and never did without an evening meal. Nor did I ever hear of a way to report my debt to them and have them rewarded. This was in contrast to Philip Stibbe who inherited his family shoemaking firm in Leicester and, when this was taken over by a larger firm, returned to Burma to give the greater part of the price to the family of the rifleman who had died under torture for his sake. His gift was given in the form of a scholarship for members of the man's family. Philip himself then became a schoolmaster, becoming a headmaster in Norwich. But what I really wanted to say and couldn't find the words for, was how very much I owed to the hill tribes, the Kachins, Karens and Shans to whom I owe my life, and to the Gurkha soldiers who made my time in Burma so pleasant. My men were a very young detachment of Rais and Limbus from the 10th Gurkhas, not the 2nd, so those who got back to India returned to their own depot. I met three of them later in Shillong. Philip Stibbe would meet some of the 20 men who did not cross the river in his Japanese prison camp.

Chapter 13

Long Walk to China – 7 Column

7 Column had been split in two when Wingate called off the crossing of the Irrawaddy at Inywa. Those who had crossed over before the Japanese arrived continued on to India, encountering numerous setbacks on the way. When the order to disperse was given by Wingate, the Column Commander, Major Ken Gilkes, would eventually decide to head for China.

When Gilkes said farewell to Major Scott and Lieutenant Colonel Cooke at Inywa, he decided to strike out into uncharted territory and try to infiltrate through areas where the Chindits had not yet stirred up a hornets' nest. By now they had been joined by a large group of around 110 men from Fergusson's 5 Column, who became separated at the battle at Hintha. Because Fergusson had not been able to keep his men fed, they were weak and tired and would have been hard pressed to keep up with Gilkes and his column. He quite rightly decided that the weaker men should be sent westwards on the shorter route back to India. For the moment they would remain with the column and try to regain their strength, but eventually they would turn west to begin the long journey to the Chindwin. Very few of them would get there.

First of all 7 Column had to cross the Shweli River. They found a good place to cross where they could walk three quarters of the way across on sand, leaving about 120 yards of fast-moving water. On 3 April, they managed to get a rope across and around 2100 hours began to cross in two dinghies secured to the sagging line. This was probably the time when Bill Smyly and his Gurkhas joined them for the crossing. The column war diary notes that they suffered the same misfortune as 8 Column and the rope broke, sending a dinghy swirling away downstream. Luckily for the occupants they made it to the bank a mile away from the forty who had already crossed over and rejoined them. This must have been the reason that Major Gilkes gave Smyly the opportunity of using the rope and the one surviving dinghy, while he led his column away to look for another crossing point. With one dinghy and in broad daylight, he would have been hard pressed to get his other 200 men across without interruption by the Japanese.

Gilkes gave George Astell and his men the option of waiting for the main body to find their way over the river, or pressing ahead on their own. They decided to get moving while the going was good and Gilkes prearranged supply drops for them. Most of Astell's party, including Flight Lieutenant Hammond and Lieutenant Smyly made their way out to Fort Hertz and were flown back to India.

Gilkes and the main body moved further east along the river and organized a good supply drop on 5 April, each man receiving seven days rations. All canned meat was given to the 5 Column personnel. They still had some mules to carry the radio equipment as well as the seriously wounded Petersen, the Fighting Dane. For the next three days, as they moved south and found water very scarce, Gilkes became very apprehensive about the ability of the column, particularly the 5 Column personnel who had been on very short rations, to survive the journey along the northern route to China.

On 9 April, it was decided to split the column up. Gilkes would take half of them east and out along the northern route. Captain Cotterill, Lieutenants Walker, Wood and Campbell-Paterson, each with twenty to thirty men, were to cross the Irrawaddy independently and then reunite for a supply dropping on the west side of the river. Lieutenant Heald would go with the parties and try to see them across the river safely, but after an hour's marching it was discovered that 5 Column's Burrifs had disappeared, therefore, with no Burmese-speaking personnel to assist in acquiring boats and discovering information about the enemy, the groups turned around and caught up with the column again.

On 10 April, with their packs and bellies full, they split up into two groups: the stronger and the weaker. Lieutenant Walker, together with Captain Aird, the 5 Column medical officer, Lieutenants Hector and Anderson Williams and twenty-five Other Ranks, went off west to cross the Irrawaddy. The column moved off south-east and after crossing the Mongmit-Myitson motor road there was a minor clash between the rearguard and a Jap patrol, with the enemy coming off worse. Sergeant O'Gorman was found to be missing, but it was thought he might have caught up with Walker's party.

Lieutenants Musgrave Wood and Campbell-Paterson each took parties of men off in different directions, intending to meet up with the column for the next supply dropping in a week's time. Gilkes was not too hopeful that they would meet up again, but considered that parties of twenty men could easily live off the land.

For the next couple of days the column moved eastwards into the hills south of the Paungkadaw Reserve Forest, seeking food in the Kachin villages to supplement their rations until the next supply drop. The Kachins were well organized with their own patrols watching Japanese movements in the area. The tribesmen were very helpful and guides took them to Nayok on the Shweli River, built rafts for them and helped them cross the river. Within three hours the whole party was across the river, complete with their mules and radio equipment. On the same day, hundreds of miles to the west, Mike Calvert and his party crossed the Chindwin and were back in India.

On 17 and 18 April, the RAF dropped two weeks supplies for Gilkes, including food, clothing and ammunition. There were also more supplies for their medical officer who was looking after Petersen. He had initially placed a sulphanilamide pack on his wound and had been reluctant to look at it since. When he did so he discovered that the Japanese bullet had ploughed a deep furrow along the side of his skull, but had not penetrated it. Bolstered by good rations and his own inner strength, Petersen was soon marching with the men again.

The following day was Easter Sunday. One contemporary report claims that while Gilkes was trying to make up his mind which way to go, he asked his radio operator to try to tune in to the BBC. He could not raise them but managed to tune in to a London church, broadcasting to the Eighth Army in Tunisia. They enjoyed the music and Gilkes was struck by the text of the sermon: 'I will lift mine eyes unto the hills from whence cometh my help', Psalm 121, Verse 6. Gilkes was a devout man and felt that he was being shown the way to go. It was at this time that he decided to take to the hills and head for China. It would take weeks longer than marching back to India, but he had 150 well-fed men and he might be able to receive help from the Kachin villages along the way. The signal was sent to IV Corps: 'Intend either contact Chinese in area Laukhaung or Mamien Pass or come out North Myitkyina. Inclined favour contact Chinese owing better local food and chance arrive before rains. Give advice state how long and in what areas you could supply us and if RV could be arranged by you for us with Chinese Army or Kachin Levies. Thanks Great Help.'

A couple of days later they were spotted by a Jap patrol of about thirty men as they were crossing the Bhamo-Siu road and the pursuit began. The column dispersed and moved into the hills where they reformed at nightfall.

As Gilkes had planned another supply dropping on 26 April, he decided to try to throw the Japs off his trail and set an ambush for them. Captain Petersen, Sergeant Thompson and some of the men lay in wait for their pursuers and when a party of fifty Japs came into view they opened fire, killing more than half of them. The rest turned and ran for their lives. The column had bought themselves a little time, but the Japs would be snapping at their heels from now on. With the help of guides they found a space on an open hillside caused by a forest fire and in the afternoon two unescorted Hudson's dropped six days' rations for each man, as well as ammunition, silver bullion and maps showing the route eastwards.

The next day information reached them from the Kachins that an enemy force 100 strong was approaching from the north. Fortunately the local villagers helped them stay one step ahead of the enemy and shepherded them through the hills during the coming weeks. As they neared the Bhamo–Lashio road they sent Kachin guides ahead to find the best crossing point. By 30 April, they were bivouacked a mile from the road when it started to rain. Their guides advised crossing under the cover of darkness as the rain would keep the Japanese lorries from using the road at night. They moved east across a chaung and found the going very difficult. They lost their last two mules due to exhaustion and their radio transmitter had to be abandoned as it was too heavy to carry. At midnight they crossed the road unseen.

As dawn was breaking on May Day a sentry brought in what they first thought was a Japanese in civilian clothes. Upon questioning it turned out he was Chinese and was very pleased to see the British officers, as he thought that the Gurkha who had apprehended him was a Japanese soldier. He spoke good Kachin and Gilkes asked him to accompany them to China and interpret for them. He agreed without question and for the next five days led the column along the valleys and over the hills, avoiding the main tracks and the Japanese outposts. They also heard that Second Lieutenant L. Tong from 7 Column's Burrif Platoon had preceded them by three weeks, heading for Kasan Bum. They decided to follow in his footsteps to obtain information on the northern and eastern routes.

They were now following the route Tinsing-Lung Hkat-Banlun and found the villages very hospitable. Guides would precede them to villages en route and they would find food waiting for them as they arrived. In several of the villages they found Burrifs, many of them on leave from their own platoons. At Banlun a Burrif Subedar gave them information on other parties that had passed through. The commander of 7 Column Burma Rifles platoon, Captain Herring, together with a Jemadar and sixteen Other Ranks went through on 20 April, having given up hope of meeting up with George Dunlop and 1 Column. Captain Buchanan, three British Other Ranks and fifty-five Gurkhas and Karens went through on 26 April, and a week prior to that Lieutenant Astell and forty-five mixed Other Ranks moved through the area. They had just missed Lieutenant Musgrave Wood and his party of fifteen men by a couple of days.

One evening their guide returned with four Chinese guerrillas clad in blue clothes and carrying rifles. They said that they had been sent by their headquarters to check on reports of British troops in the area. They were in contact with the Chinese central armies and assumed that the information about British troops had come from Chungking. They offered to take the party to their headquarters several days march away and that evening crossed the Taiping River into China. It was 6 May 1943.

Whereas the Kachin tribesmen had provided food and support for the column and warned them of the presence of Japanese patrols, Gilkes wondered whether they would receive the same support from the stocky, opium-smoking

Yunnanese. They soon discovered that they were not to be disappointed, when they entered the first village and asked for rice. The villagers refused payment as did the other villages that they passed through, despite the fact that silver was so highly prized in China. As they continued their journey they came across villages and farms burnt out by the invading Japanese, the surviving occupants fleeing to join the guerrilla forces.

Finally they reached the headquarters of the guerrillas, camouflaged deep in the mountain forests. The guerrilla chiefs turned out the guard for Gilkes to inspect and in turn the Column Commander strapped on a Kachin dah in lieu of a ceremonial sword and, after the inspection was over, saluted in best Guards fashion. As he sheathed his dah and stepped back he lost his footing and fell into a stream to the great amusement of his hosts.

Many of the guerrillas were former soldiers who had served with the Chinese Fifth Army during the Burma campaign and had been stranded in Yunnan on the way out. Others were locals who knew every inch of the country in which they fought. They laid on a huge meal for the hungry Chindits and settled down to await the return of the guerrilla commander the next morning. Many of the British soldiers passed around photographs of their loved ones, inspiring admiration from the family oriented Chinese who marvelled at the men who had left their families and travelled halfway around the world to help fight the Japanese.

The following morning Gilkes and the guerrilla commander discussed their options and decided that the best course of action was for Gilkes and a small support party to take the shorter route to contact the regular Chinese forces operating south of the Salween. Major Gilkes, Captain Blackburn and ten others left on 10 May to take the direct route to Lunghwankiang. The main body of the column under Captain Pickering would take the safer but longer route to the north-west via Fort Morton, Fort Harrison and Wawchon.

Gilkes and his party had not travelled very far when news reached them of a Japanese attack towards the Mamien Pass and they were advised to wait a couple of days until the Chinese had thrown them back. He sent Captain Blackburn and his escort back to rejoin the column near the headquarters of all the guerrillas in south-west Yunnan. Their commander was a veteran of seven years fighting against the Japs, and had been wounded four times in battle. His men offered the usual hospitality to their guests, although their peace and quiet was disturbed by two days and nights of mourning. A sentry had shot the husband of the cook when he failed to answer his challenge and the clanging of gongs and wailing of relatives kept the men awake.

By 23 May, the column was reunited with its commander at Tamza-Pa. A message had been sent to the nearest Chinese Divisional Headquarters and a couple of days later the reply came back that three officers should proceed to the headquarters and make arrangements for the movement of the rest of the column. Gilkes decided to take Captain Petersen and Captain Cotterill with him and before he left he gave Commander Wong, the guerrilla commander, a present of 30 rifles, two tommy guns, a revolver, 1,500 rounds of ammunition and ten grenades. The old veteran was very pleased as his men only had one rifle between every six men. As his men were now under Chinese protection, Gilkes considered it only reasonable to help their Allies in view of the food and assistance given to them. Before they departed the commander told them, 'We are glad to meet Allied officers who neither have creases in their trousers, nor ask for beds on which to sleep.'

The journey was beginning to take its toll on some of the men and Lance Corporals Brown and Short, and Privates Allnutt, Dwyer, Rowley, Perrett and McArthur were left at Tamza-Pa to recover. The next day Sergeant Thompson, Privates Coulson, Rubbock, Sykes and Thornton were left at Hou-Tien under Lieutenant Heald who was suffering recurrent bouts of fever.

On 29 May, the column, now 127 strong, arrived at Chiao-Tou where they met Captain Mah, an English-speaking officer with the 36th Chinese Division. His men appeared fit and determined and it was clear that the Chindits were now in safe hands. The following day they crossed the Mamien Pass. At 10,500 feet above sea level it was the stiffest climb and descent of the campaign, but the men did well, and billets and food were waiting for them at the end. On 31 May, they were ferried across the Salween River and the next day arrived at Wen-Shang, headquarters of a Chinese cavalry regiment, where they all received a shave and a haircut for the first time in months.

They left Waufangi at 0730 hours on 3 June, and after a strenuous march of 32 miles they finally reached Paoshan at 1945 hours. They were greeted with flags flying and a band playing military music, and were lodged in the best building in town. They were given baths, new clothes and haircuts, and the Chinese General even advanced Gilkes enough money to pay his men. Then followed a grand feast, given by the General commanding Seventy-First Chinese Army.

The men began the last leg of their journey home on 5 June when they boarded lorries for a drive along the Burma Road to Kunming and thence to Yunani where the American Air Force offered to fly them to Assam at once. On 9 June, Major Gilkes stepped off the train at Manipur Road, heading for Brigade Headquarters, while the rest of his men carried on to Shillong for a well-deserved rest.

Eventually the survivors of the 13th King's would reassemble at Karachi where they spent the rest of the year recuperating and training. In March 1944, Field Marshal Wavell, now the Viceroy of India, would hold a private ceremony to decorate those to whom awards had been made and to express to the whole battalion his own and the whole Army's admiration of their exploits.

Sadly, not all of Gilkes's men had made it home. One man from 7 Column who did not make it to China was Private Leon Frank:

I was in a group of thirty men under a Lieutenant from the Sherwood Foresters [Musgrave Wood?] and we decided to make our way northwards to Fort Hertz which was still in British hands. The idea was that we would take some guides from a village, who could take us on to the next village, and so on. We did this successfully for a while, then we had these two guides who were leading us up a hill towards a cross-shaped junction of tracks. Suddenly one dived left and the other right and disappeared into the jungle. In front of us across the track was a Japanese patrol. Well, we just melted into the jungle either side, but the Japs had spotted us. We hoped that if we were quiet enough they would just go away, but one of our chaps looked up and for no apparent reason shouted 'Japs!' and gave our position away. They started to open fire on us, so we turned and rolled and scrambled down the hill. We did everything we could to put them off our tracks and eventually eluded them. We realised that our party was too large and too obvious a target, so our Lieutenant told us it was every man for himself. Myself and five others, including Lance Corporal Jordan, decided to go east and try to get into China.

We became like bandits; we would go into villages and demand rice and food at gunpoint. We eventually came to a hillside with a hut on the side of it and a stream below and and settled down to rest. Someone should have been on guard but we were very exhausted. Next thing we knew the door burst open and in came a Jap soldier with a fixed bayonet and stabbed Jordan in the hand. He was about to have another go when an officer called him off. We walked outside to find a half moon circle of Japanese soldiers with a machine-gun in the centre, pointing at us. I remember turning around and saying, 'The bastards are going to shoot us in cold blood!' Fortunately we had been captured by the Imperial Guard, who were professional soldiers. They tied our hands and led us to their camp. We were fed and given various jobs to do around the camp. I was made a batman to one of the Japanese officers and had to sleep with five other Japanese batmen. One of the soldiers could speak English. He had been a barber in Tokyo and asked me to go to his hut for supper one night. He gave me some rice and kidneys to eat and invited me to go to Tokyo after the war and meet his family.

After about ten days we were put on a truck and sent to Maymyo. On the way we stopped at another jungle camp and our escort left us in the hands of the camp's personnel. We were taken into a hut and made to kneel in the execution position with our hands tied behind our back. A big Japanese officer came in whirling his sword and we thought our time had come. However, it was just a sick joke. When we got to Maymyo we were beaten up by the Korean guards, who were just as bad, if not worse than, the Japanese. Eventually we were sent to Rangoon by train, crammed into cattle trucks for the three-day trip. I remember when we stopped at Mandalay the door was opened and we saw one of the big six-foot Imperial guardsmen who had captured us. He went away and came back with a bunch of bananas which he gave to us. Our next stop was block number six, Rangoon jail. I was the only one of the six of us to survive.

Leon Frank was joined in Rangoon jail by another 7 Column member, Fred Morgan. He was among the two platoons of the column that had already crossed the Irrawaddy at Inywa when the Japanese intervened. Apparently he was not with Charles Aves and R.V. Hyner and their party and was soon bagged by the enemy. He told the author:

As soon as we landed a decision was made to move off in small groups as quickly as possible, since we did not want to attract too much attention to ourselves. After all, we had no idea as to the strength of the Jap patrol. The small group I was with was led by Lieutenant Stock.

We had paused for a while, resting our heads on our packs, when all of a sudden a number of Japs came tearing up the hillside towards us. Needless to say we beat a hasty retreat up the hill. Somehow the Bren gun was left behind and I handed my rifle to someone and went back for it. I grabbed it, but found the magazine was empty and therefore useless. On the way up I started to strip the gun and began throwing the pieces to the four winds. I finally caught up with Lieutenant Stock and found he was in possession of a revolver, but no ammunition. I think we had words with one another over that omission. We eventually lost contact with each other and I met up with him again in Rangoon jail.

Now I was all by myself. I was alone, tired and frightened. I found myself climbing a very large hill and when I reached the top I started down the other side and began to cross a paddy field. No sooner had I got to the centre of the field when I heard shouting and what appeared to be animal noises. I stopped and turned around to see three Japanese running towards me. One of them had a sword and the other two had fixed bayonets and they started to prod me in the stomach. The Jap with the sword slapped my face and then knocked me to the ground. My hands were tied behind my back and I was marched back to what must have been an advanced post, complete with a look-out tower, situated just outside Wuntho. I was interrogated by a very tall Japanese officer, who asked me all sorts of military questions about the strengths and whereabouts of the British Army in India. I replied that that sort of information was not available to an ordinary NCO. I was accused of lying and beaten up again!

Along with a number of other Chindits I was taken to Maymyo, in which there was a Japanese field prison. Here we were made to learn their language, in particular the various words of command. It behove us all to learn as quickly as possible in order to avoid being beaten up. At the end of the working day, which was spent digging air raid shelters and repairing houses, we had to stand around a flag pole with the Japanese 'Rising Sun' flag fluttering in the breeze. We had to bow towards the east in honour of their Emperor. After this charade we had to have a sing-song. Much to the amusement of the guards, a mate of mine, Sergeant Gilbert Josling, and myself used to sing Max Miller's song 'I fell in love with Mary from the dairy'. Sadly, Sergeant Josling did not make it home from Rangoon jail. Our compound was surrounded by very heavy iron railings and the Japanese guards used to patrol around this perimeter. Every time the guard passed by, we had to stop what we were doing and bow. At this time I was sitting on the ground with Sergeant Josling's head in my lap, because he was very ill with beri-beri, so I did not get up and bow. The Jap saw me and started shouting obscenities at me, so I laid Josling's head down gently and went over to the fence and bowed. The Jap thrust his rifle through the railings butt first and belted me in the stomach and testicles for not bowing to him in the first place. When I returned to Josling he had passed away.

When the crossing of the Irrawaddy at Inywa was abandoned, Private Hyner found himself on the wrong side of the river with sixty-four other men. Shortly afterwards their bivouac was attacked by the Japs and the party fragmented again. In the weeks that followed more men decided to leave his party to try to make their way back to India, although none of them were heard of again. They were now a frightening sight, with tattered clothing, long matted hair and unkempt beards; the seams of their shirts alive with lice. He later wrote:

By now no food was left and we were getting weaker every day. Not only did we have to cope with the journey but we had to conceal ourselves from the enemy, and also hack our way through the undergrowth wherever necessary. We were now down to about 20 men. We tried to make better time by walking by moonlight, but we found it impossible to keep up as the moonlight was playing tricks with our eyes. We imagined trees that weren't there and walked into trees that were there. As we were in the heart of the jungle we decided to rest. We didn't post any guards as everyone was too tired and weary. When it was dawn we found, to our amazement, that we had been sleeping on a jungle motor road which had the telltale marks of Japanese lorry tyres. We covered up our own tracks as quickly as possible and headed up the hills, out of the way of the Japs, as our only objective now was to get out.

  Water was impossible to find by now. There were no rivers or ponds from which to fill our bottles. We didn't know which berries to eat or any other things growing in the jungle as we had not had any training on jungle survival. We suddenly came across a wild banana tree with beautiful stems of bananas. We cut some down, only to find they were full of black pips. We were very disappointed as we were very hungry. We then hacked out the roots of the banana tree and were able to moisten our lips with the sap.

By now we were making our way along the side of the mountain, marching by the only compass we had and keeping due west. Our stomachs had forgotten about food; our problem now was water, or the lack of it. Private Randall was so thirsty he passed his own urine into his mug and drank it. Within seconds of his doing this someone shouted 'water'. A finger-wide trickle was coming down the mountain. We rested there while we all had our first drink for some time and filled our water bottles.

Our journey continued to the top of the mountain. We followed elephant droppings as they would ensure a clear path. After a few days we saw, in the valley below, a river, which we decided to make for, still going west all the time. Private Rackham had not discarded his 'iron lung', a frame used for carrying equipment, and he got it caught in some trees and fell over the side of the mountain. We all went down to him to see what we could do for him. He was so badly injured and unable to walk that the officer asked for a volunteer to shoot him, as he, the officer, couldn't do it; nor could any of us. We made him comfortable and decided to try to get help from a village half a mile away.

We made our way very slowly down the ravine towards the river, sliding down shiny boulders of stone. We weren't sure if the village was friendly, so we went into open formation, stepping out of the river bed, when machine guns opened up. When mortars began to fall we knew this was not a friendly village. Orders were given for everyone to use five rounds of rapid fire. I went to fire but found I couldn't as my rifle was jammed. The officer ordered us back up the mountains. We could do no more for Private Rackham.

As we continued down there were more mountains; in fact we seemed to be surrounded by mountains. During one of those days we came across a thick bamboo pipe with pure mountain water running through it. There were four bamboo cups on a small bamboo mat next to the pipe with a notice written in English saying 'You have enjoyed this drink, please replace the cups for fellow travellers.' We had a good drink and filled our water bottles and continued down the mountain. By this time I had fixed my dagger to the side of my rifle to use as a bayonet.

We came to a village where we were given rice wrapped in banana leaves, eggs, bananas and dried fish. I was also given uncooked rice which I put in my last pair of new socks, tied them together and slung them round my neck. We collected as many rupees as we could spare and gave them to the villagers. The head man drew a child-like drawing of a boat and river in the dirt and pointed towards the direction we were to take. We followed the path and within a couple of hours we came across another village with a few market type stalls and a native sitting on one. I was the last man to enter and noticed that the native seemed to be counting us in. I reported this to the officer and we decided he may well be an informer for the Japs so we went straight through and into the jungle again. It was quicker to go through the villages but not safe as the Japs would surely be using the same trail.

Progress through the jungle was now very hard and slow as we had not had any food for three days. The lice on our bodies were beginning to really worry us. Each time we made a halt we picked them out. We did this by running a twig up the front of our bush shirts, tearing them off like a line of white cotton in the seams. We could also pick them out of our beards. We noticed our Sergeant was missing, so Randall and I went back down the path and found him not far away. He told us to leave him as he could not go on any further because he was so tired and weak. We told him not to be a 'silly bugger' and we helped him to stand up. With one of us on either side of him we walked him back up the path. He never forgot the help we gave him. Later, when we got back to India he never wanted us to go on either lectures or schemes as he knew we had been through it all and only wanted new recruits.

By now, no one looked like a British soldier; we looked more like pirates. One chap had lost his bush hat and had a piece of black cloth round his head, hanging down at the back. I had a dah, which I had got from a village, which took the place of my bayonet. Some of the men had knives hanging down as well.

On reaching the next village we saw three Burmese men who ran away as we approached. We shouted to them to halt or we would fire and they stopped in their tracks. They stood and watched us helping ourselves to large green vegetables which looked like marrows and tasted like cucumbers. One of them offered to act as a guide for us, which he did for a day. Three British planes flew very low over a clearing we were just entering. This frightened the life out of our Burmese guide and he ran like hell into the jungle and we never saw him again. This made one of our chaps openly break down and cry when he saw we had lost our guide.

All our spirits were very low by now and we were still slogging along when we hit the next village. This was the largest village we had yet come across. I walked across to a woman who was standing outside her hut, holding a baby in her arms. I made a fuss of the baby and began talking to her in English, telling her I was hungry and asking if she had any food to spare. She returned from her hut with a few bananas and a packet of cooked rice in a banana leaf. I put a couple of silver coins in the baby's hand and thanked her very much. Other villagers came out of their huts and straw mats were laid in the centre of the village on the ground. About 14 troops sat on the ground and food and drink were put on the mats, which we thoroughly appreciated. It was the best village we had ever entered. We had our fill, too much really because our stomachs were swollen and then we realised we had stayed too long.

The village was almost on the top of a hill and you could see for miles. Suddenly a woman working in the field shouted out Japanese! Japanese!' We looked in the direction she had indicated and we saw a column of dust, which we knew was coming from the enemy. We estimated there were about 300 Japs coming about half a day or more away from us. The villagers quickly rolled up their mats and covered up all signs that British soldiers had been there. We thanked them and said to the head man that British forces would be returning soon and we would tell them of the help they had given to us.

Somehow, we had gone in the wrong direction. When the officer checked his compass he found we had not been going due west. We came across a fork in the path. In the distance we could see three gold domes which we presumed meant there was a burial ground there. I had seen these three domes before in a dream many years before, when I was about 14 years old. I just knew which way to go, so we took the right-hand path. We could see a river shining in the sunlight in the distance and made our way towards it. We filled our water bottles and had a good drink but didn't hang around as we were in low country.

The leading man, Corporal Risedale, started going uphill, which was hard going. We were all very tired when we got to the top. We asked the officer why the bloody hell we had come up the hill, to which he replied, 'Corporal Risedale was leading.' We told him we thought he was in charge, to which he replied, 'I feel like shooting myself,' and we said, 'Shoot your bloody self, as long as you don't shoot any of us.' We said this because we had lost respect for him ages ago.

We did continue to climb and during the evening sunset we could see from the top of the mountain a thin silver line in the distance, which we knew to be the Chindwin. We decided to rest for the night, but the mosquitoes would not let me. I put my bush hat over my face, handkerchief round my neck, made a pillow of my socks with the rice in and went to sleep the best way I could. When we arose we were in better spirits as we could see the Chindwin in the distance. We also spotted smoke from Japanese cooking fires at least half a day behind us. So our journey towards the Chindwin began, which we thought would take about three days. Those three days turned into a week because we hadn't reckoned on the dead ground in between.

Coming down from this mountain we could see in the distance a village, half of which seemed to be on fire with thick black smoke rising. We cautiously approached the right-hand side which wasn't burning. I was the leading man that day and the first thing I saw was an old lady sitting at the doorway of her hut. I asked her if there were any Japanese about, to which she replied 'No'. I asked her if there were any eggs and she put her frail hand into a very small brass vase and brought out two eggs. This was after I had made a noise like a chicken. The other men did the same thing and there must have been a hole in the floor, because eggs kept on coming out. She was paid for these eggs with silver coins as paper notes were no good to the Burmese. The only other signs there were footprints of Japanese soldiers in considerable number.

We had gone round a small bend where I picked up an empty packet of Victory V's. I began to wonder if we were near our own front line. Farther round this bend was a small footbridge over a river and, to my surprise, I saw a short Seaforth Highlander approaching me through the water, not using the footbridge. I did the same and met him in the middle. We shook hands and he said, 'You lot are bloody lucky. The village you have just come from has been occupied by about 7,000 Japs.' His patrol had been keeping them under observation and the last of the Japs had only left about half an hour before we had entered. They had gone to the left and we had kept to the right. We had been dead lucky and the old lady had told the truth that there were no Japs there then, but had not mentioned that they had just left. She must have been very bewildered.

We reported that we were still being followed by approximately 300 Japs. It was decided that we should make our way to the Seaforth Highlanders B Company where we were made very welcome and given K rations and mugs of tea and cigarettes. The medics came round to us and bandaged up my jungle sores until I looked like a mummy. We were to be sent back to Tamu immediately. The 14 of us who had come out were put into a canoe carved out of a tree trunk and two fit natives paddled us up the River Chindwin at last. We came to a landing where we disembarked next to a road which had about half a dozen huts on it. As I got out of the boat I filled my water bottle with the intention of making a cup of tea from my K rations. I made a small fire out of a few dried twigs and began to boil the water. Suddenly, an officer from the Seaforths was standing over me and he said, 'Put out that bloody fire, don't you know the enemy is over the other side.' I looked him straight in the eyes and put my tea bag in the hot water. I said nothing to him. His next words were, 'Sorry, sorry'. He must have realised that I had just come from the other side myself and had been over there for some considerable time. I had lost all sense of days and time myself.

We were told to strip and burn our old clothes and were issued with new jungle green uniforms. We were given enough food to last two or three days and sat down in a clearing and made tea in our old biscuit tins. We had the best grub we'd had for a long while of corned beef, tinned fruit and hard tack biscuits. We were then told a truck was being sent to take us down to Imphal. The truck arrived with two Indian drivers and we began to travel down the treacherous roads which we had previously walked up when they were only elephant tracks. It was now a complete motor road which the Yanks had built with bulldozers while we had been in action.

From the back of the lorry we could see for miles over the countryside as we were so high up in the hills. We stopped at a place where there was pure water running down the mountains through a bamboo pipe. We had a good drink and filled our bottles. The two Indian drivers started to argue when we got back in the truck and continued to argue. We saw so many smashed up vehicles we wondered if they were paying enough attention to their driving. Suddenly the lorry swerved and we went over the side. Luckily we only turned over once. I grabbed the rail above and simply stood up on the Sergeant who was on the deck and I walked off the lorry. We were lucky a tree had stopped us turning over. Anywhere else and we would have gone straight over the side. Another lorry following us took us into civilization, where there was a YMCA and a hospital.

Next morning I went into Imphal hospital for a check up. I weighed only seven stone instead of my normal 12 stone. A nursing sister called me into a room as she wanted to tend my wounds, which only consisted of 30 or 40 jungle sores. She asked me why there were no seriously wounded amongst our lot. I replied, 'If you couldn't walk you were left. We all knew this before we went into action.' She then broke down and cried her eyes out and had to leave the room. The next day I was admitted to hospital suffering from malaria.

Charles Aves, who had parted company with Hyner after their bivouac was attacked following their crossing of the Irrawaddy, also reached home safely:

There was one village where they laid on a real feast for us – meat and vegetables, rice and fruit – and we spent quite a time with them. We augmented our food a couple of times by throwing grenades into lakes and bringing out the concussed fish, stewing and eating them. Eventually we found our way to the Chindwin without too much alarm, although our boots and socks were worn out and our feet were suffering badly. We were almost in sight of the Chindwin when to our great pleasure we ran into a patrol of Seaforth Highlanders. Their role was to be on the lookout for us and help us get boats over the Chindwin. A patrol of Japs a few days previously had inflicted some damage on a Seaforth patrol and this group who had met us were going out to look for them. After seeing we were fed they led us to the boats and we proceeded up the river for a couple of hours to a point of safety on the west bank where we were greeted by another patrol. We still had quite a bit of trekking to get over the escarpment where there was transport to get us to Imphal. We eventually arrived in Imphal some three months after we had left and were taken to hospital where we had luxury baths, new clothing and good food. Then most of us collapsed with malaria; I was delirious for forty-eight hours but came to in chastened mood. A couple of days later Wingate came to visit us. When I mentioned my feelings about the two officers running away and leaving maps and money behind, he became serious and said, 'We won't wash our dirty linen in public, will we?' I never have until now.

The officer who led us out became quite morose and did not seem to want to acknowledge any of the party that came out with him. It was strange as we had all been so close and we all did our share of helping him as well as him helping us. Some time later we understood that he had received a letter from his wife, who was a stage actress at the London Palladium, to the effect that she had fallen in love with somebody else. Later he blew himself up when demonstrating a new form of plastic grenade.

The pride of we survivors in our accomplishment at being the first to hit back at the Japs after all our reverses along with our faith and belief in our leader was paramount. General Wingates descendants can be immensely proud of his individuality, bravery, foresight, technical brilliance, unorthodoxy and understanding of his ordinary troops.

Chapter 14

Plane Land Here Now – 8 Column

Major Walter Scott and 8 Column joined up with Headquarters Northern Group and its commander, Lieutenant Colonel Sam Cooke, for the journey home. Scott wanted to try to take his column home intact, so they could all benefit from supply drops. They marched northwards towards Fort Hertz and reached the banks of the Shweli River on 1 April. They managed to get a line across the river and began to cross in two dinghies, lashed to the line to prevent them being carried away. Captain Williams, Lieutenants Hobday and Horton and twenty-nine men of 18 Platoon had reached the far bank safely when Sergeant Scrutton's dinghy carrying a dozen men got into difficulties mid-stream, and they foolishly cut through a knot in the main rope and the two dinghies, and their occupants swirled away downriver with the curses of their comrades ringing in their ears. They would never see India again. Captain Williams and his party set off on their own, but were ambushed on the way and only one of their party survived.

The next day the column began to construct rafts and prepared to try again that afternoon. However Major Conron and his dispersal group arrived and informed them that they had tried to cross earlier using banana tree rafts, but the attempt was a failure. The current was simply too strong for the type of rafts they had made, so a signal was sent requesting more dinghies. Conron was invited to join 8 Column for a supply drop two days hence, but his party moved on and no further contact was made with them. It is believed that they were later ambushed while trying to cross the river and the majority, including Conron, perished.

On 3 April, the RAF dropped four more dinghies to the column as well as 200 lifebelts and two days rations, and the whole column and their two surviving mules crossed the river that night. They found a wounded Burma Rifleman on the bank who had been shot through the knee two days earlier and took him along on a stretcher.

The long-awaited supply drop arrived on 7 April but because they were in thick jungle many of the statachutes landed in the tops of the trees. Fortunately the Gurkhas and Burrifs were excellent tree climbers and most of the baskets were recovered. Rations for ten days had been dropped as well as boots, canvas shoes, ropes, a charged wireless battery and a bag of grain for the one remaining mule. The other mule had died of exhaustion and the wireless battery charging engine had to be abandoned, so the battery dropped by the RAF was urgently needed in order to maintain contact with India and arrange more drops.

The column continued north towards Katha and Bhamo on the Irrawaddy. They had been advised that a Japanese battalion was at Bhamo with posts scattered around the area, but the routes north of the River Uyu appeared to be clear. It was hard going over the next few days due to pouring rain and problems finding the correct route to take through the forests. They were also being plagued by lice and bamboo ticks which had an annoying habit of getting into the most private parts of a man's anatomy. It was arduous work for the stretcher party carrying the wounded Burrif.

On 12 April, the front of the column was approaching a newly built bamboo bridge over a chaung when they bumped into a couple of Japs who turned and bolted back into the jungle. Intense firing broke out and Sergeant Bridgeman and Private Beard were killed, while Privates Lawton and Witheridge were both seriously wounded. Most of the column turned around and disappeared along the track they had come down, leaving Major Scott and a small party isolated. It was not until the evening that the column reassembled and it was discovered that Lieutenant Horncastle of the Burrif Platoon and 14 others were missing. It was thought that they might have moved off as a separate party.

The column was up and moving at 0430 hours the next morning. The going was quite good but they now had three wounded on stretchers to carry with them. Major Scott and Lieutenant Colonel Cooke held an officers' conference and it was decided that they would request one last supply drop before breaking up into dispersal groups to cross the Irrawaddy.

The dispersal groups were arranged as follows; Lieutenant Colonel Cooke, Lieutenant Borrow and half of Group Headquarters; Lieutenants Pickering, Pearce and Bennett and the other half of Group Headquarters; Major Scott with Column Headquarters, 17 Platoon and two sections of 16 Platoon; Captain Whitehead and his Burrifs less those already allocated to assist the dispersal groups, plus Flying Officer Wheately and a section of 16 Platoon; Lieutenants Carroll, Hamilton-Bryan with Support Group and 19 Platoon; Lieutenants Neill and Sprague with the Gurkha Platoon and 142 Commando Platoon.

On 15 April, Captain Whitehead and his dispersal group, together with the stretcher party under Sergeant Parsons and the MO, Captain Heathcote, left the column. They planned to move to the east of Bhamo, thence north of Myitkyina to Fort Hertz. If this plan failed they would cross the Irrawaddy north of Bhamo and then go west towards the Chindwin. On the way they intended to leave the stretcher cases at a friendly Kachin village.

Captain Whitehead's party had great difficulty getting down the eastern slopes of the mountains to the Bhamo Plain and the first villages they visited were deserted. The escort party under Lieutenant Hamilton-Bryan returned after a couple of days, anxious not to lose contact with the column. The decision of the MO to remain with Whitehead's group was rather controversial as it left the bulk of the column without a doctor. It was also a fateful decision as the party would be ambushed by the Japs on their journey and Whitehead would end up in Rangoon Jail suffering from numerous gunshot wounds. The fate of the stretcher party is unknown.

Meanwhile the column received their supply drop on 17 April: four days' rations, corned beef and mutton, and another charged radio battery. The following day Lieutenants Neill, Sprague and Gillow left with their dispersal group, intending to drop on to the plain before heading for Myale where they proposed to cross the Irrawaddy. Lieutenants Pickering, Pearce and Bennett and their group left for Watto on the Irrawaddy, and half an hour later Major Scott and the rest of the column continued on their journey to Sinkan. It had been decided that Lieutenant Colonel Cooke's dispersal group, together with that of Lieutenant Carroll, would remain with Scott for the time being, making a large party of six officers and 170 men, plus one mule with the wireless set.

On 19 April, they reached the Irrawaddy and lay up in a gorge near the river. There they found a hoard of rice in Japanese petrol tins in a cave. They took enough to give each man a meal and placed a silver coin in the bottom of each tin. Then they began to construct rafts with the intention of crossing over the next night. The river at the head of the Zinbon Gorge was about 350 yards wide. The water banked up in the funnel of the gorge and on the northern side it was flowing upstream, with whirlpools and many unpleasant currents below the surface. However, it was thought that they would have a good chance of crossing on rafts at that particular spot.

Around 0930 hours three small boats were seen moving up the far bank of the river, followed some distance away by a junk. The three boats crossed over to the near bank, quite close to where the Chindits lay in wait. It was not known at the time, but they were full of Japanese soldiers, escorting the junk which was carrying supplies.

As the junk moved over to the near bank it grounded on a sandbank a mere hundred yards away from the bivouac. A quick decision was made to capture the junk and Major Scott, Lieutenant Borrow and Havildar Lanval rushed from cover and climbed aboard like pirates. Ten minutes later the first load of sixty troops was on its way across the river, with non-swimmers inside and swimmers hanging on to the sides. One and a half hours later the column was across the river, to the relief of all concerned. The serang sailed his junk onwards trying to catch up with his escorts, grinning as he jingled the bag of silver coins in his hand.

Private Dennis 'Topper' Brown managed to keep a diary of the trek home. He recorded the speech that Lieutenant Colonel Cooke made to the men, the day after they crossed the river:

> It was not very encouraging. The gist of it was that he had orders from HQ to make the return journey to India, but that if he had his way, we would fight on to the last man and last bullet! You can image how that went down with the rank and file! I did hear that at one time he suggested that the RAF should drop soap, towels and razors, until it was pointed out that you can't eat them! The next day, our last mule, carrying the radio, keeled over and died. We radioed for one last supply drop, smashed the set and continued on our journey.

On 23 April, Corporal Worsley fell by the side of the track. Suffering from acute jungle sores and with legs swollen to twice their normal size he could go no further. His platoon stayed behind to guide him to the next bivouac, but he would not budge and was left to follow in his own time. By now the troops were completely out of rations and water was becoming scarce. The next day Corporal Walker fell out from exhaustion. He had been suffering from dysentery for the past two weeks. Three Gurkhas fell out with him.

Company Quartermaster Sergeant Duncan Bett later recalled:

> We were all scared of being left behind. When we dropped down exhausted at night it was so dark under the jungle canopy that you could not see your hand at the end of your nose. It was like the tomb. I remember waking up suddenly once and I couldn't see a thing or hear a sound. No mules, no sentries, nothing. I thought I had been left behind when the column moved on before dawn. I scrabbled around in a panic, feeling for another body and the relief was indescribable when I felt someone else there on the ground. It seems hard to believe, but several men were left behind in the dark. Presumably they were so exhausted they didn't wake up and were not missed in the confusion when the column moved off.

The rendezvous for the next supply drop was a clearing near Bhamo, a large town 150 miles behind Japanese lines. As he marched along through the dark jungle, Major Scott noticed that the track ahead of him was growing lighter, as if he were approaching the end of a tunnel. Soon he was standing at the edge of the jungle, looking out on what was probably the largest patch of open ground in northern Burma.

The following day, 25 April, the Chindits scanned the sky, praying for a supply drop. Captain Johnny Carroll, the Support Group Commander, was one of them:

Colonel Cooke agreed that we should work out the best area for a supply drop using white maps and socks. I suggested that we mark out PLANE LAND HERE NOW. Colonel Cooke said that we could not issue orders to the RAF and should therefore mark out REQUEST PLANE LAND HERE NOW. As the noise of a supply plane could already be heard, I suggested we start without the word REQUEST and add it later if time permitted.

The planes came over and dropped supplies to the waiting Chindits. Tommy guns, waterproof capes, bully beef, cheese and chocolate, and five days rations floated to the ground.

One of the planes circled lower and saw the message. Flying Officer 'Lumme' Lord lowered his undercarriage and tried to land, but the area was too short and too rough to put down safely. The plane then made off to the west in a great hurry. Shortly afterwards a thunderstorm burst upon them, hailstones the size of marbles fell and the troops started collecting them to eat. Only half of the rations had arrived, so the Chindits moved into bivouac to cook what they had and hope that the planes would return later.

At 0600 hours the next day the planes returned and dropped enough rations for five more days. Another charged battery arrived, but there was no wireless now to send messages. They were also in desperate need of new clothing as their shirts and trousers were dropping to pieces. Many men had no sleeves to their shirts and no seats to their trousers, and many pairs of trousers had been cut down as shorts, with the result that at night the men were pestered by mosquitoes. During the day the men were sent down to a nearby stream to bathe and to try to remove some of the lice which plagued them.

On 27 April, a message was dropped to the men: 'Mark out 1,200 yard landing ground to hold twelve-ton transport.' A second message gave details of the route taken by Major Fergusson of 5 Column who had by now found his way back to India.

At dawn on 28 April, the Dakota rescue plane took off, escorted by eight Mohawk fighters. Flying Officer Michael Vlasto and his crew had been given a pair of Army boots each to walk home in if the plane did not land safely. When he reached the clearing, a white line was marked out on the field, together with a message: 'LAND ON WHITE LINE. GROUND THERE V.G.' The crew braced themselves as Vlasto made his approach. They touched down and the pilot hit the brakes, coming to a halt just at the end of the strip. The plane was soon surrounded by bearded, malnourished men. Who would go out in the plane? There was only one answer: the wounded would go out first – Corporal Jimmy Walker of 7 Column, who had dropped out of the column with dysentery and an infected hip, but had dragged himself along behind them; Private Jim Suddery who had been shot in the back, the bullet going right through him; and Private Robert Hulse, shaken every couple of hours by violent fits of vomiting. Lieutenant Colonel Cooke also went aboard. This was a controversial decision which provoked much discussion among those left behind. A photographer on the plane took a picture of the Colonel smiling and reading Punch magazine, in contrast to the looks of suffering, emaciation and profound relief on the faces of the others. Fifty years later on one of those who walked out remarked to the author: 'A round of bread and jam would have been more use to them than a read of Punch magazine. If you want my opinion it wasn't a case of wangling a seat, but that Scotty was glad and eager to get rid of him! And of course there were more deserving cases who should have gone.' One of those was Topper Brown, who staggered on to the Chindwin while suffering with dysentery, after escaping death when they were ambushed at the Kaukkwe Chaung, and then came down with typhus fever and had to be carried 70 miles on a stretcher by Naga tribesmen to the Imphal Road.

Eighteen men were counted into the plane and the cargo door was closed behind them. One of them, Corporal Bert Fitton, who played left half in the company football team, helped Lieutenant Colonel Cooke and the sick and wounded into the plane, only to find himself locked in and about to take off and had to plead with the pilot to let him out. Back on the ground he told Major Scott, 'I came in on my feet and I'd like to go out the same way,' and rejoined his comrades. Michael Vlasto gripped the control column as the end of the field rushed towards his plane. The runway was too short and they were overloaded. With knuckles white and his face dripping with sweat, he pulled back on the stick and the plane staggered into the air, brushing the treetops below. 'God bless number eighteen,' he said. Sadly, number eighteen was later killed.

For the record, in addition to those mentioned above, the lucky ones included Privates Lambert, Walsh (7 Col), Yates, Wilson and Crowhurst; Lance Corporals Nightingale and Rogerson; Sergeants Flowers, Aubrey, McElroy, Whittaker and Berry; Rifleman Tun Tin one of the Burrifs, suffering from malaria and Rifleman Kulbahadur of the Gurkhas.

The Chindits hoped that more planes would be sent to take them all home and divided themselves into groups in anticipation. But it was not to be. After receiving reports from Lieutenant Colonel Cooke and the pilot of the Dakota, the commander of IV Corps decided it was too risky to repeat the operation. Major Scott had been relieved of his wounded and they had enough supplies to last them three weeks. They also had Fergusson's details of his escape route, so they were in a much better position to walk out. The next day a plane appeared overhead and dropped a message to Major Scott, which read:

> After very careful consideration I have reluctantly decided not to allow the pilot to take the risk of attempting to land his plane again. Apart from the actual landing risks there is considerable danger of interference from Japanese land and air forces. This must, I realise, be a very great

disappointment to you and all your men. We will do all in our power to help you and patrols are now operating east of the Chindwin to meet you. I have no doubt at all that you will be able to reach the Chindwin safely by one of the two routes given you by Fergusson. Have just heard Wingate crossed the Chindwin today. Hope to see you soon. G. Scoones, Major General, Corps HQ. 29 April 1943.

Before the plane departed it parachuted more supplies to the men, including a large bundle of boots. The column, now down to 159 disappointed men, shouldered their bulging packs and continued their journey.

The next day, 30 April, was a fateful day for 8 Column. They reached the Kaukkwe Chaung, halting a mile south-east of the village of Okthaik. The men began crossing on two rafts that had been constructed out of lifebelts. The Burrifs were across first and Havildar Lan Val went into Okthaik and arranged for the headman to guide them on to Pumhpyu. The bridgehead expanded as more men crossed the river and a heavy thunderstorm began as the column started to form up.

Unknown to the drenched Chindits, a strong enemy force had crept up under cover of the storm and heavy firing suddenly broke out around them. CQMS Duncan Bett was one of the men who retired to the cover of the river bank:

On reaching the river bank, which was very high and steep, I sank over my knees in the mud with the weight of my pack, which weighed about seventy pounds. I was forced to slip it off and it rolled down the bank and disappeared in the muddy water with all my newly acquired food and gear. I was left with what I stood up in, a rifle and a bandolier of .303 ammunition.

Company Sergeant Major Cheevers reported to Major Scott that he had knocked out two Japanese machine-gun positions on the west side of the perimeter and the RSM was ordered to lead the dispersal groups off in that direction, keeping to the lower banks of the chaung. While this was taking place the Japanese put in a bayonet charge from the south, but they were driven back by 17 Platoon's Bren gun. Lieutenant Rowland was hit in the chest and was last seen crawling towards the river bank.

As Major Scott collected up the stragglers in the area he came across Colour Sergeant Glasgow who had had his knee shattered. He refused all offers of help and asked Scott and others in the area to shoot him as he knew the Japanese would not bother to take him prisoner if he was unable to walk. Scott told him to lie low until darkness but he told the Column Commander not to bother coming back for him as he intended finishing himself off. He was never seen again.

At this point the Burrifs were seen in the chaung, trying to swim back to the far bank. Two Japanese then appeared on the top of the bank and began dropping grenades into the water. These two were shot by Sergeant Delaney before he joined the Major and the column melting away into the jungle. The firing died away but flared up again fifteen minutes later from the direction of Okthaik village where some of the scattered Chindits had made contact with the Japs again. In the meantime Major Scott and his party put 5 miles of jungle between themselves and the chaung and bivouacked for the night. They discovered that out of the fifty-seven men in the party, only seven had kept their packs. The bulk of the supplies dropped to the column a day or two earlier had been lost during the fighting.

Without Burrifs it would be difficult obtaining food from the villages en route, but one or two of the men knew a few words of Burmese which enabled them to buy rice and obtain guides to help them on their way. As they neared the railway a group of twenty-one at the rear of the column lost contact and continued on their way alone, leaving Major Scott with thirty-five others. They finally crossed the railway at 0245 hours on 3 May, not far from Kadu railway station where a train was unloading Japanese reinforcements. Nine days later, on 12 May, they reached the Chindwin and crossed over. The missing party of twenty-one, led by Sergeants Puckett and Saxton, arrived ten days later and by early June the majority of the 100 men missing after the Okthaik battle had reached the Chindwin.

Not all the dispersal groups had an easy time crossing the railway. CQMS Bett recalled:

As we neared the railway we picked up a Burmese who offered to lead us across the railway between Japanese posts. Although we were very suspicious he led us safely across at night and, just as dawn was breaking, to the entrance to a village. The Lieutenant in charge of our party placed a Sergeant and the men in some cover a short distance away while he, a warrant officer and myself leant against an earth bank outside the entrance to await the return of the Burmese. Meanwhile a large covered bullock cart trundled past within touching distance, on its way to the paddy fields. After some time firing broke out where we had placed the rest of the men. The bullock cart had obviously been full of Japs and if we had tried to see what was in the cart we would not be here now. We ran into the village, which was deserted, and in the centre of an open area was a dugout with a sloping ramp and the Burmese was hiding inside. I tried to put a round up the spout of my rifle to shoot him, but it jammed. I did not have a bayonet or a grenade and as I was being fired on from the other side of the village I reluctantly had to leave him and run for cover. I then got stuck in the tangled undergrowth, still being fired at, before breaking free and getting away from the village. From then on there were only the three of us. We had a map which was of little use, but we knew if we kept going west we would eventually reach India, picking up food in villages on the way.

Just after dark we once went into a hut and obtained a chicken which had its neck wrung by the villager, who folded it over and bound it with some fine bamboo. It was deposited in a bamboo basket which I slung on my back before we went on our way in the brilliant moonlight. After a while we heard sounds of revelry in the distance and hastily dodged off the track and lay down behind a small bank in the dry paddy fields. It was a number of villagers who had obviously been celebrating in the next village. Just as they drew level there was a tremendous fluttering from my pack. The chicken was not dead and it was making frantic efforts to escape. I got the pack off and tried to wring its neck, but instead pulled its head off and it ran around headless in circles making what seemed to us to be a tremendous noise until I managed to fall on it and quieten it. We could not believe we hadn't been noticed and they must have been very drunk on the local rice beer.

We successfully avoided any Jap patrols and crossed the Chindwin in a dugout canoe we found hidden at the river bank. After spending the night in a woodcutter's hut on the Indian side of the Chindwin we set off up a track towards Somra in the Naga Hills. After a time a voice shouted 'Tairo' ('Halt' in Urdu) and we ran into a machine-gun post manned by the Assam Rifles. We were escorted to their headquarters several miles back and, after being fed and sleeping for about twenty-four hours, carried on towards Kohima. We were put in the Somra District Officer's bungalow the following night, when suddenly shots rang out and we thought 'Japs!' but it was the D.O. firing at rats with his revolver. We did not appreciate his efforts, but put it down to his being round the bend' being stuck in such a place for years.

Two other dispersal parties had left the column, prior to the crossing of the Irrawaddy. Lance Corporal George Bell was with the second party to leave the column:

Our party under Lieutenant Pearce, about fifty strong, went north-north-west. Before splitting up we shook hands with our pals in other parties, several of them we would never see again. Our party included three officers and two Burmese who were in the Burma Rifles and could speak both English and Burmese. They saved our lives, as they were able to enter villages and obtain information about the whereabouts of the Japs. Apart from one occasion when they got drunk as newts in one village on rice wine!

After leaving the other parties we made for a small village on the Irrawaddy, only to find as we arrived there about dusk there were only two Burmese there. The village had been moved to the other bank several years before. It transpired that our maps were dated 1912! We decided, although it was pitch black, to make for another village several miles north. Fortunately as it turned out we got bogged down in the thick jungle and halted and slept for a few hours. When eventually our two Burmese lads went into the village the following day, they found a large party of Japs had been there that night. After that lucky escape I always felt that someone above was looking after me and the lads for the rest of the campaign.

As soon as it was dark I, together with my section and a villager rowing, crossed the river, in a boat similar to that used in the Oxford and Cambridge boat race. I can still vividly remember the water came up to a few inches from the top. I couldn't swim and was I pleased when we reached the other side, despite not knowing whether the Japs would be there. Fortunately they weren't. Throughout the night the boat crossed and recrossed until everyone was over. By that time we had no means of contacting our air base and had to rely on rice bought from the villages. Boiled rice, no salt, for breakfast, lunch and dinner! Having had no change of clothes for some time we all became lousy. After a couple of days we forgot all about it. We had more important things to worry about. Leeches were another problem. They got everywhere and I mean everywhere. We had been told that if you stubbed them with a lighted cigarette they would drop off. That advice presupposed we had cigarettes. We hadn't. I was lucky being a non-smoker, but to those heavy smokers the lack of a cigarette was almost as bad as the lack of food. We called into a small village one day where some of the lads bought some tobacco. But how to smoke it? We had no paper. That also brought other minor problems! One of our lads had carried a bible throughout the campaign and had a heart-searching battle with his conscience as to whether to tear a few pages from it. He still had a few matches left and the desire to smoke was greater than his religious convictions and he rolled a couple of cigarettes. A few puffs was all he managed, but it sufficed.

We marched on about twenty to twenty-five miles per day, with little food, crossing the railway line and two minor rivers. One day, marching along a track in thick jungle, we picked up a Burmese who could speak some English. What he told us didn't ring true, so we decided to take him along with us. The following day our two Burmese lads went into a village and when we followed them the headman stated that our prisoner had been there with Japs a few days before and was probably a Jap spy. It was decided it was too dangerous to let him go and that he should be shot that evening. My section took him away from the others and one of the Burmese shot him through the head. I had never seen anyone killed like that at short range and as he slipped to the ground he gazed at us with such a look of surprise and condemnation. Unfortunately the shot hadn't killed him and the Burmese finished him off with a machete. Much later it struck me that we had been judge, jury and executioner. That night we had difficulty in sleeping, not because of what we had seen, but because of a swarm of small insects buzzing round all night. An omen?

A few days later, calling into another village, we found a villager with a British rifle, which he could not account for. We decided he should suffer a similar fate, but later the saner councils prevailed and after taking him along for a couple of days we let him go. I don't think he realised how lucky he was.

The rest of the campaign was a steady slog, with only a couple of incidents of note. We set off early one morning with no food in our packs. I had brewed up with a tea bag which had been used at least twenty times before. Around midday we were walking along a dried-up river bed when we saw some parachutes in the trees to the right. We went carefully towards them in case it might be a Jap ambush, but it was a definite ration dropping, presumably for some other party. We found enough for eight days' rations per man and left some behind in case of any stragglers. Exactly eight days later when we had almost finished our rations, we were in a small village when a British plane came over and, having seen us, the pilot dropped a small canister in which he had scrawled a note asking whether we were some of Wingate's lads and, if so, did we want a ration dropping? We marked out on the ground using strips of parachute how many there were of us and where we wanted the drop. We waited almost a couple of days but nothing happened and knowing the dangers of hanging around too long, we reluctantly moved on with no rations.

About this time we stopped at a small stream for a brew up. Two of our lads, whose feet were in a shocking condition, were bathing their feet in the water when the order was given to move off. They said they would stay a short while and catch us up. A few hundred yards down the track we ran into a villager who told us that there was a large force of Japs nearby looking for us. We sharply turned down a small track away from the village and a few minutes later realised the two lads were not with us. A section was sent back to the stream, but could find no sign of them. We heard later that two British soldiers had been killed in that village. They were the only two casualties in our small party since we crossed the Irrawaddy.

We pushed on, eventually reaching the Chindwin, where we walked down the east bank for some time and then found some boats in a village. Some Burmese ferried us across to the other side, just north of Tamanthi which we did not enter as Jap patrols often stayed there. We continued westwards over mountains 8,000 feet high until we reached an Assam Rifles outpost. Here we shaved off our beards, realising how thin we were. Most of us had lost two or three stone. After a few days' rest we set off again on foot, knowing that we were safe. Remarkably that made matters worse. Our incentive to keep going was no longer there. Physiologically and mentally we were in poorer condition and myself and two others were told to stay behind to try to keep them going. Rather hard work! Eventually we hit the road and were transported to the hospital at Kohima. Sadly Lieutenant Pickering and Private Sullivan died there. After all our privations it was heartbreaking.

Looking back at the age of seventy-seven, I am glad I was in the 1943 expedition. It taught me self-confidence, not to take the ordinary things of life for granted, and the enjoyment of a comradeship which is sadly lacking in our society today.

Lieutenant Nick Neill, the Animal Transport Officer, led the first party to break away from 8 Column. He had witnessed Wingate's actions at Inywa when he abandoned the crossing of the Irrawaddy and ordered the columns to disperse and make their way back to India. He later wrote:

I asked Lieutenant Tag Sprague, who commanded the column's commando/demolitions section from 142 Company, if he and his small band of commandos might like to join my Gurkhas and I for the return journey. Much to my pleasure and relief he agreed readily to my suggestion. He was four years older than me and had fought in Norway with 1 Commando. We have remained friends to this day.

Scotty gave us the map co-ordinates of a number of DZs to the north where the RAF would be dropping supplies and to which we could go if we required further supplies during our withdrawal. He then issued us with maps and compasses, the first time I had been given such navigation aids! Now in the middle of the wilderness, with the same poor knowledge of map reading as before, I was being required to take my small group of ill-trained Gurkhas over hundreds of miles of inhospitable terrain and through the whole of the Japanese 33rd Division, who were already searching for us with the intention of preventing our escape. It is perhaps not surprising that I should have been so critical of Wingate's training methods and battle tactics.

So, in the early part of April, Tag and I, with my fifty-two Gurkhas and his dozen or so BORs, split from 8 Column to begin our long march back to the Chindwin. We crammed ten days' bulky rations into our packs, the only supplies we would have unless we could buy some from villages on the way. I was given 400 silver rupees for this purpose and I put them into one of the two basic pouches on my web belt. They weighed a ton, as did my pack, and I nearly fell over as I put it on. The only way I could stand up straight was to place my rifle butt on the ground behind me and poke the muzzle underneath the pack to take the weight. But carry it I did. A man's pack from that day on carried very literally his lifeblood and it was never, ever to be discarded.

Tag and I decided to march in a northerly direction to try to recross the vast Irrawaddy somewhere along its stretch where it flows east-west between the big villages of Bhamo and Katha. We would have to avoid Shwegu though, as that village contained a Jap garrison. Every escape group had been given a few soldiers from Nigel Whitehead's platoon of 2 Burrif and we were delighted to find that we had Naik Tun Tin and four riflemen attached to us.

An outstanding NCO, Tun Tin and his men were Karens and he had been educated at a mission school. He was very intelligent and spoke excellent English and was to prove to be of tremendous assistance to us. Sadly, however, we were soon parted from him. It took four days to reach the Irrawaddy, near the village of Zibyugon. The sal trees were in blossom; they smelt like a wet flannel and whenever I scent such a smell my mind goes back to that day at Zibyugon, and our brief stay there while we searched for boats to take us across the river. Tun Tin and two of his men changed into civilian clothes and went into Zibyugon to try to find boats to carry us across. He was successful and on the night of 11/12 April four or five boats appeared and ferried all of us across the river.

We made camp four miles from the Irrawaddy. We had crossed the major river obstacle between us and safety. We still had to cross the Chindwin and other smaller rivers, but they should present us with little difficulty, providing we crossed them before the monsoon rains broke in late May or early June. We had over 200 miles to cover before reaching the Chindwin. By the morning of 14 April we had crossed the Kaukkwe Chaung, a north–south flowing river which joined the Irrawaddy and entered the village of Thayetta. Tun Tin was arranging the purchase of rice, chicken and vegetables while I sat down to remove my boots and examine my sore feet. I noticed briefly a villager leaving the village on a bicycle and heading north. I thought nothing of this at the time and did not realise the significance until later in the morning.

We had not gone far from the village when, totally out of the blue, an ambush exploded abruptly to my immediate left. I can remember roaring out to my men 'Dahine tira sut!' (Take cover, right!) before diving for cover myself into the bushes to the right of the track. I remember I wasn't actually frightened – which surprised me – but I was totally and utterly shocked. Never, ever, during any of my previous training had I been taught any of the approved contact drills; certainly the counter-ambush drill was unknown to me. I was utterly appalled to realise that I simply did not know what to do to extract myself and my men from our predicament. A Jap gunner was firing his LMG immediately opposite me from the jungle on the far side of the track and another was firing at the men who were behind me. I could see the smoke rising from his gun muzzle and his bursts of fire were hitting the trees and bushes above my head. When the Jap gunner stopped firing to change magazines I roared above the noise of the continuing rifle fire, 'Sabai jana ut! Mero pachhi aija!' (Everybody up! Follow me!). I leapt to my feet, turned away from the track and crashed through the jungle, calling to my men to follow. I looked around and saw some of my Gurkhas and Tag's men running parallel to me. When we halted, there were only twenty of us. Tag and I, eleven Gurkhas, six of Tag's men and one Burma Rifleman. I did not believe that many of the others had been killed, but those missing were without maps and compasses. My guilt at not being able to do better for them in the ambush, and being unable to maintain contact with them afterwards, hung very heavy on my conscience and still does to this day.

It was clear that the villager who had left Thayetta on his bicycle had gone straight to the nearest Japanese outpost to alert them. The survivors of the ambush had to put as much distance between them and the village as possible, before making camp for the night. The next day they set a course westwards for the Chindwin, straight across country. They did not see a track again for three weeks. It was a good tactical decision; through bitter experience soldiers learnt to avoid the high ground, tracks, roads, streams and rivers for that was where the enemy waited for them. Much better to take a compass bearing and break a new trail through the jungle. It might be harder going but it was a safer way to travel. After a couple of days, Sergeant Sennett and the five other British commandos asked Tag Sprague if they could turn about and head east for China. They planned to make for one of the pre-arranged drop zones, collect some rations and then make for China. Tag told them frankly that they were mad to go to the DZ area, as the enemy would probably be waiting there by this time and by going towards China they would be heading into the unknown. They were adamant, however, and with reluctance Tag gave them a map and compass and allowed them to go. They were never seen again.

As the days passed, the men got weaker. Fortunately the Gurkhas' knowledge of what wild plants and fungi to eat helped eke out their meagre supply of rice. Food was so scarce that Nick never cleaned his mess tin at all. Any residue would harden on the sides of the tin, to soften next time a meal was cooked, before being scraped off with his spoon and eaten. They were now infested with lice which lived in their shirt seams and socks. They did not bother them during the day, but made them itch so much at night that they slept without clothes. Any scratches quickly turned into sores.

Eventually they reached the Mawhun-Mawlu road, which ran parallel to the Myitkyina-Rangoon railway a couple of hundred yards away. They crossed without delay and entered the Mawhun Reserve Forest. They had 18 miles to go, as the crow flies, to the Meza River. When they got there, the river was only 50 yards wide and with little water in its bed. From there it was another 22 miles to the Zibyu Taungdan Escarpment. It would be hard going. Nick recalls:

During one part of the journey, my tired mind, with its sights set forever on the Chindwin, recalled a time from the past when my mother used to sit me on her knee and, bouncing me up and down, she would sing the old American negro spiritual hymn, 'One More River', the words from which so aptly fitted both my frame of mind and our ultimate aim:

> One more river, that's the River of Jordan,
> One more river, that's the river to cross,
> One more river, that's the River of Jordan,
> One more river, that's the river for me.

The Jordan of the hymn became the Chindwin of my thoughts and prayers. It helped me push my tired legs ever westwards.

Sleep at night did not come easily at this time. We were only using game trails, but at night we would move as far from the trail as possible and, like hunted animals, seek the thickest cover available. My blanket was used during the day as a pad between my pack and my back and by nightfall it would be soaked through by my sweat. It was a pretty chilly thing to wrap around me, particularly if we were on very high ground. Then one night it rained very hard. It was on this night, with the rain water soaking through my already damp blanket and running down the slope either side of where I lay, that I really started to pray to God for deliverance. I suspect that many a soldier, in times of grave danger and misfortune, has prayed to his Maker for help, just as I did in those dark days. Then we met the buffaloes in the Namma Reserve Forest and I began to think that some of my prayers were being heard!

Each day two of my riflemen, 107871 Bandilal Limbu and 107524 Dhanbahadur Rai, would volunteer to scout ahead of our small party. Tag or I would follow behind them and concentrate on reading our compasses. Suddenly on the morning after the heavy rainfall, Bandilal turned to me and whispered, 'Bhainsi, sahib. Hanum, ki?' (Buffalo, Sir. Shall I shoot?) Sure enough, there were four village buffaloes wallowing in the water of a fairly deep-sided chaung just ahead of us. Manna from Heaven! Tag and I looked at each other. Should we take the risk, or would the firing of a shot alert a hostile villager? We were nearly starving and had to take the risk.

Tag took Bandilal's rifle, aimed carefully at the nearest buffalo and killed the unfortunate beast cleanly with one shot. The other buffaloes scattered in panic at the sound of the shot, which I hoped was muffled by the steepness of the chaung banks. The men dragged the buffalo out of the chaung and proceeded to butcher it on the spot. Soon a large fire was built from the driest wood, to minimise smoke, and the meat was smoked and roasted in the fire in no time at all. We were so hungry that many of us ate quite a number of pieces of meat before they were properly cooked through, with the blood running down our chins. Soon the buffalo had disappeared. Our stomachs were full to bursting and we had some left over to carry with us on our journey.

It was now the middle of May and they still had another month to go before reaching the Chindwin. They crossed the Zibyu Taungdan, the escarpment, by struggling along a very prominent river called the Chaunggyi, shaped, in its course, like a dog's leg. It cut through the escarpment via a pass, then continued its journey west to flow into the Uyu River, which in turn flowed west to join the Chindwin about 2 miles south of the big village of Homalin where there was a large Japanese garrison. The 10-mile stretch was to take them three days, through ankle-deep soft sand and knee-deep water.

Another Gurkha rifleman was lost during an encounter with a truck full of Japanese, which curiously was being pulled by an elephant. By now they were all very weak and Naik Harkabahadur had gone down with a severe bout of malaria. They took his equipment from him and he staggered along without a word of complaint. They were now just 16 miles from the Chindwin.

Nick Neill, Tag and their eleven riflemen took ten days to cover the 16 miles to the village of Sahpa on the east bank of the Chindwin. They had passed through the area in February after crossing the river with 8 Column and hoped to find a friendly villager to help them across the river. Upon reaching the village they discovered that the Japanese had recently collected every single boat from all of the villages on the east bank of the river and taken them north, to be guarded by the garrison at Homalin. Neill recalls:

Suddenly we saw again the Chindwin, the River of Jordan of my hymn. At this point it was some 250 yards across and fast flowing. Tag and I could probably have swum it without arms and equipment, but none of my men could swim and we would not leave them. I went to stand on a little open rise on the bank of the river and gazed longingly across to the safety of the other side. Suddenly I heard a shout from the far side, 'Ko ho?' I could not believe it, I was being hailed in Nepalese. I shouted back at once, 'Hami Thard Sikin Gorka haun. Tyahan dunga chha, ki? Yatapatti rahenachha.' (We are the Third Second Gurkhas. Is there a boat over there? We find there is none on this side). Immediately the reply came: 'Euta chha, ma pathaidinchhu. Parkhanu hos, hai!' (There is one, I will send it. Please wait!)

I stood the men to, and we took up defensive positions with our backs to the river. Most of our rifles were rusty due to the lack of oil, although my tommy gun was still in working order. I prayed to God that the Japs would not jump us at this eleventh hour. Eventually a small dug-out type boat appeared, being paddled upstream against the strong current by a single boatman. It could only take four men at a time, so I sent Havildar Budhiman, the sick Harkabahadur and two riflemen in the first boat. It took twenty minutes for the return journey and three more trips before Tag and I clambered down the steep track to the river's edge, placed our packs in the centre of the dug-out and carefully climbed aboard. We rounded the bend in the river and saw a tiny encampment on the west bank. It was the V-Force post at Hwemate and we could see the smiling faces of the others waiting to greet us, together with the British officer commanding the post. We had made it! We would live to fight another day!

They did not realize just how lucky they had been when they reached safety on the west bank of the Chindwin at 1400 hours on 6 June 1943. A V-Force reconnaissance patrol crossed the river the next day and went to the village of Sahpa. There they learnt that a Japanese patrol of fighting strength had been tracking Tag and Neill's party for a week. They had been very close on their heels and had arrived at their crossing point on the bank of the Chindwin a mere half hour after they had crossed.

Chapter 15

A Near Run Thing – Brigade Headquarters

As 7 and 8 Columns moved off to find their own way back to safety, Wingate divided his own brigade headquarters column into five dispersal parties: the Brigadier's party, mostly commandos, some RAF and Lieutenant Spurlock; a party of Gurkhas, mostly muleteers, under Major Conron; a party of Burma Rifles from the propaganda section and some Gurkha muleteers under Lieutenant Molesworth; a party of British other ranks under Major Ramsay, the MO and Captain Moxham; and a party of British Other Ranks under Captain Hosegood and Lieutenant Wilding. Wilding's party was about thirty strong. He recalled:

We were instructed to go north, cross the Shweli, swing west and go home, a distance of some 200 miles. First of all we received an enormous drop by the RAF. This included some rum and some chocolate bars, a gift from the RAF station, bless them. We were very grateful, but when I opened my rations I found that every bar of chocolate and every cigarette had been stolen, presumably by the packers. How mean can you get?

We withdrew from the drop area for a few miles and just at nightfall we had the grisly job of killing our remaining mule. To maintain silence we had to cut his throat, a difficult and literally bloody job. I suppose we should have eaten him, but he had been with us for many miles and we were fond of him. It was 30 March 1943.

We reached the Shweli on 1 April. It was only about 200 yards wide and not very swift flowing. I was sure that any competent swimmer could manage it. However, only about eight men could swim and that included the officers. This was a blow. We made rough rafts from dead bamboo, but when we launched the first after moonset we were greeted with heavy fire from the north bank. We withdrew. I wonder if this rather supine behaviour was the product of slinking about behind enemy lines for six weeks and, perhaps, very inadequate rations. We had become furtive and had lost our aggression. Had it been possible to arrange a reasonably bloodless (on our part) battle early on, it might have helped. We had two choices. The swimmers could cross that night and the rest could make their own arrangements, or we could stick together. It is arguable that the proper course was to get the swimmers over and back to India, but I suggest this might win battles, but will not win wars. The men had a right to leadership and we decided to stick together. I think it was the correct decision, but only three (including myself) who could have swum survived.

Wilding's party spent the next couple of weeks resting and preparing for another attempt to cross the Irrawaddy. One of the Burmese jemadars was wounded and captured during a recce to Inywa and a British private got lost while out searching for water and was presumed captured. The party made some more rafts and set out for the Irrawaddy. However they found themselves in a mangrove swamp and could not get through. They then decided to try to go east, cross the Shweli where it was but a stream, swing north and go into the Kachin hills and there sweat out the monsoon. It was only 80 miles, but they had hardly any supplies left, so they decided to find a village and obtain some food. There was not much food to be found, but the headsman offered to put them over the river for a consideration, a very considerable consideration. Wilding continues:

That evening, 21 April, he and his 'brother' took us at racing speed to the river. It was night and we were not exactly sure where we were. We embarked, paddled round one island and disembarked, handed over nearly all of our money and set out for the hills to the west. Alas we found a wide stretch of water between us and the hills; it was the main river. We had literally been sold up the river.

The next six days are very confused in my mind. We searched the island, it was about a mile long and half a mile wide. We found a village and persuaded the villagers to sell us a meal, but this only occurred once. I had two black-outs which were alarming. When travelling in a hot country beware when the sweat getting in your eyes stops stinging – this denotes that you need salt.

On 29 April we found a boat that floated. We decided that Second Lieutenant Pat Gordon, Lance Corporal Purdie and Signalman Belcher, with Burma Riflemen Orlando and Tunnion as paddlers, should make the first trip. They reached the other side, then we heard Pat rallying his men and a good deal of firing and then silence. Orlando and Tunnion survived but the others were all killed. I was very sad. I thought that the first boat load would have the best chance, but I was wrong.

We split up into small groups and hid in the elephant grass, but on 2 May the Japs, or possibly the Burmese police, set fire to it. The flames came very close, but I was not burnt. We then rendezvoused and discovered that only one rifle was serviceable, the one belonging to Lance Corporal Willis. Since leaving Imphal eleven or twelve weeks before, nobody had thought of having more rifle oil dropped and now you could hardly move the bolts. Lance Corporal Willis had used mosquito repellent cream, and it worked. I would ask the reader if he would order his men to attack a well-armed enemy with rifles that would not work. We didn't even have bayonets. And so, alone and very frightened, I went into the village – and that was that. The Japs were away searching for us and the Burmese tied my wrists rather cruelly tight with a sort of bark string, the scars are still just visible. In spite of this discomfort, when the men arrived I curled up and slept for hours. It is a frightful thing to be a PoW. You have failed. You have lost your liberty and you have a nagging feeling that you should have done better. When the Japs returned to the village they were really quite decent. They released me from the very tight bonds on my wrists and let me sleep for twenty-four hours.

We proceeded to Tygiang where we lived in what must have been the school house and were given three meals of curried chicken and rice each day. Shortly afterwards we set out for Wuntho, then Maymyo, where the missing Private Simons rejoined us. Our time in Maymyo was pretty ghastly. I think we were there for about a fortnight, it seemed like years. Then another quite horrible railway journey to Rangoon. Our party when the brigade broke up was thirty strong. Twenty-four of us arrived in Rangoon. Seven of us survived. Captain Hosegood was a great personal friend, a very gentle and very good man. I never heard him say anything unkind about anyone, even a Jap. He died in Rangoon in April 1945, of a heart attack I think. Two hundred and ten Chindits, including our party, arrived in Rangoon. By the time we were liberated two years later, 168 of the 210 had died or were deliberately killed, a survival rate of about one in five. Even taking into consideration the fact that we had rather a rough time before capture, eighty per cent casualties among prisoners of war shames the Japanese Imperial Army.

Wingate's dispersal group comprised the Brigadier, Major Anderson, Major Jefferies, Lieutenant Kenneth Spurlock, Lieutenant Rose, Squadron Leader Longmore, Flight Lieutenant Tooth, Captain Aung Thin and Captain Katju. In addition he had thirty-four other ranks from 142 Company, 2nd Burrifs, Gurkhas and other followers. They still had eight mules and one horse, and retained their wireless set for the time being.

After Wingate divided his headquarters column into dispersal groups and sent them on their way, he took his party of forty-three deep into the jungle, where they bivouacked near the Tokpan Chaung for almost week while they regained their strength and waited for the situation at the Irrawaddy to calm down. Perhaps it would be uncharitable to suggest that Wingate waited for a week in order to allow the Japanese to set off in pursuit of the other columns and groups before he set off to make his home run. If this was his plan he was taking a big gamble, for he finally made it home by the skin of his teeth. While they waited they sent a final message to Corps then used the radio to monitor the news until the battery finally ran down.

The remaining mules were killed by having their throats cut rather than risking the sound of rifle shots. This was done to prevent them giving their position away and to fill the bellies of the men before they began the long trek home. For six days they ate mule for breakfast, mule for lunch and mule for dinner. On the seventh day they ate the horse.

Major Anderson later recalled that after forty-eight hours the stench became somewhat disagreeable and they were glad to leave the bivouac. There was a shortage of water as well and they had to dig for it in a nearby dried-up chaung. During the night elephants were continually trumpeting nearby and they always had fires ready to light at short notice to try to scare them off. One day, when walking with Wingate a short distance from the bivouac, they observed a large herd of elephants with their young some 50 yards away.

On 7 April, Wingate made a second attempt at crossing the Irrawaddy, 25 miles south of Inywa. For two days they searched the bank for boats, but Captain Aung Thin of the Burma Rifles could only find one boat and it would take but seven people at a time. They began crossing late in the afternoon, but when half of the party was over automatic fire was heard from the north and the native boatman made off with the boat, leaving the other half of the party stranded on the east bank. Those who successfully made it across the river included the Brigadier, Majors Anderson and Jefferies, Captains Aung Thin and Katju, and twenty-four Other Ranks.

They were not, however, on the west bank of the river yet. They were, in fact, on an island and they immediately moved on towards Nyaungbintha where they found a large boat and crossed over at dusk. They moved on for a couple of miles and lay up for the night. The mosquitoes were intolerable and they got little sleep.

Signaller Eric Hutchins was in the last party waiting to cross the river, together with Squadron Leader Longmore, Flight Lieutenant Tooth, Flight Sergeant Fidler, Lieutenant Rose of the Gurkhas, Private Dermody and Private Weston of the King's. He told the author:

The first six boat parties made their way safely to the opposite bank. Eventually the boat returned for us, but when we reached the opposite bank we could find no trace of the others. Wingate's excuse when we met him later, was he 'thought' we had been captured by the Japanese, whereas he had abandoned us without maps or any means of finding our way back to our own lines. Such is my regard for a commander who later became world famous.

So we set out west only to find we were on an island in the middle of the river. Our problems now really began, because we could not find a suitable boat. Eventually we found a boat that had seen better days and decided to take a chance crossing at night, using our rifles as oars. Of course the inevitable happened and the boat capsized. I and others swam to the west shore, where we had to rescue two of our party who were clutching a floating plant because they could not swim. At light of day we found that Squadron Leader Longmore was missing. Later at the end of the war I found out that he had remained clutching the boat and floated down river and was eventually captured.

We found we were on another island and right opposite a very large village and most of the inhabitants walked across the shallow water to the island, presumably out of curiosity. We had lost everything when the boat capsized and had no arms to defend ourselves, except that I still had a hand grenade. We went with the villagers and enjoyed a meal of rice and obtained two sacks of rice, cooking pans, a flint stone to make a fire, salt and juggery, the latter unrefined sugar. Suddenly there was a commotion in the village and the locals started to disperse, which was a signal to us that the Japs had arrived. We made a quick retreat and proceeded to climb the hills behind the village and make our way westwards.

Our progress after that was mainly at night, avoiding paths and villages. I remember the beautiful clear moonlit nights with the stars to guide us. I often look for a constellation set at dead 270 degrees which we used as our direction arrow as we kept walking westwards. Daytime was spent trying to sleep in the intense heat with no water, setting out at dusk to find water and cook a meal. I was suffering severely from dysentery, but somehow raised the strength to carry on.

As we neared the Chindwin we found we found a small chaung in which were some pools of water containing fish. We caught one by swimming under water, but then became greedy and thought if we threw my grenade into the water we could have a real feast. This was not to be because the grenade failed to explode as I had forgotten to prime it. On seeing the river valley of the Chindwin we now became over-confident and started to abandon our policy of avoiding footpaths. On rounding a bend we ran into a Japanese sentry guarding the path. We immediately plunged into the jungle to our left, but Weston was captured because he was too weak to react quickly. We were forced to stand in a marsh for thirty-six hours while the Japs set fire to it to try to draw us out. Meanwhile we could hear the screams of Weston as they slowly tortured him to death with their bayonets.

On the second night we came out of the marsh only to walk straight through the Jap-occupied village. We walked on down the path leading to the Chindwin and then, practising the usual dispersal drill on leaving a path, hid in the jungle nearby. Within fifteen minutes a party of Japs came down the track, following our footprints by torch light. Fortunately for us they hesitated where our footprints finished and then carried on. This was our cue and we retreated deeper into the jungle. Within half an hour they were back searching the spot we had left. We were now under real pressure and headed for the Chindwin, but could not find a boat to cross. We were walking along the path on the river bank and came to a small clearing with Lieutenant Rose leading. He suddenly turned round and yelled 'Japs' and in the sudden rush to retreat I fell over. I scrambled to my feet, leaving behind the rice sack I was carrying. The others had a good fifty yards' start on me and machine-gun bullets were whizzing all around. I think I broke the world record for 200 yards and reached the jungle on the opposite side of the clearing before the others. Here we lost Lieutenant Rose and I heard after the war he was later captured and also survived the prison camp.

We decided to regain the hills and walk northwards hoping there would be fewer Japs to encounter in that direction. We came upon a hut in the middle of a paddy field and found a native sitting inside. He immediately beckoned us to lie down in the paddy and pointed to a road about fifty yards away where Jap lorries were moving. He indicated to follow him crawling on our bellies to a small copse, where the miracle occurred! He brought us food twice a day for three days while we got our strength back. He could not get us a boat but when we drew bamboo poles he understood and on each night visit he brought two bamboo poles. Finally we had enough to make a raft and took them down to the river at the dead of night and our saviour tied them together. We had no money and could not reward him, but gave him a note saying how he had helped us and that he should be rewarded by the British if he produced the document. This man, a complete stranger, possibly a Buddhist, displayed all the ethics of a Good Samaritan and has remained in my deepest thoughts all my life. That day in 1943 on the banks of the Chindwin I learned to believe in miracles.

I was the only strong swimmer and pushed the raft from the rear. Some of the other survivors were too weak to swim and had to be hauled back on the raft. Eventually we reached the other side and rested for the night. In the morning we walked into the nearest village which was occupied by Gurkhas.

Wingate was my hero before the campaign, but after his deliberate abandonment on the east bank of the Irrawaddy I know he only considered his own safety and not others. He would deliberately abandon anyone whom he considered to be a handicap. This was proved later when our signals officer, Ken Spurlock, who was in Wingate's boat party, was abandoned in a village not far from the Chindwin because he was weak with dysentery. I was weak with dysentery but my companions never abandoned me.

Another survivor commented to the author that 'Wingate HAD to survive or else all the lessons we learnt so painfully would have been lost – who would have listened to surviving column commanders?' There are two sides to every story and only those who were there have the right to pass opinion.

After crossing the Irrawaddy, Wingate's party faced the obstacle of the railway. It was heavily patrolled and every bridge and station was guarded. They decided to cross over near the Nankan Railway Station. The jungle petered out 10 yards from the line, but Japanese soldiers were on guard duty 400 yards away to their right and left. They closed up together and all crossed in one rush, disappearing into the jungle on the far side. They put 5 more miles between themselves and the line before stopping for a rest. The next day they entered a village, obtained a small buffalo and some chickens, and lay up for a day and night to eat and gather their strength for the next stage.

For the next several days they marched through the Mangin Mountains between the railway and the escarpment. Their boots began to fall apart and diarrhoea, dysentery and jungle sores began to take a heavy toll. Men began to fall by the side of the track and there was nothing that could be done for them. On 16 April, Lieutenant Ken Spurlock, who had been suffering from dysentery since eating mule meat that was 'off' and had been getting weaker as the days passed, finally had to fall out near Kyingi.

Amazingly Wingate took the decision to wait and see if Spurlock would recover enough to carry on. Forty-eight hours later, with Spurlock still unable to continue, Wingate reluctantly ordered his party to move on. He later wrote to Spurlock's father:

> I was one of the last people to see your son in Burma. He had been throughout the Campaign absolutely invaluable to me as my principal Signals Officer. As you may well imagine the success of the campaign was largely due to the excellent signals work of your son and his subordinates. It was for this reason I decided to keep him with me in my own party when we broke up into small groups in order to regain India. To start with all went well, we recrossed the Irrawaddy and were almost in sight of home when to my great unhappiness your son announced his inability to continue. He had always been so strong I had not realised that the greatly reduced diet had told more heavily on his big body than on the smaller ones. We waited two days in the hope he would regain strength, and then were compelled in the interest of the whole party to set out again. He was suffering from aggravated diarrhoea and the wait did nothing to improve matters. We had provided him with food, money and a compass in case this should happen. I had a long talk with him that morning about the advisability of surrendering to the Japanese. He was against this but I pointed out to him that he could escape when he had regained his strength. As he was quite incapable of self-defence, there was no

question of dishonour. I cannot say, however, that he appeared convinced by my arguments. For the rest I told him to wait a day after we had passed, then to enter the nearest village where he could have a bed and be looked after. I expect he did this, and hope that he was either taken care of by kindly Burmans or that he is a prisoner in the hands of the Japanese.

Wingate was unaware of it at the time, but Spurlock did exactly as he was advised – he waited for a day and then set off in search of a friendly village. He did not know it but the Japanese were offering a reward to the villagers for bringing in Wingate's men, dead or alive. Suddenly a group of natives appeared on the track and, seeing Spurlock in front of them, brought up their crossbows and let fly at the startled officer. Spurlock took to his heels and dived behind cover, drawing his revolver as he did so. He aimed at one of the attackers and pulled the trigger, looking quickly around him as the native clutched at his stomach and fell to the ground. As the other attackers sought cover, Spurlock ran back into the jungle and finally lost his pursuers.

Eventually Spurlock found his way to a village and saw what he thought was a group of friendly natives sitting around a fire, dressed in loincloths. Smiling he walked closer only to discover that they were Japanese soldiers. One of them jumped to his feet and ran into a hut, returning with his rifle and bayonet fixed. He thrust the weapon at Spurlock and ran the bayonet through his chest, under his left armpit and then struck him on the head with the rifle butt. He collapsed in a heap on the ground.

When Spurlock came to he opened his eyes very slowly and discovered that he was peering down the barrel of a machine gun. He was in fact being used as the top row of sandbags on a machine gun emplacement. The Japanese must have thought that more men were coming along behind Spurlock and took cover ready to repel an attack. Half an hour later they must have decided that he was alone, dragged him upright and bound his arms behind his back. The other end of the rope was tied around his neck, so that if he struggled he would slowly throttle himself. Finally subdued, the officer was sat on the ground and his captors fed him. Spurlock decided that the front line troops were not so bad after all. His troubles would really start once he reached the prisoner-of-war camp in Rangoon.

Meanwhile, the survivors of Wingate's party stumbled onwards towards the Chindwin. Wingate drove his men on, urging them not to fall out of the column even for diarrhoea. 'Don't worry about your trousers, just keep on marching,' he told them. They kept going only by sheer will-power and faith in Wingate.

The next dangerous stretch was a 20-mile strip in the Mu River Valley between Pinlebu and Pinbon, Japanese garrison villages that had been attacked by 4 and 7 Columns on the way in. They crossed the valley by night and reached the foot of the Zibyu Taungdan Escarpment where they were faced with a sheer wall of rock 1,500 feet high. Few tracks crossed the escarpment and it was likely that the Japanese would be patrolling them. Before they attempted the climb, the desperately hungry men ventured into a village to buy food. As they were leaving a small Burmese ran after them and offered to guide them across the escarpment using a little-known track. Fifty years later, Arthur Willshaw the RAF radioman recalled:

> Crossing the Mu River we faced the last sixty miles over almost impossible country to the Chindwin. It was here that we met an old Burmese Buddhist hermit, who appeared one evening just out of nowhere. He explained, via the interpreters, that he had been sent to lead to safety a party of white strangers who were coming into his area. He was asked who had sent him and his only answer was that his God had warned him. It was a risk we had to take, especially as we knew from information of friendly villagers that the Japs, now wise to our escape plan, were watching every road and track from the Mu to the Chindwin. Day after day he led us along animal trails and elephant tracks, sometimes wading for a day at a time through waist-high mountain streams. At one point on a very high peak we saw, way in the distance, a thin blue ribbon – the Chindwin. What added spirit this gave our flagging bodies and spent energies! All our supplies were gone and we were really living on what we could find. A kind of lethargy was taking its toll, we just couldn't care less one way or the other – it made no difference to us. The old hermit took us to within a few miles of the Chindwin and disappeared as strangely as he had appeared.

At noon on 23 April, Wingate's party reached the other side of the escarpment and gazed upon the Chindwin Valley. Arthur Willshaw continues his story:

> A villager we stopped on the tracks told us that the Japanese were everywhere, that it would be impossible to get boats to cross the river as they had it so well guarded. Wingate selected five swimmers who would, with himself, attempt to get to the Chindwin, swim it and send back boats to an agreed rendezvous with the others. These swimmers were Brigadier Wingate, Captain Aung Thin of the Burma Rifles, Captain Jefferies, Sergeant Carey of the Commandos, Private Boardman of the 13th King's, and myself.
>   At four a.m. on the morning of 29 April 1943 the six of us set out for the river. Soon we struck a terrible stretch of elephant grass, seven or eight feet high and with an edge like a razor. We reconnoitred along it but could see no end to it, and no track through it, so the decision was made – 'into it'. Each man in turn dived headlong into it while the others pushed him flat; after a few minutes another took his place at the front. In four hours we had covered

about 300 yards and were making such a noise that we feared the Japanese would be waiting when we broke out of it. We pushed our way into a small clearing and collapsed – I couldn't have gone another foot and I know that we all had the same sickening thought. After all we had been through, how could we find the strength to go on? Then Wingate crawled to a gap in the grass and disappeared, only to reappear within minutes beckoning us to join him. We pushed our way another few feet and there it was – the Chindwin – right under our noses. Arms and legs streaming with blood, we decided to chance the Japs and swim for it right away.

Among the many things I asked for on my stocking-up visit to Drigh Road at Karachi was a number of 'Mae West' lifejackets. I had carried mine throughout the whole of the expedition; I wore it as a waistcoat, used it as a pillow, used it to ford rivers and streams – and I still have it! It was to save my life and that of Aung Thin that day. Blowing it up, I explained that I would swim last and that if anybody got into difficulties they could hang on to me, and we would drift downstream if necessary. How I feared that crossing – even though the Mae West was filthy and muddy it would soon wash clean in the water – and what a bright orange coloured target it would make for the waiting Japs! And so into the water – ten yards, twenty yards, fifty, one hundred, now almost just drifting, thoroughly exhausted. Aung Thin with a last despairing effort made it to my side and together we struggled the remaining fifty yards to the other bank. We dragged ourselves up the bank and into cover – I still relive those fifteen minutes waiting for the burst of machine-gun fire that didn't come.

Major John Jefferies almost did not make it. After swimming about 40 yards he had to let go of his boots and rifle and at about 100 yards from the bank the tattered shreds of his shirt sleeves wound themselves tightly around his arms completely imprisoning them. He kicked out desperately with his legs and forged towards the bank. He began to swallow mouthfuls of water and his kicks grew feebler. He felt an enormous weariness and began to lose consciousness. Then his feet touched bottom and he dragged himself through the shallows and collapsed on the beach. Wingate was waiting for them. He had strapped his Wolseley helmet to his chest, where the thick canvas made an airtight and waterproof float and did much to support him during his swim. The hat would remain with him until his death.

The exhausted men struggled on for 5 more miles to the nearest British outpost, where a group of British officers were sitting on ration tins drinking tea. They were given hot sweet tea with condensed milk, bully-beef stew, rum and cigarettes.

A day or so later Major Gim Anderson and the rest of Wingate's party were carried across the Chindwin, narrowly escaping capture by a platoon of

Japanese from the 114th Infantry Regiment who had been tracking them. Captain Katju MC, the Indian Army observer, was not with them. He had entered a small village looking for their Burrif havildar who was trying to arrange boats and was shot and killed.

Arthur Willshaw was now back in the Promised Land:

> And so on to Tamu, Imphal, Dimapur and into hospital. We were looked after by Matron Agnes McGeary, a charitable lady who had won a medal for gallantry at Dunkirk. I went into Burma nine stones in weight and came out a mere five and a half stones. After a month in hospital the adventure was over for me. Later by air to Delhi and Bombay and then the first boat home via the Cape. Air Marshal D'Albiac certainly kept his promise!

Of Wingate's five dispersal groups, only two made their way back to safety: the Brigadier's and the Gurkha Defence Platoon. The other parties were broken up and the men killed or captured by the Japanese. Major Ramsay, Captain Hosegood, Lieutenants Wilding, Rose and Spurlock would all meet again in Rangoon Jail.

PART 3 – Success or Failure

Chapter 16

Prisoners of War

Second Lieutenant Alec Gibson was one of three young officers from the 8th Gurkha Rifles sent to join 3/2nd Gurkhas only days before Wingate's expedition set off for Burma. Together with Harold James he joined Mike Calvert's 3 Column, while nineteen-year-old Ian MacHorton joined George Dunlop's 1 Column. Both Harold and Ian found their way back to India, but Alec Gibson found himself a guest of the Emperor:

**'MISSING FROM 4th APRIL –
LAST SEEN SWIMMING THE IRRAWADDY.'**

That was the message sent to my parents in July 1943. They were to hear nothing more from me until I was reported recovered from the enemy on 30 April 1945.

Following Wingate's dispersal order we were trapped on the east side of the Irrawaddy and my party was unable to find boats, so swimming was the only alternative. After two abortive attempts I found myself alone with one Gurkha when we were jumped by eight Burmese Independent Army soldiers who tied us up and dragged us to the nearest Jap outpost some five miles away. At Maymyo we had to learn Japanese drill; commands were shouted at us in Japanese and we were expected to understand them. If we got it wrong we were knocked down with rifle butts, pick handles or bamboo canes. We managed to learn in about two days! As a deliberate policy of humiliation we were lined up at least once a day and subjected to considerable face slapping by the Jap guards. Every now and then one of the prisoners would be called out for interrogation and you knew that you would have to undergo considerable punishment before you got back again.

At this camp I met one of our Gurkha Subedars wearing an armband with the Jap Rising Sun, the sign of the Indian National Army. I asked him how he could do this and he replied, 'Do not worry Sahib – I have plans to get out of here.' I heard later that after training with the Japs he and the rest of the

Gurkhas were given arms and sent to the front where they promptly killed the Japs with them and then went straight across to the Allied troops.

From Maymyo we were taken to the Central Jail at Rangoon and on arrival we were put into solitary confinement. The cells were about nine feet square and with one small window, dark and gloomy, with only the stone floor to sleep on. We were given one blanket each. We could not speak to one another and were only taken out for interrogation. I was only there for a couple of weeks, but some prisoners spent months there. I was then transferred to one of the open blocks of the jail. The officers were in two rooms on the upper floor, about twenty-six of us to each room. There was no glass in the windows so in the monsoon period the rain poured in. We slept on the floor with our one blanket and used anything else we had as a pillow. As the Japs took everything we had from us when we were captured, we had little other than the clothes we had been wearing since leaving India in February 1943. Most of the time we only wore a fandoshi or loincloth made up of a rectangle of cloth and a piece of string. As our boots fell apart we walked barefoot and soon our feet got pretty tough.

Everyone including the officers had to work. We worked on the railway, dug up unexploded bombs, repaired roads and bridges, unloaded stores at the docks and cleared up damage after air raids. If anything went wrong the man concerned and the officer in charge would be beaten up. Some men were permanently on cooking duties and did their best with the rations we were give, chiefly rice and vegetables with occasional pieces of meat we scrounged from outside, or a pigeon caught inside. Sometimes we had a sort of porridge made from ground-up husks of rice. It tasted horrible but contained Vitamin B1 and was a great help against beri-beri. We also had tea, or rather hot water with a few leaves thrown in, no milk and no sugar.

The one thing which really worried us was being injured or becoming ill as medical treatment was almost non-existent. We had several medical officers with us as prisoners, but they had virtually nothing in the way of medicines or equipment. Jungle sores or ulcers were treated with copper sulphate crystals, dysentery with charcoal and creosote tablets, beri-beri with grain husks. Incredibly, two successful amputations were carried out with the crudest of instruments and no anaesthetics. Most of us suffered from ulcers, dysentery, beri-beri, dengue fever etc. at some time, but if it developed into a serious condition it was usually terminal. Two-thirds of the complement of the camp died.

When Lieutenant Allen Wilding arrived at Rangoon Jail, there were plenty of familiar faces to greet him. Ken Spurlock was there from Wingate's party, so was Johnny Nealon, last seen by George Dunlop when he went into a village to look for food during 1 Column's trek home. From 5 Column were John Kerr, left behind wounded at Kyaikin, and David Whitehead who had been led into an ambush by a Burmese which left him with seven bullet holes in his body and five in his clothes. For those poor souls who were sick or wounded, there was little succour to be found in the jail. Allen Wilding recalled:

The 'hospital' was an old bug-ridden building situated in the compound of Block 6. There was a sort of 'greenhouse' staging made of wood all round, on which the sick lay and alas often died. To give some idea of the infestation of bed bugs, we took the staging on one side down and the floor seemed literally to move with the bugs crawling to the other side. For those fortunate to have never encountered a bed bug, they are brown but otherwise resemble a ladybird and they smell awful when crushed. There were no beds or sick room equipment of any kind, not even bed-pans. There was an empty lime drum which dysentery patients could use if they had the strength and resolve; otherwise – well, to wash a dysentery patient's blanket when you have no tub, no soap or hot water, just cold water and a bit of concrete to bash it on, is rather unpleasant! I know, I have done it.

At first the 'hospital' came under the care of Lieutenant Brian Horncastle (King's Regiment). He was a wonderfully kind chap and worked really hard to make the 'hospital' work. After his death, American Second Lieutenant Waldo Cotten (USAAF) took over and he did his best too, but neither had any medical knowledge, just common sense and compassion. Then our brigade senior medical officer, Major Raymond Ramsay (RAMC), was released from solitary. It was a disgrace that he was kept there so long while our poor chaps died at the rate of at least one a day. Words cannot convey enough praise for his work, his devotion, his gentleness and his ability. After the war they gave him an MBE just as if he had been a Beatle, or me. Never was a man's work so grossly undervalued and rewarded in such a niggardly way by 'The Brass!' He was NEVER undervalued by us!

Through all these changes, one man soldiered on: Sergeant Scrutton of the King's. He was a jewel. He knew nothing of medicine, he was a bricklayer's labourer in civilian life, but he had a fund of common sense. Sadly he died, worn out with the work and, I suspect, frustrated because he could do so little for his charges. A surprising number of people were prepared to take a turn at dressing tropical ulcers. In particular I remember Sergeant Jock Masterson and a huge Colour Sergeant named Beatie who had been a 'loom turner' from Hawick. I have vivid memories of Jock dressing, very gently, an enormous sore high up on the thigh of a youngster of nineteen. So deep was it that you could see the femoral artery pulsing, so Jock had to be extra careful. Despite Jock's devoted care the poor boy died. One of the Chindit officers had a jungle sore which became gangrenous. The smell was so bad that, at his own request, he was moved out of 'hospital' for the sake of the other sick. I liked him very much but found that a half hour visit was all I could manage. A friend of his, a Canadian Flight Lieutenant named Wheatley, used to sit with him for hours, although on at least one occasion he was physically sick when he left. When the patient (and never was the word so appropriate) died, Ken was there to hold his hand. What more can you do for a friend?

The Japs did provide an equally comfortless hut for the cholera patients. In spite of Major Ramsay's heroic work, it proved impossible to save any of them or Corporal Brown of the KOYLI, a brave chap who volunteered to nurse them. So did the 'cultured' Japanese care for those unfortunates who were ill when under their care. Even allowing for their belief that to become a prisoner was a lasting shame, their behaviour was disgraceful. To the average Westerner, the Japanese are a polite race, good at miniaturisation, making television sets and motor cars and motor cycles which are expensive to repair, and who are much addicted to making money, buying golf courses, folding paper, arranging flowers and torturing trees into unnatural shapes. To the average serviceman who has experience of them, they are admirably brave and well disciplined, very noisy and shockingly bad shots. To a Far Eastern prisoner of war, they are cruel, callous, brutal, unhygienic and really rather incompetent administrators.

It is difficult to describe really serious inhumanities without risk of hurting widows, children and friends of those who died in Japanese hands and this is a risk I will not take. They had one nasty habit of making a prisoner stand for hours in the sun without headgear, sometimes holding a heavy stone over his head. One poor chap was made to stand on his head. This might have done him real harm so I shouted to him to collapse and with a couple of chaps rushed out and made a great to-do about taking him into the 'hospital'. He survived. They kept people in solitary for too long. The record once stood at 100 days, but this was greatly exceeded. The cells were small and often shared by two or three people. There was no exercise period and the only facility was an old ammunition box, usually leaking, for use as a latrine. After the bombing of Tokyo all flying personnel captured were kept in solitary confinement. I am aware of at least three men who were deliberately killed.

Lieutenant Denis Gudgeon duly arrived at Rangoon and was promptly put in solitary confinement in Number 5 Block, which was the norm for all officers. They were supposed not to talk, but did; an Edinburgh Beaufighter pilot named MacDonald kept watch by the main gate and would whistle 'The Campbells are Coming' when the guards paid their many visits day and night, and 'Intermezzo' when the coast was clear. Denis spent five weeks in the cooler and was released shortly after his twenty-second birthday.

Denis was then transferred to the top floor of the two-storey communal Number 6 Block, where he became seriously ill with dysentery. The only medicine he was given for it was charcoal and creosote pills. The food was always inadequate and they had no Red Cross parcels to fall back on as had the European prisoners of war. Their staple diet was rice and Denis was permanently hungry. He later recalled:

> We received neither milk nor bread. The meat ration, generally of pork, was very irregular and we never got more than two issues a week. Indeed it was only during the final year that we had a proper meat ration, beans, grain and fish. Prior to that our meat ration used to be a few bones slung at us. The fresh vegetables consisted of aubergines, pumpkins, marrow and sweet potatoes. But in spite of these meagre rations our own cooks used to do wonders turning out pork pies, Yorkshire puddings, curried puffs, cakes, chutney, jam and sausage rolls. We had a pair of mill stones and were able to grind our own flour. There was a fairly large 'Jock' contingent and on each 25 January we had porridge for breakfast rounded off on Burn's night by a haggis concoction.
>
> A contractor used to come round every ten days and from him I used to purchase Burmese cheroots, duck eggs, jaggery balls (a coarse brown sugar made from toddy palm sap) and rice toffee. Also I used to acquire cheroots on working parties and would barter them for duck eggs. Conditions in the goal were not good at all. The communal block had no glass windows and the monsoon rain just poured in. There was no electric lighting and we slept on the floor, coping with bed bugs, lice, ants and mosquitoes. Washing and drinking facilities were from a long trough, but the water was frequently turned off due to the reservoir being bombed. I well remember one day in November 1943 when I was pouring out mugs of tea at lunchtime that the camp was hit by a stick of four 500 pound bombs. The American bomber had been hit by the Japs and had to jettison its load which fell right across the jail killing 14 prisoners of war. Tenko took place at sun-up and sundown. We paraded in the yard and were brought to attention (kiotsuke) and then ordered to number (bango) ichi, ni, san (1, 2, 3). This used to go on for hours sometimes as the British other ranks would deliberately muddle up the numbers. I received pay, that for a Second Lieutenant was Rs 41 per week but after a hefty amount of this was put into a Jap Savings Bank, two further deductions and an appropriation, what was left over, which was not much in my case, went into a general messing fund to bolster the money the other ranks received on working parties.

Denis spent much of his time as a prisoner working in the Rangoon docks. He had to carry sacks of rice weighing up to 200 pounds, a back-breaking task that necessitated extensive spinal surgery twenty-five years later. He was once sent out in charge of a working party to build an air-raid shelter for the Japanese.

The guard carefully paced out the area to be dug, then left Denis and his team to perform the task while he attended to another matter. Denis quickly moved the markers in at both ends, thus dramatically reducing the area to be evacuated. This backfired, however, as the guard was so pleased that the group was always chosen to dig air-raid shelters.

The officers went on working parties doing very heavy work such as unloading rice sacks from barges to godowns, building air-raid shelters and gun emplacements, sweeping the streets and gardening. The working parties used to steal books from private houses and high schools and smuggle them into the jail. They had a library of over 200 books at the end.

We were fortunate in having several RAMC doctors including Major Raymond Ramsay, senior medical officer of the brigade and a very dour Scot Colonel K.P. MacKenzie, ADMS of the 17th Division who would later write a book about his experiences. There was not a lot that our medicos could do for the sick and wounded with the minimum amount of medical facilities available to them. The stock treatment for jungle sores was blue stone or copper sulphate. When someone died his remains were sewn into a jute rice sack by a Jewish tailor. We all stood at attention in the compound whilst the funeral party marched past at the slow march. The body was then taken in a tonga to the English Cemetery which was next door to the zoo. I took several services amid the roars of the lions and tigers and trumpeting of elephants and the Jap guards telling me to hurry up all the time. The clothing we wore was of a very scant nature and consisted just of a 'G' string and our prison number tag, with no footwear. I lost my number tag once and was put on a charge for doing so. I received a sentence of 36 hours in solitary confinement without food or water. We had to bow from the waist down to all Japs we passed. We had nicknames for all our guards. Some of them were – the Ape, the Kicker, the Gorilla, the Chimp, the Green Linnet, the Runt, the Farmer's Boy, the Bulldozer, Creeping Jesus, Paranorma Pete, Death Warmed Up and Sanitary Dan. In Japanese eyes it was a total disgrace for us to have been taken prisoner. The guards used to turn nasty to us at the slightest provocation, especially after Allied air raids. Their favourite method of humiliation was to slap us across the face as hard as they could with both hands or on occasion with a bamboo cane. Several men were badly beaten up with rifle butts. We had a very efficient news gathering service even though we did not possess a radio. The sources included a newspaper the Japanese published in English called 'Greater Asia' which was a propaganda sheet but we were able to read between the lines. I well remember the guards rushing into our block the day after the Chindit leader was killed, with banner headlines about his death and shouting 'Wingate Shinde' (is dead). We also gleaned information from friendly Burmese on working parties, indiscreet guards, and recently captured prisoners of war. All this was collated by a Squadron Leader Duckenfield on a war map concealed in the false bottom of a wooden box. He used to shade in the areas which had been re-taken in the East or West.

One of the few Royal Air Force Chindits to survive captivity was Flight Lieutenant Edmunds. He was last seen carrying a wounded Lieutenant Colonel Alexander amidst a hail of mortar explosions following the scattering of Dunlop's party just east of the Mu River near the village of Okkan. His fellow RAF colleague Sergeant Kenneth Wyse was with him. Amazingly a record of their fate was kept by Edmunds, scribbled on the back of photographs belonging to Wyse. Eventually they found their way back to the Wyse family at the end of the war and they tell a sad story.

On the rear of a photograph of Wyse and his girlfriend was written:

Both Ken and myself and Colonel Alexander wounded – Colonel A seriously wounded in thigh and bleeding badly – Ken has slight wound in hip and two bullets through stomach. We managed to carry Colonel Alexander several hundred yards, but we were too weak to go further. Colonel Alexander died. We hid in some long grass, intending to make our getaway after dark. Our wounds stiffened up, neither of us could walk and we were very thirsty. We heard the Japs searching for us. Ken said his mother will know he is wounded. Japs pass within ten feet of us and our chances look very slim. Ken appeared unconscious – no hat – sun very hot. Would give anything for a drink. Shots being fired near and a good deal of.

It is presumed that Edmunds and Wyse were captured soon after Lieutenant Colonel Alexander died. On the back of a photograph of Wyse's mother Edmunds had written; "Japs plug our wounds and give us water and food. They are very young and fanatical. Ken is capable of walking but is in pain. Interrogated three times at Munya.' The next four lines were very faint but were followed with: 'Five days in cattle truck. Japs more hostile. Am still unable to walk. Ken much better. Kalaw. Midnight interrogation by candlelight. Food very poor. Guards rough. Maymyo. Am being taken to Rangoon tomorrow. Ken being left here.'

When Edmunds arrived at Rangoon he continued his record on the rear of a photograph of Sergeant Wyes's sister Mary:

Am in Cell 82 – filthy conditions. Somebody died last night of dysentery, unable to get any medical treatment or a wash. Cell searched and Ken's wallet and photos taken. I made a complaint and said photo was picture of my wife and got it back. Hope Ken's sister won't mind! Several prisoners very sick with dysentery. Ken arrives from Maymyo. Has recovered from wounds. Has frequent doses of malaria – no quinine. Was experimented on by Japs with fever (?) August 20 Ken very bad with high fever – unable to get any quinine. Unconscious, rambling in speech, talks of family. Appears to think he is in France. Seems to recognise me at times – unconscious again and I do not think he will live tonight. August 21 Ken died. One of the bravest chaps that I have seen in this war. Buried in Rangoon.

On the reverse of a fourth photograph, Edmunds wrote:

August 21 1943. Buried Ken today in Rangoon. Held short service, but I could not remember much of it, so had to make most of it up. Japanese gave us very little time. They are afraid of RAF bombers. Hope to be out of here by Christmas. Six have died in last twelve weeks and many more will die unless we get more food and some medical supplies – no Red Cross. Jap's very confident of victory.

And there the record came to an end. However Edmunds kept the photographs safe and he survived until the end of the war when he returned the photographs and notes to Ken's family. Forty years later they were deposited for safekeeping in the Imperial War Museum.

Chapter 17

An Unexpected Ally

Wingate crossed the Chindwin on 29 April, rested for a day at the Gurkha post on the west side of the river and then marched on to the road where he and his companions obtained transport to Imphal, arriving on 3 May. He reported to Lieutenant General Scoones, the IV Corps Commander, and a brief report on the Brigade's activities was sent on to Wavell. He was vocal in his praise for Calvert, Fergusson and the RAF elements that accompanied the columns. However, the fate of 7 and 8 Columns as well as George Dunlop's 1 Column was not known at that time. Wingate's party was only the fourth to reach India; Calvert's men had crossed over first, on 15 April, followed by Fergusson's party on the 25th, and Lieutenant Colonel Cooke and sixteen men from Scott's 8 Column had been flown home on 28 April.

Out of Wingate's dispersal group of forty-three men, thirty-four of them reached safety. From the other four dispersal groups from Brigade Headquarters only one, the Defence Platoon, got back to India, at the end of May. On 13 May, the remainder of Scott's 8 Column crossed the Upper Chindwin at Tamanthi and the Headquarters of the Burma Rifles reached Fort Hertz at the same time. George Dunlop's 1 Column was the last to reach the west bank of the Chindwin, recrossing near the place where they had crossed over three months previously. They had covered more ground than the other columns and were in a far worse state. Last of all, on 3 June, Ken Gilkes and 7 Column walked into the Chinese town of Paoshan.

Calculating the number of survivors from the expedition is no easy feat and depends on which source one consults. Official figures suggest that 77 Brigade entered Burma just over 3,000 strong, comprising seven columns, Brigade Headquarters, two group headquarters and the Burma Rifles headquarters. Just over 2,000 had apparently re-entered India by the first week of June; 2,180 was the final figure. The rest, around a third of the Brigade were either dead or in captivity.

At the time of Wingate's return at the end of April, only one report had been received by the Corps Commander. Written by Major Fergusson, it had been handed in on 1 May and dealt mainly with the fate of 5 Column. It did however include criticism of Wingate's handling of his force in the Shweli loop. Wingate was very annoyed with Fergusson, but accepted his explanation that something had to be recorded in case Wingate did not make it home.

On 6 May, General Irwin, the Army Commander, arrived with the Army Group Commander Sir George Giffard, and visited Wingate and other Chindits at Number 19 Clearing Station where many of the men were recovering from exhaustion, wounds, jungle sores, malaria and other ailments. The following day Wingate returned with them to Delhi.

For more than a fortnight Wingate stayed in Maiden's Hotel, with occasional forays to brief the Chief of the General Staff and other high-ranking officers. His Patron, the Commander-in-Chief Sir Archibald Wavell, had left India and it was generally known that he would not return. He had had enough faith in Wingate's ideas, though, to order the formation of 111 Brigade, but whether it would ever be used for Long Range Penetration was another matter.

The Acting Commander-in-Chief was Sir Claude Auchinleck and he was less enthusiastic than Wavell, believing that Long Range Penetration Groups could accomplish little more than an extension of patrol work. The change of commander did not bode well for the future of the Chindits, especially as so few men of 77 Brigade had so far returned to India.

The situation began to change in Wingate's favour from 12 May onwards when the press arrived in force at Imphal. They visited the men in hospital and with Auchinleck's blessing released their stories in a blaze of publicity, making the headlines in every newspaper in England and India. The Chindit expedition behind the enemy lines was the only success to report in the Far East and Auchinleck wanted to attract attention away from the recent reverse in the fighting in the Arakan. The news raised the spirits of the men in the Army who had come to think of themselves as being outclassed by the Japanese in jungle fighting.

At the end of the month Wingate left Delhi for Calcutta where he supervised the sending of the survivors of his brigade away on five weeks leave: the 13th King's and 142 Company to Bombay, the Gurkhas to the regimental centre at Dehra Dun; and the Burma Rifles to Hoshiarpur and Karachi. By 5 June, the men had all gone away for rest and relaxation, with the exception of Major Gilkes and 7 Column who were still marching out through China, and Brigade Headquarters which left Imphal on 18 June.

Matron Agnes MacGeary ran the 19th Military Clearing Station at Imphal and did her best to restore the exhausted Chindits to health again. When Wingate visited the hospital she took him under her wing, installed him in two empty rooms in one of the wings and monitored his health and recuperation while he put pen to paper to write a report on the expedition. It was quite an undertaking, but it was a very comprehensive record of the activities of his brigade and the lessons learned during the expedition.

When the report and its sixteen appendices were finished Wingate obtained the approval of Lieutenant General Scoones and flew back to Delhi to arrange the printing and distribution of his manuscript. From 23 June to 6 July, Wingate was mainly occupied in compiling citations for awards for his men, including the DSO for Calvert and Fergusson. On the morning of 6 July, the copies of his report were delivered from the Government of India official press and Wingate sent copies straight away to the office of the Director of Military Operations. He was not aware that typed draft copies of his report, sent originally to IV Corps and General Irwin, had found their way to General Headquarters where they were being scrutinized by Wingate's detractors. When the official copies of the report began to arrive his enemies showed their hand.

The following morning the Chief of the General Staff ordered all copies of the report to be withdrawn, until they had been re-examined by IV Corps and approved by General Irwin. It was a blow to Wingate who realized what was going on. By delaying the release of the report for weeks or indeed months, it would prevent any chance of Wingate leading a second expedition in 1944.

Fate now took a hand in Wingate's future with the release by the censor of photographs of the participants of the expedition. There were pictures of Major Scott's men being flown out of the jungle clearing, of Bernard Fergusson and his monocle and of the Brigade Commander himself with his thick dark beard and brooding eyes staring from under his sun helmet. His opponents were unaware that Wingate was fast becoming a national hero.

Wingate had also sent a copy of his report to Mr Amery, the Secretary of State for India, and although he did not know it at the time, by doing so he had completely outmanoeuvred his opponents. The report landed on Amery's desk in the middle of July and within days he had sent it on to his friend and chief, Prime Minister Winston Churchill.

At that time Churchill was in discussion with his Service Chiefs and General Auchinleck over their suggestions to put in effect decisions taken at the Trident Conference in Washington in May. The Prime Minister felt that the generals in India were being too cautious and the exploits of Wingate and his Chindits fired his enthusiasm. On 25 July he sent for Wingate.

Clearly out of favour in India, the summons to England was welcomed by Wingate as an opportunity to see Mr Amery, one of his few but powerful supporters, and also to see his wife Lorna. It was 4 August when Wingate finally set foot in England; he was met by a personal representative of the Chief of the Imperial General Staff and learned that he was to meet the Chief himself that afternoon. Sir Alan Brooke listened to Wingate's proposal that he be sent behind Japanese lines again, but this time with much larger and better forces. He wanted the best men, NCOs and officers available, the best equipment and much more air support. The CIGS gave him a number of contacts to obtain what he wanted, but before he could do so he was summoned to Downing Street.

Wingate appeared at the door of 10, Downing Street on the evening of 4 August just as the Prime Minister was sitting down for dinner. He was invited to join Mr Churchill who later recorded:

We had not talked for half an hour before I felt myself in the presence of a man of the highest quality. He plunged at once into his theme of how the Japanese could be mastered in jungle warfare by long range penetration groups landed by air behind the enemy lines. This interested me greatly. I wished to hear much more about it, and also to let him tell his tale to the Chiefs of Staff. I decided at once to take him with me on the voyage.

The Prime Minister and the Chiefs of Staff were to sail the next day to Quebec to meet President Roosevelt and the American Chiefs of Staff at the Quadrant Conference. When Wingate mentioned that his wife Lorna was on her way from Scotland to London the Prime Minister gave orders to intercept her train. She would be going to Canada too.

The next day they set sail on the Queen Mary and Wingate found himself with a captive audience comprising the very people who could convert his theories into practice. During discussions with Sir Alan Brooke and his staff it was agreed that future Chindit operations must take place in conjunction with an advance into Burma by the Army, or Wingate would merely invite the wrath of the Japanese divisions that had failed to capture him the last time. Wingate asked for six brigades this time – three for offensive roles and three to man and defend strongholds around landing fields in enemy territory. He made a good impression and the General Staff began to consider his proposals as a part of their overall plan to further the war against Japan.

When the Queen Mary docked in Canada the British party had three days before their American counterparts were due to arrive. During that time Wingate outlined his proposals to the British Joint Planning Staff. He suggested that three groups, each of eight columns enter Burma from different directions in conjunction with advances by the Army in Assam, by Stilwell's Chinese-American force and by the Chinese forces in Yunnan. He would require 26,000 men in all. The Service Chiefs decided to back Wingate's plans and three signals were sent to the Commander-in-Chief in India. The first informed him that they planned to adopt Wingate's proposals, the second was to confirm the details as expounded by Wingate and the third described how Wingate's new force was to be raised.

Over the next few days Wingate described his plans not only to the Combined Chiefs of Staff, but to President Roosevelt as well. His ideas received support from the very highest echelons of power, much to the consternation of his detractors at GHQ in India, who had no option but to dust off Wingate's previously withdrawn report and put it into circulation without delay.

Chapter 18

Wingate's Censored Report

The note was written in New Delhi on 18 August 1943 by none other than General Auchinleck, the Commander-in-Chief in India. Attached to Wingate's post-expedition report and stamped SECRET, it read:

I wish to emphasise that this is the report of the Commander 77 Indian Infantry Brigade to the Commander IV Corps. It contains opinions with which I am not necessarily in full agreement. Certain remarks which are unsuitable in a report of this nature have been deleted. While passages of questionable propriety remain, I have decided to sanction a limited distribution in order that Commanders should have without delay the benefits of the great quantity of valuable information which it contains.

Auchinleck went on to set out the true functions, as he considered them, of Long Range Penetration Groups, as well as the actual results achieved by the operations of Wingate's brigade.

As far as Long Range Penetration Groups were concerned, Auchinleck believed that they must be considered in their proper perspective. He considered that they were detachments from the main forces and their operations should be governed by the same principles as all other detachments. If they contained superior forces away from the main effort, or if their operations had an effect on the enemy's conduct of the main battle, then they were of value. The Groups should be as few in number and as small in size as was consistent with the achievement of this object; and their commanders must direct and subordinate their actions to the achievement of success by the main effort.

Auchinleck went on to state that the use of Long Range Penetration Groups alone and unsupported was unlikely to achieve results commensurate with the almost certain loss of a large proportion of these highly trained and specialized troops. It followed therefore that the groups should operate in conjunction with, even if widely separated from, the main effort; and the plans of the two must be closely coordinated and co-related. This would require the most careful timing so that the effect of the groups could be felt at the right time during the execution of the main plan.

Unfortunately for Wingate, the 'main plan' had not been put into effect when he took his brigade into Burma and he did lose a large proportion of his troops as a result, but as far as Auchinleck was concerned, it was worth the effort. There were five positive results of the operation:

1. The ability of the British to re-enter Burma, and the inability of the Japanese to stop it was demonstrated to the Burmese.
2. The Mandalay–Myitkyina railway was put out of action for a period of four weeks and the Japanese were forced to use the longer and more limited river and road lines of communications via Bhamo.
3. Between six and eight Japanese battalions were drawn off from any other operations which the Japanese might have contemplated; and the activities of 77 Brigade might have prevented them continuing their advance beyond Sumprabum.
4. Much valuable information, both as regards the topography of the country and conditions of life in occupied Burma, was gained.
5. The operations had a good moral effect on our own troops generally and on the public, both in India and abroad.

It was the last result which was to thrust Wingate into the limelight and lead to his return to India as a major general, with orders in his pocket to raise a Chindit Division and send it back into Burma in 1944. But we will come to that later.

And what of Wingate's censored report? Many copies were circulated, individually numbered and many found their way into various archives after the war. The author's copy was Number 38, lodged with the India Office and yes, it did contain passages blacked out with the censor's ink. Finally, in 2008, an uncensored copy was tracked down in the National Archives in Kew and the author had an opportunity to discover which comments Auchinleck considered to be inappropriate. They have been added to the text in **bold** and provide an interesting insight into the mind of the great man.

On Page 4 of the report, 142 Company was the first unit to receive disapproval. The first paragraph, with censored comment, read as follows; '142 company was at first to have been a battalion. Its function was to provide each column with squad of fighting saboteurs. The training for this is highly specialised and I know of only three officers qualified to give it. The first to join the 142 Company were members of a draft of Commando personnel destined for 204 Mission. About 75 per cent of these were high category personnel who proved invaluable to us in action. The remaining 25 percent were misfit or **shirkers** who left us before concentration.

Why the censor left 'misfits' in but left 'shirkers' out is not known. Most units have their share of shirkers and misfits and 142 Company was probably no different from the others.

Training was described on Page 6 of the report, with Wingate lamenting the lack of experienced instructors. There were only two, with Wingate on the tactical and strategic side and Major Calvert on the demolition side. He went on to say: 'I attach great importance to tactical exercises on sand pits of large scale. **Stupidity and laziness prevented this excellent method being pursued, but** it is undoubtedly the only way in which junior leaders can obtain the necessary volume of experience in the solution of tactical problems.' One wonders at first who the stupid and lazy were that Wingate referred to, but it becomes clear as he continues:

> The average infantry officer does not know how to put out a road block or an ambush, how to place a Bren gun in position with due regard to the circumstances, how to post a sentry, how to direct and control fire, or a hundred other elementary points. It is regrettable to find that not one senior officer in ten could pass an examination on these points with credit. The reason is that not one in a hundred officers have had any experience of real fighting; that is of fighting, not as cogs in a machine as in the Great War, and perhaps to some extent in the Desert now, but as individuals trying to kill their enemy, while avoiding destruction themselves. This is what warfare against the Japanese is, and all sloppiness and ignorance are instantly punished. Only thought over a long period gives the sort of instinctive reaction that is required. Such thought cannot start too early. Only an accurately constructed sand pit with carefully controlled movement can provide the necessary volume of experience in the brief time available.

Page 7 of the report saw the first of Wingate's barbed comments regarding the lack of help from the upper echelons of the Indian Army. He stated:

> Training started in July, and followed a rational progress, until the somewhat late arrival of mules made full-scale Column exercises possible. The assistance given by Central Command was invaluable and unfailing and the presence of the Commander-in-Chief at exercises did much to stimulate enthusiasm and produce the change of heart referred to. **It is regrettable however, to have to record that the Military Training Directorate took not the slightest**

interest either at the start or at any other time in what was happening, in spite of an attempt by me to obtain its assistance.

Wingate went on to mention that on 20 November he flew in a Blenheim over what proved to be the exact path of his subsequent operation and was thereafter able to tell the Commander-in-Chief that the plan was feasible. He also set a number of measures in progress, including arrangements for the transit of the Brigade through IV Corps area, discussion with Commander IV Corps and the preparation for a number of reconnaissance parties through IV Corps front. He commented in his report: 'To implement these and other preliminary measures, I despatched an Advance Headquarters to IV Corps area consisting of an acting Brigade Major, Staff Captain, Intelligence Officer and various other elements. **Although in theory, the General Staff organization makes such measures redundant, in practice they are vitally necessary and failure is the reward for yielding to the prejudices of the clerical soldier.**'

Wingate was equally outspoken on the subject of Royal Air Force Co-operation. This section began with the paragraph;

Although the presence of RAF sections with Columns gave earnest RAF support, all those concerned with training were greatly worried at this stage by the almost complete lack of experience in Supply Dropping and analogous air problems. As the result only of oft repeated efforts and representations, a few unrealistic exercises by Lysanders were forthcoming, and these were all we had until the eve of entry. Even then, a realistic exercise only took place owing to the personal interest of Air Vice Marshal Williams. **The reason for this neglect is not incidental but of a universal character. It is owing to the fact that the Army and Air Officers responsible for the vital liaison are inferior in quality. Resentment or ignorance of this fact will merely result in so many more dead and wounded. The right answer is the much closer and more intimate type of co-operation that inevitably ensues when RAF officers with fighting experience are employed to fight the air arm from the ground. The difference to a Column Commander between having one of our RAF fighting officers to consult on air problems, or having the usual semi-educated liaison officers is the difference between confidence and uncertainty, between efficiency and incompetence, between vitality and emasculation.**

The censor had removed this part of the report in an attempt to avoid offending said liaison officers, but Wingate was quite correct in his observations. The experienced RAF NCOs and officers who marched with the columns were worth their weight in gold and Wingate was advocating a new way of fighting, with men supplied by air rather than long lines of communication. Within a year the whole army would be adopting his ideas.

Wingate continued to point the finger at those who he felt had been less than helpful with the organization and equipment for the operation. On the subject of Signals, Wingate contended:

> These are vital elements in an LRPG. I was fortunate in having Lieutenant Spurlock as my Signals Officer and Captain Wilding as Cipher Officer. The Signals Section of an LRPG carries out an incomparably more important role than in the case of a normal Brigade. The whole operation depends on good signals and it is the height of folly to be pinchbeck in their provision. **This however was the error made by the Signals Section of GDS almost until the time of entry**. Although the normal responsibility rested upon Lieutenant Spurlock he was a Subaltern instead of the normal Captain. He had no deputy although vulnerable to fire.

It is almost certain that Spurlock would have had his own observations to add to Wingate's, but unfortunately at the time Wingate dictated his report Spurlock was a prisoner of war in Rangoon Jail, along with Captain Wilding. Ken Spurlock would finally have a chance to dictate his comments on the expedition to the author from the comfort of his own sofa sixty-three years later in February 2009.

On Page 13 of his report Wingate justified the launching of LONGCLOTH even though his men would receive no support from other troops. It also gave an interesting insight into his views regarding the casualties suffered by his brigade.

> Had we not gone in, the following would have happened:- Firstly, the vast majority of staff officers who denied the theory would have continued to deny it. Secondly, the Brigade would at once have gone off colour. Thirdly, our ignorance of Japanese methods and reactions would have remained profound. Fourthly, the Japanese campaign against the Kachin levies would have been pursued beyond Fort Hertz. Fifthly, the projected Japanese infiltration over the Chindwin would have taken place. Sixthly, the serious interruption of enemy plans and confusion in his military economy throughout Burma, which our penetration caused, would have left him free to develop offensive intentions.
>
> On the whole, therefore, the decision may be said to have been justified. The argument that one third of the personnel have been lost is of little weight. **90 per cent of the personnel were in any case unfit for this type of operation and should not therefore be used again. Most of the priceless ten per cent are among the seventy per cent who are back in India**. If properly used, the experience gained can be worth the loss of many brigades.

When one reflects that up to fifteen times this number of troops is lost every monsoon through disease on purely defensive duties of routine nature, the exceedingly profitable character of these operations is realized. But their real value lies in the development they have made possible in waging war against the Japanese.

Wingate begins to describe the activities of his Northern Force between 18 and 23 February on Page 27 of his report. As the Japanese begin to withdraw their patrols following news of the Brigade's arrival in the area, the five columns labour through forest and marsh towards Tonmakeng. Wingate complained that:

We had taken six days to march there, owing mainly to the bad going and the inexperience of officers in march discipline. It is no use saying that they should have had experience. They had many times as much experience as any officers of their service in this theatre of war, but it wasn't nearly enough. **This was due to the abysmal ignorance with which they started and a poor standard of intelligence that prevails among wartime officers, with of course many notable exceptions**. For example, every officer had marched with his Column not less than 300 miles on exercises and a further 300 since Manipur Road. Yet many had still everything to learn. This was due to the great dearth of experienced officers in the Brigade and could largely be corrected. Anyway, their march discipline was bad. Columns made a trail through jungle of cigarette cartons and other packings that would have been too liberal for a paper chase. Big gaps occurred in the Column snake that did not correspond with tactical divisions. Getting into and out of bivouacs occupied thrice the necessary time and the rules for security in bivouac were almost universally broken. I do not record these painful facts to damn those concerned, but to point out what happens when personnel are not selected in accordance with the principles discussed. Whenever opportunity occurred in the course of the approach march to the railway, I personally lectured all officers on these and other points. The improvement was slight but steady.

Improvement was clearly not happening quick enough as far as 4 Column was concerned. On 1 March Wingate bivouacked not far from Pinbon.

On this day I was compelled to remove Major Conron from command of 4 Column, replacing him with by the Brigade Major – Bromhead. The latter's place was taken by Major Anderson, commander of 6 Column, represented in the field only by a Headquarters. Finding Pinbon and neighbourhood strongly held and patrolled I ordered 4 Column to ambush the Mansi motor road and seek to by-pass Pinbon through the mountains, while the remaining Columns marched down the Mu Valley on Pinlebu.

Bromhead later wrote that the reason Wingate replaced Conron was that he had allowed his radio batteries to run down as he could not stand the sound of the charging engine. At any rate the replacement of Conron could not save 4 Column when it was ambushed three days later. The radios would be lost, as would Conron on the way back to India.

The fate of 4 Column occupies a mere half a page in Wingate's report, but it was censored in three places nevertheless. Wingate records in 'Disaster to 4 Column' that he ordered Bromhead and 4 Column to join him before he proceeded to Wuntho. They started out on 4 March and early in the morning they encountered an enemy force of unknown strength, in the neighbourhood of Nyaungwun.

There followed what can only be described as a disgraceful exhibition of panic by the Gurkha Rifles; both the Burma Rifles and the British troops remaining firm and endeavouring to obey their commander and restore order. The brilliant history of the Gurkha Rifles in war, and indeed the splendid performance of 3 Column in these operations, makes it all the more necessary to tell the truth about what occurred on the March, but this is not the place for a post mortem.

It is sufficient to say that after repeated attempts to rally the column and counter-attack, the Column Commander did ultimately collect the greater part of his force at his Operational Rendezvous. Here, I must point out that without the use of a Rendezvous to be used on dispersal, this Column would have broken up and few indeed would have returned.

In the panic, the cipher had been lost, and it was quite impossible for me to send a R.V. in clear although a cryptic message was sent from which it was hoped the general line of my advance could be deduced. This message did not reach the Column Commander. The latter who was now without supplies or means of obtaining them, had lost much indispensable equipment, and was separated from the Brigade Group by strong enemy forces, rightly decided to march back to the Chindwin. I have no adverse comment to pass on the conduct which showed judgement and courage throughout. **The faults of 4 Column are those of others**.

Despite General Auchinleck's disapproval of Wingate's inappropriate comments he did not spare the individual when it came to criticism. Following on from 'Disaster to 4 Column' came 'Disaster to 2 Column'. Wingate was extremely critical of Major Emmett's tactics stating: 'The disaster that happened to 2 Column was easily avoidable and would never have taken place had the Commander concerned understood the doctrines of Penetration.' It would have been acceptable to march down the railway line in darkness only, or to have used the line for one swift march, melting away into the jungle and then attacking from a different direction.

> What he actually did was to march in broad daylight from the 6th milestone to within three miles of Kyaikthin. Here he bivouacked within two hundred yards of the line. In this bivouac he remained from 1730 to 2130 hours. The enemy used this interval to bring up a company of infantry to the immediate neighbourhood of the bivouac. When the force began to file out to carry out the attack on the railway it was ambushed.

Wingate then described the techniques of night fighting before continuing:

> On this occasion the bulk of the force would have been saved but for a blunder on the part of the Column Commander. Towards the end of the fight he altered the Operational R.V. deciding to go back and not forward. Very few indeed of his men even heard of the alteration and he was not in fact joined at his Rear R.V. by a single man. Meanwhile the parties that went forward found no Commander at the R.V. Some went right on the Irrawaddy and crossed it in the hope of meeting other Columns. The majority straggled back to the Chindwin whither the Column Commander also marched. **The Commander of 2 Column was Major Emmett, a Gurkha Rifle officer, with excellent knowledge of Gurkhali but unfit to command men.**

The censor finally gave up his efforts on Page 33 of the report, after removing the following line from Major Calvert's report of his attack on the railway; '**As we reached the station, Captain MacKenzie was crazy enough to open fire at the telegraph wires with his Tommy Gun as a feu de joie.**' Whether or not the remark deserved to be removed is open to conjecture. The other seventy-odd pages of the report escaped censure. Was it right to censor the report before it was distributed? I will let the reader decide.

Chapter 19

The Second Chindit Expedition

The aim of the Quadrant Conference was to decide future Allied global strategy, of which Burma was but a minor part. However, in the eyes of the United States, Burma was of far greater importance. President Roosevelt wanted to elevate China to the status of a great power within the American sphere of influence, whilst simultaneously using China as a base from which to conduct air and ground operations against the Japanese. Their priority was the re-opening of the overland route from India to China via northern Burma. The Burma Road from Mandalay was under Japanese control and although the new Ledo Road was being built by US Army Engineers, the main supply route was now by air over 'the Hump' – the Himalayan Mountains. As Great Britain stood to lose from such a development, Churchill was against it.

Relations between Great Britain and China had soured in 1940 when they closed the Burma Road, the land supply route to China, in order to placate the Japanese. In return China's General Chiang Kai-shek had declared his support for Gandhi's National Congress Party, whose aim was the throw the British out of India while the war was still in progress. At that time the war in Europe was of greater importance to the British and Churchill wanted the help of the United States to defeat Germany.

A compromise was reached and Churchill summoned Wingate to explain his proposal for the recapture of northern Burma by using long-range penetration brigades together with a southwards advance of Chinese troops under US General 'Vinegar Joe' Stilwell, and an eastwards advance by British troops in India. It was just what the Americans wanted to hear. This time, though, there would be six brigades of Chindits with a greatly increased air supply capability, provided by the Americans.

Although he put the wheels in motion, as directed by the British leaders in Canada, General Sir Claude Auchinleck, the Commander-in-Chief, India, did not agree with Wingate's proposals. He did not think that the British supply lines could support an invasion of Burma and had little faith in co-operation from the Chinese. He certainly did not agree with the breaking up of the 70th

Division in order to provide three of the six brigades of Wingate's new Special Force. The resentment of GHQ India was compounded when it was announced that a South East Asia Command (SEAC) was to be established, with Lord Louis Mountbatten as Supreme Commander. The new command would take direction of the war in Burma out of the hands of GHQ India and so, it was hoped, provide new energy and new operational efficiency.

The ground forces of SEAC would be organised into 11th Army Group, under which would come the troops of General Slim's Fourteenth Army. General Stilwell would become Mountbatten's deputy and one of his many responsibilities would be persuading the Chinese to move their forces into northern Burma. Auchinleck and GHQ India would take on the responsibility of training and equipping the Indian Army and developing India as a base for operations. Although GHQ India would try to thwart Wingate's plans, despite their approval by Churchill, Wingate would fight them tooth and nail, even resorting to a privileged direct line to Churchill via Mountbatten.

Wingate now had a cause, if not a crusade, from which only death could divert him. His disciples rallied to his call to arms – Fergusson, Calvert and Scott would each command a brigade and many other officers and selected personnel from the first expedition would join them. This time, though, things would be different because they would be assisted by brave men from the United States Army Air Force.

One of the biggest weaknesses of the first Chindit expedition was the need to abandon the wounded in the jungle. However, as Major Scott had discovered on his walk out, there were many clearings and open spaces where an aircraft might land, especially something light and small. The Americans had just the thing in the shape of L-1 and L-5 light aircraft that could carry one or two stretcher cases and could land and take off over short distances.

In August 1943, Lord Mountbatten met with US General 'Hap' Arnold to discuss plans for American support of the long-range penetration brigades. A new unit was to be formed, known as the 1st Air Commando Group. It would include a squadron of Douglas C-47 Dakota transport aircraft to be used for air supply of the many Chindit columns, a squadron of North American P-51 Mustang fighters to escort the transports and attack targets on the ground, and finally a squadron of North American B-25 Mitchell bombers.

The Air Commandos would be commanded by two veteran American pilots, Lieutenant Colonel Philip G. Cochran and Lieutenant Colonel John R. Allison. When they discussed Wingate's ideas with him they came up with another addition to the force: one hundred Waco gliders, capable of carrying fifteen troops each. The next time the Chindits went into Burma, did they really have to walk, or could they fly in?

Wingate's plan was for 16 Brigade under Brigadier Fergusson to walk in from Ledo to Indaw and capture its two airfields. If all went well Wingate could provide Churchill with an all-weather airfield into which a British division could be flown. 111 Brigade was to fly in by glider and Dakota and then operate south of Indaw, blowing up bridges and ambushing the roads. Mike Calvert would fly by glider with 77 Brigade into two jungle clearings nicknamed 'Broadway' and 'Piccadilly' and then establish a fortress block across the road and railway running northwards to supply the Japanese troops opposing Stilwell. 'Piccadilly' was the clearing from which Scott's men had been flown out during the march back to India in 1943. The other three brigades would be held in reserve, to relieve the 16, 77 and 111 Brigades after the ninety-day limit which Wingate considered to be the maximum time they could exist before exhaustion overtook them.

Wingate seriously doubted that the Chinese would play their part and the Chindits would be left as before, at the mercy of the Japanese divisions occupying Burma, unless of course something happened to occupy them elsewhere. That something, Wingate knew, could be a Japanese invasion of India and there were signs that a Japanese offensive was in the making. Wingate, indeed, was counting on it.

Within days of the launch of Operation THURSDAY on 5 March 1944, three Japanese Divisions had crossed the Chindwin at several points, attacked the 17th Indian Division at Tiddim and were marching in strength towards Imphal and Kohima. The reason for the Japanese invasion was directly related to Wingate's expedition the previous year. Up to that time the Japanese Army Command had thought that the countryside just east of the Chindwin was impassable for any substantial force of troops and had adopted a policy of defence. Wingate had proved them wrong and caused a rethink of Japanese plans. If one brigade could invade Burma in 1943, perhaps the whole British Army would come in 1944? Maybe it was better to invade India first?

After landing at 'Broadway' Calvert established a block across the main road and railway at Mawlu, named 'White City' from the parachutes which festooned the trees. The stronghold was held against all-comers, and later a second stronghold was established at 'Aberdeen' from which the Chindit columns roamed far and wide. Unfortunately Wingate would not see his plans come to fruition. He flew in to 'Broadway' on 24 March to inform Mike Calvert that he was to be awarded a bar to his Distinguished Service Order. He later flew on to Imphal to see Air Marshal Sir John Baldwin and then boarded his B-25 at 1700 hours for a flight to Assam. A couple of hours later the aircraft crashed into the ground in the hills west of Imphal, killing all on board.

Following the death of Wingate a new commander was appointed: Brigadier William 'Joe' Lentaigne, the commander of 111 Brigade who would not have been Wingate's first choice. Calvert would have been Wingate's logical choice, but he was too much like his controversial leader for many in higher command.

Then to add insult to injury, command of the force was transferred to the American General Stilwell, whose advance on Myitkyina by his Chinese-American army had been held up by stubborn Japanese resistance. By the second week in July the Chindits had reached the limit of their endurance, but Stilwell would not let them come out. It was not until August that the last Chindits returned to India, having taken 5,000 casualties during the campaign.

The ensuing battles are beyond the scope of this book, but suffice to say that the Japanese invasion was finally halted and defeated. The British Army then proceeded to clear the Japanese out of Burma and eventually recaptured Rangoon, the capital, where the surviving Chindit prisoners of war were still clinging to life.

Chapter 20

Home at Last

By April 1945, there were signs that the Japanese occupation of Rangoon Jail did not have long to run. The air raids were becoming heavier and work parties began to report a large exodus of troops and Japanese civilians from the city. Friendly civilians and even members of the Japanese-sponsored Indian National Army were telling them, 'It won't be long now.' The Allied bombing had put the water system out of action and the Japs began to move stocks of food and firewood into the jail for safe keeping. Soon rioting and looting began to take place, and the sounds of shooting and columns of smoke could be seen all over Rangoon.

Finally, around midday on 25 April, the inmates were told that all fit British and American prisoners would be leaving that afternoon. They were not told their destination, but they would have to march there as no transport was available. The cooks were allowed to draw as much food as they could cook before the march and some men were even issued with new clothing and boots. Denis Gudgeon recalled that his share of this bounty was a pair of Navy shorts, but no boots. He and many others would be going barefoot.

There was an air of despondency as those selected for the march wondered whether they could stand the pace after months of inactivity, while those who would remain discussed whether they would be killed by the Japs before they departed, or bombed or shelled by the British when they tried to recapture the city. John Kerr was one of those staying behind and Philip Stibbe gave him a note for his parents just in case the worst happened.

It began to rain when the march began in the late afternoon. The cooks were pushing handcarts piled high with rice and other stores, and the men were carrying their meagre belongings in bundles wrapped in rice sacks. Stibbe trudged along behind Brigadier Hobson (the senior officer at Rangoon Jail) carrying a bamboo pole between them, their bundles of belongings suspended from it. They marched in columns of threes with the Japs walking along beside them.

Over the next two nights they were passed by streams of Japanese trucks and cars carrying Japanese and Indian National Army troops. In their weakened condition, however, men started to fall out and several were loaded on the carts, including Colonel Mackenzie, the senior medical officer who had refused to stay behind, despite his age. There was also the persistent risk of attack from the air and the Japanese decided to lie up by day and march at nightfall.

The prisoners had no idea where they were going. The most likely guess was that they were heading north to cross the Sittang Bridge, which is the most southerly route to Moulmein and Thailand. This was confirmed on the night of the 26th when they reached the junction where the Prome Road goes to the left and the Pegu Road to the right. They took the road to Pegu.

As the night wore on the Japanese appeared to be suffering from nervous strain and became very irritable. Word reached the Brigadier that one of the officers had been taken ill and had fallen out. Why he did not ask to be carried on a cart no one knows, but he was never seen again. It appears that this was Lieutenant Arthur Best from Dunlop's 1 Column. He had been marching with Denis Gudgeon and he said to him, 'I can't go on, Gudge, I shall have to fall out.'

Denis was horrified and replied, 'No, keep going, or they will kill you!'

It was no good though and it is believed that the Japanese murdered him with their bayonets.

Another day and night passed and the men began to discuss the idea of escaping from the column. There were 400 prisoners and only fifty guards – could they be overpowered or were the men too weak now? As they formed up at dusk for the march through Pegu they noticed that about thirty men were missing. To their astonishment the Japs did not seem surprised and there were no reprisals.

The men were told to leave their hand carts behind and the Japanese started to abandon much of their kit. The sick could no longer ride on the carts and had to be helped along by their friends which made the Japs impatient because they could not keep up. They were understandably nervous because Pegu had been bombed the previous night and they feared that they might return again. The place was in ruins and only the framework of the larger building remained. As they crossed the Pegu bridge they saw the Japanese sappers preparing it for demolition and about an hour later they heard the explosion as it blew up behind them.

Now and then, men fell by the wayside. Thirst was a major problem and the men staggered along in a daze. Colonel Mackenzie was in such a poor state that two of the cooks, Sergeants Martin and Hansell, volunteered to carry him between them. Amazingly Brigadier Hobson had found a new source of energy and kept encouraging the men to keep going. When the column stopped for a break he would walk around, enquire how the men were doing and cajole their captors into giving them a drink. Surprisingly one or two of the Japanese handed round their water bottles.

Finally, in the early hours of the morning, the Brigadier went to see the Japanese Commandant and told him that they could not go on any further. The men needed rest, water and food, and were at the end of their tether. The reaction was not what they expected – the Commandant agreed to send one of his men ahead to look for a suitable place to lie up for the day, and an hour and a half later they stopped in a village at the side of the railway line which led to the Sittang Bridge. They had marched 70 miles from Rangoon.

The men were exhausted, collapsed under cover of the trees and tried to sleep. In the meantime their guards began to slip away. Suddenly someone shouted out that the Brigadier wanted to make an announcement and the weary men looked towards an empty space in the middle of the village where their senior officer stood. In a clear, loud voice he announced, 'At last I can tell you something that you have been waiting to hear for years; we are all free men!' A few seconds passed while the news sunk in and then the men sprang to their feet, shouting, laughing and slapping one another on the back. Some shed tears of joy and relief.

When they arrived in the village the Japanese Commandant had sent for the Brigadier and informed him that they were going to release them. He advised them to stay where they were until the British troops advancing from the north arrived and gave them a note to say that they had been officially liberated. This was to show to any other Japanese troops who crossed their path and who might not be so merciful. In fact there were rumours that the Japanese second-in-command wanted to shoot them, rather than allow them to go free. Such was the fate of other prisoners of war in other some of the far-flung Japanese prisoner-of-war camps.

The men were now free, but there was still great danger around them. The air was thick with Allied fighters and some of the RAF prisoners laid out a ground strip in a nearby paddy field, using white clothing from the prisoners. They also put together a Union Jack and laid it alongside.

Before long some of the inhabitants of a nearby village approached them and offered them food. They also told them that there were many Jap stragglers in the area and the villagers were hunting them down. In the distance an artillery barrage began against a target a mile or two away. The battle was getting closer.

Some men set fire to a haystack and tried flashing mirrors in the sun to attract the attention of the passing aircraft. It may have been a great mistake. The men were crowding around the village well when the first aircraft flew low over the area. In the paddy field the RAF men waved pieces of cloth as the planes flew lower. Suddenly there was a burst of cannon fire and a small bomb exploded in the centre of the village. The planes were lining up to strafe the village.

Panicking figures ran in every direction as shells and bullets ploughed up the ground and tore through the trees. Some found cover behind thick tree trunks while others sought holes in the ground and clung to the earth and prayed. At last the planes flew away and the dust began to settle. Amazingly, out of the 400 men in the village only one had been hit – the Brigadier had established his headquarters in a house in the village and a burst of bullets came through the roof and killed him outright. It was a terrible tragedy and a bitter irony that they had come so far only for their leader to be killed by his own side.

The men had scattered when the attack came in and they were loath to return to the village. Many gathered at the nearby railway station and prayed that the planes would keep away until nightfall. Philip Stibbe and Colour Sergeant Beatty of the King's took four men and organized sentry posts to look out for marauding Japs. Friendly natives told them that all the villages along the railway line were being bombed, but they were welcome to spend the night in a village about three quarters of a mile away. They were only too pleased to accept.

As darkness fell the men feasted on rice and curry, their first decent food for a long time. They had just settled down to sleep when Major Lutz, one of the American prisoners from Block 6 appeared with some good news. After the strafing that morning he had disguised himself as a Burman and with the help of a guide had made his way to the nearest British lines. He told them that the village was full of freed prisoners of war and the planned bombardment of the village was postponed. He was told to return to the prisoners and arrange for them to meet a British patrol later that night.

Sleep was forgotten as the men thanked their hosts and made their way back along the railway line to the village where they had been strafed that morning. They found a large group of prisoners already hiding in the dark and after a while they all moved off across the countryside towards the north. They passed through another village and had just started to climb up a gentle slope when a challenge rang out. It was a patrol of Indian soldiers from the Frontier Force with a Scottish officer in charge of them. Smiling Indian faces emerged from the darkness and began to shake their hands. Now at last they were truly free.

A short walk later and they came to some waiting lorries, and half an hour later they were deposited with officers and men from the West Yorkshire Regiment. There another meal awaited them, followed by mugs of real tea, complete with milk and sugar. They were given blankets and settled down for their first night of freedom. At long last they were home.

Well, most of them, that is. Some, like Ken Spurlock and Johnnie Nealon were still on the last leg of the journey. Ken had long been concerned that, as an officer, he might be made to pay with his life if any of his men escaped. So when Johnnie Nealon and four Australian NCOs told him they were making a break for it and would he like to come, there was no other answer than 'Yes'! At that time the column was being strafed again and the Japanese guards were taking cover. The escapees decided to split up and make their way individually past the cordon of guards and in true Chindit dispersal fashion, meet up again at a hill in the distance.

Ken Spurlock began to breathe easier once the cordon of guards was behind him, but as he walked along a track he noticed the distinctive footprint of a Japanese army boot, which has the big toe separate to the others. Thinking that their escape had been discovered he took to the jungle, and slowly and quietly crept towards the rendezvous. Unknown to him, four of the other escapers were doing the same thing as they had also seen the boot prints. Johnnie Nealon, however, was quite unconcerned, as he was the man wearing the boots, having stolen them earlier in the march.

Eventually the six men were reunited and sat down to consider their options. Ken Spurlock was the senior man present and, convinced that the British would be invading Burma from the west, argued that they should head in that direction. Unbeknown to him they were in fact coming down from the north and would be heading away from friendly forces. However, although they were tired and hungry they were now free again. They got to their feet and began to trek to the west.

After about a week they came to a village occupied by refugee tribesmen who took them in and fed and hid them from the Japanese. The tribesmen contacted a Burma Rifles Naik who had been dropped behind the lines to organize resistance against the Japanese, and he informed them that the liberating forces were in fact coming down from the north, not the west. So the weary men retraced their steps back to where they had left their fellow prisoners and found the area under the control of British troops. They would be the last of the party that had walked out of Rangoon Jail to find their way back to freedom.

Lieutenant Denis Gudgeon wrote to his family on 30 April, their first notification that he was safe:

WHOOPEE, WHOOPEE, WHOOPEE. I AM FREE AND WELL IN BRITISH HANDS. I feel absolutely overjoyed. I hope to be flown out to India very soon. I will probably be put in hospital first, as the Japs did not treat me very well. I lived on a bowl of rice three times a day for the two years and eight days of my captivity. I was captured on April 20 1943 and was in Major General Wingate's Brigade. I very nearly got back to India, in fact I reached the banks of the Chindwin River, only to be betrayed by Burmese civilians to the Japs. I was absolutely on my last legs, suffering from thirst, hunger and exhaustion. I don't think I could have gone another day. I had a rather unpleasant time being interrogated, as I refused to talk at first, just giving name, rank and number. They threatened to cut my head off with a sword and all the time during my questioning, this Jap officer had his sword pointed at my throat. On April 26 I arrived at the Central Gaol, Rangoon and was immediately put into solitary confinement for 35 days. When I came out of that I was in a building with other prisoners. I had a very bad do of dysentery just coming out of solitary, but made miraculous recovery. The only 'medicine' I was given for it was charcoal and creosote pills. Present weight is 143 pounds, so will have to put on between two and three stone to get back to normal. Never make me a rice pudding again, Mummy.

One week later Denis was a resident of 17 Ward, 74 General Hospital in India. He wrote home again:

I saw a casualty return yesterday and notice I was reported missing on April 20 which was the day on which I was captured, so the 12 Gurkhas I had with me must have got out. George Wort tells me that Captain Silcock the 2nd i/c of my column very kindly wrote to you about me. He unfortunately died later under tragic circumstances. After we retook a certain place he was sleeping in a house and had a night move and jumped out of the window and broke his spine. I am given three Vitamin B and two Vitamin C tablets with every meal. I tasted my first sausages and bacon for two years for breakfast this morning.

There was a lot to catch up on. There was news of family and friends and sadness as the fate of comrades was discovered. Arthur Best, the ATO with George Dunlop's column, had been bayoneted to death on the march from Rangoon to Pegu because he could not keep up owing to a bad leg. Graham Hosegood the Brigade Intelligence Officer died of beri-beri two months before the march out of the jail. He was Denis's best friend and one of the nicest men he had ever met. He was twenty-four years old.

Chapter 21

Postscript

How does history judge Wingate? He certainly made mistakes during Operation LONGCLOTH and one of these was neglecting to supply Captain 'Fish' Herring with a long- range wireless transmitter for his mission to the Kachin Hills. In March 1943, Herring travelled to the Sinlumkaba Hill Tracts and told the Kachin elders that he had come into the hills to raise the Kachins to fight against the Japanese. Their tactics were to be guerrilla tactics consisting of the destruction of the several small Japanese garrisons and line of communication guards in the Bhamo area, the ambushing of parties of enemy using the main hill tracks and the disruption of the Japanese lines of communication between Namhkam, Bhamo and Myitkyina. They would be supplied with arms and ammunition by air. The same message was sent to the Kachins in the Kodaung Hill Tracts, and the Lashio and Kutkai districts; the scheme was well received. Herring believed that as many as 2,500 men could be called up as the districts were rich in retired and serving Burma Rifle and Burma Frontier Force personnel, the vast majority of whom saw active service during the operations in Burma in 1941/42.

The Japanese discovered that Herring and his platoon were in the area and he was hunted for the duration of the six weeks he was in the hills. Despite this he made his way as arranged to the rendezvous point and waited from 25 to 29 March. Whether Gilkes and 7 Column or Dunlop with 1 Column were tasked with meeting Herring and communicating his success by radio to Wingate, the fact is that neither of them arrived on time. Thus Wingate was deprived of the chance of joining up with Herring and finding sanctuary and allies in the Kachin Hills.

On 18 April, Herring made contact with the Headquarters of 2nd Burma Rifles and learnt that the Brigade had been broken up into small parties. Had he had a powerful wireless transmitter he could have reported on the favourable situation in the Kachin Hills where many could have found asylum. Disappointed, he headed for China, reaching the Kachin Levy HQ at La Awng Ga on 11 May.

An account of the activities of 1 Column, together with letters written in 1951 by Major Dunlop to Colonel Barton helped explain why he was late at the rendezvous and cast doubts on whether raising rebellion amongst the Kachins would have succeeded. Like Herring, he too was having problems with communicating with Brigade Headquarters:

> Unlike the rest of the Brigade we were a detached force and did not enjoy the information which they passed to each other. We were on a different wireless net and could only communicate with Brigade – when Brigade chose to communicate with us! Herring must have painted a very rosy picture about conditions in the Kachin Hills. He cannot have had much to do with the area around Mongmit, where the inhabitants were very far from wanting to rebel. This is not surprising when one considers that the Japanese were in Mongmit and also in the Baldwin Mines area. Furthermore the people were terrified of the Japanese, as well they might be. As it was the Sawba (Prince) of Mongmit was executed as a result of our unwanted visit.
>
> The inhabitants were: Burmans in the low ground who had no love for us; Burma-Gurkhas, descended from the former garrisons in the Maymyo area who were rather timid; Shans who were quite ineffective; Palaungs of whom it is said 'they can't keep anything to themselves' who did, in fact, inform on us; and Kachins who were helpful and friendly, providing us with useful information. These people were spread evenly over the country we traversed and no large area could be said to belong to any one race. We, of course, discovered all this as we went along. Had Wingate had this information he could hardly have expected us to raise rebellion. He would, of course, have still sent us to the Mongmit area for by going there we must have aided the withdrawal of the rest of the brigade.

By leaving Dunlop and the remains of Southern Group out on a limb, Wingate was probably trying to fool the Japanese into thinking that the Brigade was continuing to advance eastwards, whereas they had turned about and were making for home. By the time George Dunlop decided to follow them they were far more exhausted than the other columns, having been 'out' a month longer. Morale was extremely low, they had few maps and not enough officers capable of leadership. Finally they discovered that they were the only British troops left in that part of Burma. Intelligence from the villagers had dried up, probably due to their fear of the Japs and the apparent collapse of the 'invasion'. As the earlier dispersal parties passed through the villages many days before, heading for India, the Burmans probably decided to hedge their bets and support the Japanese. Thus were many parties betrayed for pieces of silver on the way home.

Dunlop did the right thing by trying to fight his column home in one piece. Not only was it a show of force to the villagers that they passed, but he knew that when faced by a large and determined force the Japanese usually withdrew. By the time he turned for home the Japs were close on their heels, they were soon appraised of their every change of direction and, knowing that they were the only people left in the field, could redeploy in large numbers to cut them off. The only reason the column got as far as it did was because they hardly ever used tracks or paths. They held together long enough, so that after they put in their last attack and the column broke up, they were close enough to the Chindwin that Chet Kin and his large party could force their way through. Dunlop was left with a small party which disintegrated near the end and he was lucky to get home.

Some of the participants of LONGCLOTH are scathing in their opinions of Wingate and his methods, and one or two of these have appeared in the narrative. It would also be fair to say that the Gurkhas were not impressed with Wingate. It is not surprising when one realizes that when the 3rd Battalion reassembled in Assam under Major Emmett, losses amounted to 446 of all ranks. Of these around 150 returned afterwards. Seventy-four were reported as prisoners of war and forty-five of them escaped after capture.

Much criticism was levelled at Wingate's training of the Gurkhas. They should have been taught not only what they had to do, but why they were doing it. Most of the British troops were mature men who could comprehend the general picture. They could understand that on occasion food would be short, that speed of movement was essential to success and that calmness was an even greater asset than courage in jungle fighting. In such a hazardous expedition the psychological factor might dictate success or failure, but it is evident that such aspects had not been fully explained to the rank and file.

Most of the Gurkha junior commanders lacked training in basic jungle warfare tactics and did not fully understand the principles of dispersal. Major Mike Calvert later wrote:

> The continued emphasis on dispersal and security in bivouac had a bad effect on Gurkha troops. They came to feel that when an alarm had been given or shots had been fired, dispersal must take place. This may have accounted for what appeared to be bad behaviour. I would never give an order for dispersal in battle except through proper channels as a military movement. I found in all cases that it was possible to control the column in that manner. In training there had been too much emphasis on caution. I used to ask the Gurkha officers for their advice and they practically always urged caution. In my opinion the whole conception of the campaign was a bold one and caution in carrying it out spelt disaster.

Language was also a problem and Mike Calvert considered that if he could have spoken Gurkhali fluently his column's morale and performance would have been twice as good. Despite this he was still very impressed with the Gurkhas of 3 Column:

> They underwent great physical endurance tests and hardships which would have tried the finest troops in the world. I cannot show too much admiration of the way these young Gurkhas marched great distances over very difficult country, bore heavy loads, carried out our rearguards religiously, were restrained at all times in matters of talk, fires etc and then fought time and again without cracking up.

Major George Dunlop later wrote that the greatest mistake had been in having commanders who could not speak directly and properly to their men. Quite apart from misunderstanding itself, there was far too great a strain on the commander. In the Gurkha columns there were men of four different races and languages, and to get them to work as a unit in times of great hardship was difficult in the extreme. Morale also had its ups and downs. The Gurkhas collapsed completely on the return journey, except for the strange restoration in the 'dispersal' battle. There were a number of reasons for this, recorded by Dunlop:

> Owing to an ill-timed exercise on training the Feast of War, 'Desera' was not properly celebrated. This matter came up frequently during operations. Also, for some reason best known to their Regiment, the request by the 3/2nd for a visit of the Regimental 'Truncheon' was refused. Thus many reinforcements from other regiments could not be sworn-in as members of the 2nd. This was extremely important and seems to have been generally overlooked.

In 1951, Lieutenant Colonel J.E.B. Barton from the Cabinet Office Historical Section in Queen Anne's Chambers, Tothill Street, London SW1 was given the job of telling the story of the expedition. Once completed, his work was to be used as a guide by the War Office historians writing the history of the Second World War.

The author eventually tracked down a copy of Barton's draft narrative. It was largely based on Wingate's original report, although the surviving senior Chindit column commanders were happy with Barton's work and his conclusions. Copies of the letters sent to and fro during the research have survived and details of two of them are reproduced below.

One of the men he exchanged letters with was Sam Cooke, former commanding officer of 13th King's and the Northern Group, and in 1951 a major general commanding a division in Jordan. Cooke wrote:

It seems to be a general impression that the troops who went into Burma with Wingate in 1943 were not quite up to the standard required for operations of the kind Wingate had planned. This has unfortunately been given prominence in many reports and people seem to think that we should have done very much better if we had had a regular battalion.

The 13th King's was raised in North Wales in 1940 from a cadre which consisted almost entirely of Warrant Officers and NCOs of the King's Own Scottish Borderers, the Royal Welch Fusiliers and the Royal Ulster Rifles. In July 1941 the Battalion Cadre moved to Glasgow where there was an intake of about a thousand recruits. These represented a cross–section of 'town–dwellers' from Liverpool and Manchester. They were by no means youngsters but many of them had found good employment, were married and with families, and most of them realized what war meant.

In October 1941, the Battalion moved from Felixstowe to Ipswich where it was employed on coastal defence duties. Months were spent in digging trenches, building breastworks and other field defences. The work was hard, the days long but those who were not already used to tough work soon became used to it.

In January 1941 the Battalion moved from Felixstowe to Ipswich where it was employed on beach defence duties, aerodrome protection etc. This form of employment went on until July, when the Battalion moved to Burford and was told to mobilise for overseas. There was a good deal of hanging about after the orders were given and it was not until the beginning of December that the Battalion finally sailed for India.

The first six months in India were spent at Secunderabad on Internal Security duties and it was during this period that the Battalion was 'milked' of many of its regular NCOs. The loss was not as great as people like to make out, but on the other hand the Battalion lost many of its experienced junior leaders.

In the middle of 1942, the Battalion was selected to form part of Wingate's Brigade and went to Saugor in the Central Provinces to start jungle training. During this period the Battalion was able to throw out all men considered unfit to take part in the operations which had been visualised. Others were taken in from the British Base Reinforcement Camp at Deolali. This process went on until the end of training and at least 300 men must have been got rid of as unsuitable, either mentally or physically, for operations with Wingate. There was not time to train replacements and so Wingate decided to disband one column – 6 Column – to keep the other three up to strength. The men who did in fact take part in the 1943 operations were the pick of the bunch and there is no doubt in my mind that they were as good as any average regular battalion. They were far above the average of the average war-time battalion that was raised.

My point about all this is that the men we took into Burma were a first class type and well up to the average which any commander can expect in war. Our handicap was, of course, in junior leaders with war experience. Civil life does not normally produce leaders of men and this was the real problem we were up against. To say that the 13th King's were a 'war-time' unit and not suitable for LRPG operations is a mistake. The troops proved they were able to withstand hardship and their story, with the possibility of one or two exceptions, has confirmed this. The absence of good junior leaders was not felt as much as might have been the case if the Battalion had been called to operate as a normal battalion in a Brigade, but I mention this later.

The 13th King's spent six months training in the jungle at Saugor. This period was in fact broken by the Monsoon which created havoc with jungle sores and a certain amount of malaria. The time was all too short and the standard of training was not what it should have been for an operation such as Wingate visualised. Much time had been spent on getting the men fit, in getting them used to the jungle, and in teaching them manoeuvres created by Wingate but which in fact were never used. It was a race against time and minor jungle tactics were sadly neglected. As it happened the Brigade, or a large portion of it, wandered around Burma with no special object in view other than to act as a decoy or as protection to Wingate's headquarters. On the occasions when they met the Jap's face to face our minor tactics were deplorable.

I did not join the 13th King's until November 1942 and spent only eight weeks with them before they went into Burma. This included only two Brigade exercises and it was painfully obvious to us all that although we had mastered Wingate's method of operating in groups and columns in the jungle we really did not know very much about fighting in the jungle. If we had, then I doubt if we should have had such little success at places like Hintha, where Bernard Fergusson ran into the Japs and at Baw where we had to call off a supply drop.

It can be said that troops are never ready or sufficiently trained for battle. I think our training was just a little too fine and lacked the reality of jungle warfare. With our lack of junior leaders to control and lead the troops it was as well we did not get involved in too many battles and kept to Wingate's 'tip and run' methods.

The following figures with regard to casualties suffered by the 13th King's are of interest. They are not official figures but I tried to keep a record of what happened to people. The figures are for Other Ranks and do not include the Officers.

Killed and missing	141
Died in Captivity	113
Released in 1945	71
Died after operations	12
Returned with columns and dispersed parties to India	384
Total	721

The 'missing' were never heard of again as far as I know. They are not included in the numbers as Died in Captivity or Released in 1945.

It was a heavy casualty list and one wonders if it was worth it to get the experience for the Second Wingate Operation, to keep the Japs engaged at rather a critical period in the Burma fighting and to give a fresh impetus to morale in that area. I like to think it was worthwhile as we lost many excellent men who were entirely spent by the lack of proper rations, excessive marching and fatigue, long before they ever came into contact with the Japs and able to fight him as man to man.

Lieutenant Colonel H.J. Lord OBE was another who put his opinions on paper in 1951, in his case from 'Q' Branch, Headquarters, British Army of the Rhine. Lord had been the Staff Captain in 1943, responsible for keeping the Brigade supplied from the air. He wrote to Barton:

It strikes me now after reading the narrative that there was too much wasted effort and insufficient concentration of forces. It is also rather surprising that no one conceived the idea, as was adopted in 1944, of using light 'Auster' type aircraft for evacuation of casualties or for flying in essential 'key' reinforcements or special equipment, e.g. wireless transmitter sets. The knowledge that casualties must necessarily be abandoned must have been very bad for morale and fighting organisation. It was pure accident that George Bromhead, the Brigade Major and I evolved a method of demanding commodities by which long signals were cut down. There never was a real planning staff and the ordinary Brigade staff were more than fully occupied with day to day problems including initial equipping of units. A proper planning staff could almost have worked out exact routes, dropping points, dates for drops, etc before the brigade even started into Burma. Headquarters IV Corps could have assisted in this but the whole operation plan was kept at too high a level and suffered from overmuch 'security'. The latter was eventually negatived by the Columns themselves leaving litter etc on their route from Imphal onwards.

The failure of particular columns to receive a supply drop was basically their own fault. Either the column had lost its W/T equipment or had allowed the batteries to run down. Drops were staggered as far as possible and in many cases aircraft were despatched on the due date to a particular column, hoping to pick up recognition signals within a radius from the previous drop. Few sitreps were received showing column positions daily and little or no attempt was made by Brigade Headquarters in the field to co-ordinate drops and if necessary lay down priorities. Some columns 'cheated' in that they displayed signals on hearing aircraft, even though the column did not necessarily require a drop until a further day or so. This was understandable and unavoidable after some columns had dispersed.

Intriguingly Lord finished his letter with the comment: 'It is rather extraordinary you received no reply from Sam Cooke who is usually rather punctilious in this respect. I believe he had a difference of opinion with Wingate and now he probably does not want to get drawn into the matter at all.' What that difference of opinion was, no one will ever know, but it may have had something to do with the fact that his regiment suffered almost 50 per cent casualties during the operation and as its commander, Cooke, would have been entitled to have strong feelings about such heavy losses.

Although this book concentrates on the first Chindit expedition and merely scratches the surface of the second, one cannot deny that, at the end of the day, Wingate did get results. He did, however, make many enemies on the way. One of them was Major General Kirby who was given the job of writing the Official History of the Burma Campaign in 1951. He had a bitter clash with Wingate in India in 1943 and was determined to do a hatchet job on the Chindit leader. By the time the Official History was published he had had his revenge. The convention of Official Histories is that there is no personal criticism of commanders in the field, but Kirby made an exception for Wingate – the commanders responsible for the loss of Singapore and Burma did not receive the destructive criticism of Wingate by Kirby. Many of Wingate's senior commanders protested at the unprofessional and biased view, as did Air Marshal Sir John Baldwin who commanded all the air forces in the campaign. As far as this author is concerned, readers would be better guided by the comments of Prime Minister Winston Churchill in the House of Commons on 2 August 1944:

We placed our hopes at Quebec in the new Supreme Commander Admiral Mountbatten and in his brilliant Lieutenant, Major General Wingate, who alas, has paid a soldier's debt. There was a man of genius who might well have become a man of destiny. He has gone, but his spirit lives on in the Long Range Penetration Groups and has underlain all these intricate and daring air operations and military operations based on air transport and on air supply.

Lord Mountbatten echoed Churchill's words when he later gave a speech at the unveiling of a memorial to Major General Wingate at Charterhouse School. Some of the extracts of the speech go a long way to describe Wingate's legacy.

> We are here today to honour the memory of a most remarkable man and leader of men. I first met Orde Wingate in August 1943 when we were together on our way to attend the Quebec Conference. At that time I had no notion that I should shortly be ordered out to South East Asia myself; but I can vividly recall the intensely exciting experience of hearing Wingate describe the operation of the 77th Indian Infantry Brigade, which he led in their operations behind the Japanese lines in Burma. We all of us felt, not only the inspiration that he exerted over everybody, but we felt that burning, fiery desire to get to grips with the enemy in a part of the world where the enemy had it all his own way.
>
> And so it isn't very surprising that when, a week later, I was suddenly appointed to the South East Asia Command, the first man I should have turned to was Wingate. Together we planned that he should carry out another operation behind the Japanese lines, but this time a much greater one; at least six times as great. His time in Burma was comparatively short, but the impact that he made on the campaign in Burma was simply terrific.
>
> Up to the time of his first Expedition, the Allies had suffered a series of unrelieved defeats for eighteen months in the Far East. The myth, the legend, had grown up, assiduously fostered by the Japanese propaganda machine, that the Japanese was a born jungle fighter, and invincible at that game. It was Wingate who proved that he was not; it was Wingate's men who went in and showed that, man to man, they were superior to the Japanese at any game.
>
> Wingate also introduced a vital new technique into the campaign in Burma. He used to say 'send us down our supplies like Father Christmas down the chimney.' The only way you could supply men operating behind the enemy lines was by air. Now, no one would claim that Wingate invented Air Supply, because it was well known. But what he did do was to prove that military ground forces could operate with no other form of supply at all, other than air supply. And those lessons were taken up; and as we got more transport aircraft, so we ended up with practically the whole of the Fourteenth Army on the air supply of which Wingate was the pioneer.
>
> Wingate was a great fighter; a fearless leader of men; a brilliant orator; and a deeply religious man.

Bernard Fergusson gave a well-balanced opinion of his friend and former leader in his book Beyond the Chindwin. It is therefore appropriate to give him the last word on Wingate in this book. He wrote:

He seemed almost to rejoice in making enemies, but he was a military genius of a grandeur and stature seen not more than once or twice in a century. Secondly, no other officer I have heard of, could have dreamed the dream, planned the plan, obtained, trained, inspired and led the force. There are men who shine at planning, or at training, or at leading; here was a man who excelled at all three, and whose vision at the council table matched his genius in the field.

The one column commander that Barton had the almost impossible job of pinning down was Mike Calvert. Now that peace had broken out he lost his war time rank of brigadier and was now a colonel. As one of the most experienced jungle fighters in the world he had been sent to Malaya to resurrect the Special Air Service to fight the Chinese insurgents in that country. He had commanded the Special Air Service in Europe after the 1944 Chindit expedition, but they had been disbanded at the end of the war. However Calvert was not a well man. Apart from exhaustion he was still suffering from the effects of illnesses contracted during his two campaigns in the jungle. He finally ended up in the military hospital at Millbank in London where Bernard Fergusson went to see him. The words that he reported to Barton are a fitting end to this book and a tribute to Mike Calvert and the Chindits who fought in both campaigns. A smiling Fergusson reported: 'He is not at all well, and will not be passed fit to go back to Malaya. I understand the doctors have said he is fit for duty on lines of communication only. "But," said Mike, "they didn't stipulate whose!"'

Awards and Decorations – Operation LONGCLOTH

Distinguished Service Order
Brig O.C. Wingate, Commander 77 Indian Infantry Brigade
Maj J.M. Calvert, Royal Engineers, CO 3 Column
Maj B.E. Fergusson, Black Watch, CO 5 Column
Maj (T/Col) L.G. Wheeler, 2nd Burma Rifles (Posthumous)
Lt (T/Capt) Aung Thin, 2nd Burma Rifles

Distinguished Conduct Medal
CSM R.S. Blain, 3 Column Sabotage Squad
CSM R.M. Cheevers, 8 Column
Sgt F.E. Pester, 5 Column Sabotage Squad
Cpl P. Dorans, 5 Column

Indian Distinguished Service Medal
Subedar Kum Sing Gurung, 3 Column Senior Gurkha Officer

Burma Gallantry Medal
Lance Naik Tun Lwin, 2nd Burma Rifles, 1 Column
Rifleman Hpau Wai La, 2nd Burma Rifles, 1 Column

Member of the British Empire
Capt (T/Maj) G.M. Anderson, Brigade Major
Capt (T/Maj) R.B.J. Bromhead, Brigade Major then CO 4 Column
Lt (T/Captain) H J Lord, Brigade Staff Captain (Air Supply OC)
Lt K.E. Spurlock Brigade HQ Signals Officer, Royal Corps of Signals
Lt Richard Allan Wilding, Brigade Cipher Officer, Manchester Regiment
Lt (T/Capt) N. Whitehead, 8 Column, OC 2nd Burma Rifles Platoon
Maj Raymond Ramsay, Brigade MO, Royal Army Medical Corps

Military Cross
Capt (T/Maj) K.D. Gilkes, 13th Bn King's, CO 7 Column
Lt (T/Capt) D.C. Herring, 2nd Burma Rifles
Lt (T/Capt) W.B.E. Petersen, 7 Column
Lt (T/Capt) P.C. Buchanan, Adjutant 2nd Burma Rifles
Lt J.G. Lockett, 3 Column Commando Squad
2 Lt H.D. James, 3 Column
Lt G.H. Borrow, 13th Bn King's, Brigade HQ Intelligence Officer
Lt D.C. Menzies, Black Watch, 5 Column Adjutant (Posthumous)
Lt (T/Capt) J.S. Pickering, 13th Bn King's, 7 Column
Lt R.S. Clarke, 1 Column
Lt (T/Capt) G.P. Carne, 2nd Burma Rifles, OC Guerrilla Platoon, 2 Column
Lt J.C. Bruce, 2nd Burma Rifles, No. 1 Group
Lt (T/Capt) J.C. Fraser, 2nd Burma Rifles, 2 i/c 5 Column
Lt (T/Capt) W.D. Griffiths, 2nd Burma Rifles, 3 Column
Lt Saw Chet Kin, 2nd Burma Rifles, 1 Column
Lt L.W. Rose, Sherwood Foresters, Brigade Headquarters
Lt W.J. Livingstone, former RSM, 13th King's

Military Medal
CSM T. Thomson, 13th Bn King's, No. 2 Group HQ
CSM J. Cairns, King's Own Scottish Borders att 13th Bn King's, 5 Column
Sgt J. Thornborrow, 13th Bn King's, 5 Column
Cpl H.H. Day, Wiltshire Regiment att 13th Bn King's, 3 Column
Pte C.N. Guest, Royal Welch Fusiliers att 13th Bn King's, 3 Column

Indian Order of Merit
Jemadar Manbahadur Gurung, 3/2nd Gurkha Rifles, 2 Column

British Empire Medal
Sgt P.R. Chivers, Royal Engineers, 3 Column
Sapper (Acting Cpl) R.W. Pike, Royal Engineers, 5 Column
Sgt R.A. Rothwell, 13th Bn King's, 5 Column

Note: The above list is not complete. It is believed that the 2nd Burma Rifles were awarded two DSOs, one MBE, one Order of Burma, seven Military Crosses, twenty-one Burma Gallantry Medals (equivalent to the Distinguished Conduct Medal or the Indian Order of Merit) and twenty-seven Mentions in Despatches. In addition to the list of awards prepared by Wingate in the summer of 1943, others such as the MBE for Ken Spurlock did not appear in the London Gazette until long after their release from captivity in June 1946. The author would be pleased to hear of any additions or amendments.

1 Column Order of Battle

Column Commander: Maj G.D. Dunlop MC
2i/c and Rifle Company Commander: Capt V. Weatherall, 3/2nd GR
2i/c Rifle Company: Lt R. Clarke, 3/2nd GR
Subaltern, GR: 2Lt Harvey, 2Lt Wormald
Animal Transport Officer: Lt J. Fowler, 6 GR
Guerrilla Platoon, 142 Company: Lt J. Watson, Black Watch, Lt J. Nealon, KOSB, replaced Watson
Burma Rifles, Recce Platoon: Capt M. Freshnie, 2Lt Chet Kin
Doctor: Capt N. Stocks, RAMC
RAF Liaison Officer: Flt Lt J. Redman
Subedar: Subedar Kulbir, 3/2nd GR

Organization
Column Headquarters comprising: Column Commander, Subedar, Orderlies, Signals Section – Corporal and four Other Ranks, Medical Section – Doctor and two Indian orderlies, RAF Signals and Liaison Section – RAF Officer, RAF Sergeant, Four RAF Other Ranks, Animal Transport Officer – HQ chargers and mules.

Rifle Company 3/2 GR comprising: Company Headquarters, Three rifle platoons of four sections each, Support platoon – 2 Vickers machine-guns, 2 x 3-inch Mortars. Each platoon also had one Boyes anti-tank rifle and each section had a grenade discharger cup.

Guerrilla Platoon (British): Platoon HQ – 2 officers and a sergeant, Three sections

Reconnaissance Platoon: Platoon HQ – 2 officers and 2 GCOs, Three sections

3 Column Order of Battle

Column Commander: Maj M. Calvert, Royal Engineers
2i/c and Rifle Company Commander: Capt G. Silcock, 3/2nd GR
2i/c Rifle Company: Lt D. Gudgeon, 3/2nd GR
Animal Transport Officer: Capt Roy McKenzie
2i/c Animal Transport Officer: Lt George Worte
Intelligence Officer: 2Lt Alec Gibson
Commando Platoon, 142 Company: Lt Jeffery Lockett
Burma Rifles, Recce Platoon: Capt Taffy Griffiths, 2Lt Ken Gourlay
Doctor: Capt Rao, RIAMC
RAF Liaison Officer: Flt Lt R. Thompson
Subedar: 3/2 GR

Organization

Column Headquarters comprising: Column Commander, Orderlies, Signals Section – Corporal and four Other Ranks, Medical section – Doctor and two Indian orderlies, RAF Signals and Liaison Section – RAF Officer, RAF, Sergeant, four RAF other ranks, Animal Transport Officer – HQ chargers and mules, Rifle Company 3/2 GR comprising: Company Commander – Subedar Kumba Sing Gurung, Three rifle platoons of four sections each, 13 Platoon – Lt Harold James/Jemadar Andaram Gurung, Support platoon – 2 Vickers machine guns, 2 x 3-inch mortars. Each platoon also had one Boyes anti-tank rifle and each section had a grenade discharger cup.

Guerrilla Platoon (British): Platoon HQ – 2 officers and a sergeant, Three sections

Reconnaissance Platoon: Platoon HQ – 2 officers and 2 GCOs, Three sections

5 Column Order of Battle

Column Headquarters
Column Commander: Maj B.E. Fergusson, Black Watch
Column Adjutant: Lt D.C. Menzies, Black Watch
Administrative Officer: Capt A.I. MacDonald, King's Regiment
Medical Officer: Capt W.S. Aird, RAMC
Air Liaison Officer: Flt Lt D.J.T. Sharp, RAF
Cipher Officer: Lt W Edge, South Wales Borderers
Animal Transport Officer: 2Lt W. Smyly, 3/2nd Gurkha Rifles
Column Sergeant Major: CSM J. Cairns, King's Own Scottish Borderers

Detachment of The Burma Rifles
Commander: Capt J.C. Fraser, Burma Rifles (also 2i/c of Column)
Second-in-command: Lt P.A.M. Heald, Burma Rifles
Officers: Subedar Ba Than, Burma Rifles
          Jemadar Aung Pe, Burma Rifles

Support Platoon
Commander: Capt T.C. Roberts, King's Regiment
Second-in-command: Lt W. Williamson, King's Regiment

Commando Platoon
Commander: Lt J.B. Harman, Gloucestershire Regiment
Second-in-command: Lt D. Whitehead, Royal Engineers

Rifle Platoons
No. 7 Platoon Commander: Lt P.G. Stibbe, Royal Sussex Regiment
No. 8 Platoon Commander: Lt J.M. Kerr, Welch Regiment
No. 9 Platoon Commander: Lt G. Roberts, Welch Regiment
Reinforcement Officer: Lt T. Blow, 14th Punjabi Regiment (8 Platoon Commander).

7 Column Order of Battle

Column Commander: Maj K.D. Gilkes
Capt H.C. Cotton
Capt J.S. Pickering
Capt H.B. Blackburne
Capt L.R. Cotterill
Capt W.B.E. Petersen
Lt Walker
Lt R.A. Williams
Lt S.F. Hector
Lt H.S. Pearce
2Lt J.T. Kelly
2Lt R. Wilkinson
Lt F. Oakes
Lt J. Musgrave-Wood
Capt A.H. Snalam, RAMC
Lt J.S. Frew, 1 Punjab (attd)
Lt T.A. Stock, 19 Hyderabad (attd)
Lt D.R. Chambers, 3 Gurkha Rifles

8 Column Order of Battle

Major W.P. Scott, Column Commander
Capt R.E. Williams
Capt J.S. F. Coughlan, ? Platoon
Capt J.R. Carroll, Support Platoon
Lt B.P. Horncastle
Lt D.M. Rowlands
Lt P.A. Bennett, 16 Platoon
Lt E.W. Hobday, Column HQ
Lt E.T. Horton
Lt A. Campbell-Patterson, Column HQ
Capt J.D.S. Heathcote, RAMC
Lt W.T. Callaghan, 18 PGR (attd)
Lt J.M. Gillow, 1/3rd Madras Regiment (attd)
Lt P. Hamilton-Bryan, 6 Lancers (attd)
Lt T. Sprague, 142 Commando Sabotage Squad
Lt Nick Neill, 3/2nd GR
Lt G. Astell, 2nd Burma Rifles Platoon
Capt Whitehead, OC 2nd Burma Rifles Platoon

The author would appreciate any additions or amendments.

Appendix 7

Letter from Wingate to Ken Spurlock's Father

GENERAL STAFF, INDIA.

Major-General O.O. Wingate
c/o General Headquarters,
INDIA.

My dear Mr. Spurlock,

I was one of the last people to
see your son in Burma. He had been throughout the
Campaign absolutely invaluable to me as my principal
Signals Officer.

As you may well imagine the
success of the Campaign was largely due to the
excellent signals work of your son and his subordinate
It was for this reason I decided to keep him with me
in my own party when we broke up into small groups in
order to regain India. To start with all went well,
we recrossed the Irrawady and we almost in sight of
home when to my great unhappiness your son announced
his inability to continue. He had always been so
strong I had not realised that the greatly reduced
diet had told more heavily on his big body than on
smaller ones. We waited two days in the hope he
would regain strength, and then were compelled in the
interest of the whole party to set out again. He was
suffering from agravated diarrhea , and the wait did
nothing to improve matters.

On the march, which took place
at night and lay through a mountainous district, he
came up to me and announced he could go no further.
We had provided him with food, money and a compass
in case this should happen. I had a long talk with
him that morning about the advisability of surrenderir
to the Japanese. He was against this but I pointed
out to him that he could escape when he had regained
his strength, as he was quite incapable of self-defence
there was no question of dishonour. I cannot say,
however, that he appeared convinced by my arguments.
Fo the rest I told him to wait a day after we had

passed, then to enter the nearest village where he could have a bed and be looked after.   I expect he did this, and hope that he was either taken care of by kindly Burmans or that he is a prisoner in the hands of the Japanese.   The prospect of the first alternative grows less hopeful with the passage of every month.   I believe it takes the Red Cross about six months to get news of prisoners of war.

Finally, I would like to say that myself, and all members of my H.Q. have the greatest respect and admiration for your son.   To this was added affection for his very likeable character.   His disappearance – which I hope is only temporary – is an irreparable loss to me.   I had the greatest opinion of his judgment, on which I always relied implicitly.

Before closing this letter I wish to express my deep sympathy with you and Mrs. Spurlock in your anxiety over the fate of such an excellent son.

Yours sincerely,

Orde Wingate

H.J. Spurlock, Esq.,
10, South View Avenue,
Walcot,
Swindon, WILTS.

Index

Rothwell, Sgt R.A., 201
Rowlands, Lt D.M., 137, 206
Rowley, Pte, 121
Rubbock, Pte, 12

Saugor, 14, 29–30, 41, 194
Saxon, Sgt, 138
Scoones, Lt Gen, 100, 137, 168–9
Scott, Capt Ray, 60
Scott, Maj Walter P., 27, 56, 80
  Baw, 81, 83, 89–90, 116, 131–47
  return to India, 168, 170, 181–2,
  206
Scrutton, Sgt, 131, 162
Sennett, Sgt, 144
Sharp, Flt Lt Denny J.T., 110, 204
Short, L/Cpl, 121
Shweli River, 59, 76–9, 94–5, 101,
  108–9, 112, 116–17, 131, 148
Silcock, Capt George, 14, 101–2, 189,
  203
Simons, Pte, 150
Sinlamaung, 56, 58
Siribhagta, Subedar, 101–2
Sittang Bridge, 16, 185
Slim, Gen William, 16, 19, 181
Smyly, Lt W., 82, 111–15, 117, 204
Snalam, Capt A.H., RAMC, 205
Southern Group, 27, 51, 61, 66, 68,
  71–2, 75, 78–9, 92, 93, 191
Sprague, Lt Tag, 132–3, 142–7, 206
Spurlock, Lt K.E., 30–1, 40, 148,
  150, 153–5, 158, 161, 176, 187–8,
  200–1, 207–8
Stewart-Jones, Lt, 59–61
Stibbe, Lt Philip G., 105–8, 111, 115,
  184, 187, 204
Stilwell, Gen Joe, 19, 171, 180–3
Stock, Lt T.A., 123, 205
Stocks, Capt N., RAMC, 31, 93, 99,
  100, 202

Suddery, Pte Jim, 135
Sullivan, Pte, 141
Sykes, Pte, 121

Tagaung, 28, 32, 49
Tamu, 29, 44, 47, 100, 128
Thapa, Rfn Lal Bahadur, 62
Thapa, Havildar Lalbahadur, 63
Thapa, Subedar Maj Siblal, 66, 96
Thompson, Sqn Ldr Robert, 101–2,
  203
Thompson, Sgt, 118, 121
Thompson, CSM T., 201
Thornborrow, Sgt J., 106, 201
Thornton, Pte, 121
Tigyaing, 65, 74
Tikajit, Subedar, 59
Tong, 2Lt L., 119
Tonhe, 27
Tonmakeng, 56, 58, 177
Tooth, Flt Lt, 41, 150–1
Tun, Lance Naik Lwin, 200
Tun, Rfn Maung, 107–8
Tun, Rfn Tin, 136, 142–3
Tunnion, Rfn, 149

Vann, Tommy, L/Cpl, 43, 45, 47
Vlasto, Michael, F/O, 135–6

Walker, Lt, 117, 205
Walker, Cpl Jimmy, 134–5, 206
Walsh, Pte, 136
Watson, Lt J., 49, 202
Wavell, FM A., 18–19, 23–4, 32–3,
  41, 48–9, 54, 121, 168–9
Weatherall, Capt Vivian, 31, 66–7, 77,
  92, 94–5, 202
Weston, Pte, 151–2
Wheatley, Flt Lt Ken, 132, 163
Wheeler, Lt Col L.G., 26–7, 81, 83,
  105, 110, 200

Note. 'Wingate', 'Chindwin River' and 'Irrawaddy River' are left out of the index as they are mentioned on so many pages it is pointless to include them all.